Survival

GLOBAL POLITICS AND STRATEGY

Volume 58 Number 6 | December 2016–January 2017

'One of the paradoxes of intelligence [is] the extraordinary precautions that have to be taken to conceal the identity of an extraordinary source versus the dangers in withholding that information from the very people who need it. In each case, it is a judgement that even King Solomon would have had to think long and hard about.'

Gordon Barrass, *Able Archer 83*: What Were the Soviets Thinking?, p. 25.

'The US-led global economic order – from 1945 to the present – has always been far more dependent on a certain constellation of geopolitical circumstances than Western leaders prefer to acknowledge. The efforts of US and EU policymakers to rid the global economic order of geopolitics appear to be failing abroad and backfiring at home, undermining the very structures they aim to protect.'

Jennifer M. Harris, America, Europe and the Necessary Geopolitics of Trade, p. 65.

'"Leadership" is an oft-used and somewhat vacuous mantra, but we are about to understand its more precise meaning by virtue of its absence from the liberal West.'

Dana H. Allin, President Trump, p. 245.

Survival

GLOBAL POLITICS AND STRATEGY

Volume 58 Number 6 | December 2016–January 2017

Contents

Cover: Jim Watson/AFP/Getty Images

On the cover
United States president-elect Donald Trump gestures after his victory speech on election night at the New York Hilton Midtown, 9 November 2016.

On the web
Visit www.iiss.org/publications/survival for brief notices on new books on Environment and Resources, the United States, Europe, and Counter-terrorism and Intelligence.

***Survival* editors' blog**
For ideas and commentary from *Survival* editors and contributors, visit www.iiss.org/politicsandstrategy.

Review Essays

Closing Argument

Survival
GLOBAL POLITICS AND STRATEGY

The International Institute for Strategic Studies
2121 K Street, NW | Suite 801 | Washington DC 20037 | USA
Tel +1 202 659 1490 Fax +1 202 659 1499 E-mail survival@iiss.org Web www.iiss.org
Arundel House | 13–15 Arundel Street | Temple Place | London | WC2R 3DX | UK
Tel +44 (0)20 7379 7676 Fax +44 (0)20 7836 3108 E-mail iiss@iiss.org
14th Floor, GBCorp Tower | Bahrain Financial Harbour | Manama | Kingdom of Bahrain
Tel +973 1718 1155 Fax +973 1710 0155 E-mail iiss-middleeast@iiss.org
9 Raffles Place | #51-01 Republic Plaza | Singapore 048619
Tel +65 6499 0055 Fax +65 6499 0059 E-mail iiss-asia@iiss.org

Survival Online www.tandfonline.com/survival and www.iiss.org/publications/survival

Aims and Scope *Survival* is one of the world's leading forums for analysis and debate of international and strategic affairs. Shaped by its editors to be both timely and forward thinking, the journal encourages writers to challenge conventional wisdom and bring fresh, often controversial, perspectives to bear on the strategic issues of the moment. With a diverse range of authors, *Survival* aims to be scholarly in depth while vivid, well written and policy-relevant in approach. Through commentary, analytical articles, case studies, forums, review essays, reviews and letters to the editor, the journal promotes lively, critical debate on issues of international politics and strategy.

Published for the IISS by
Routledge Journals, an imprint of Taylor & Francis, an Informa business.

About the IISS The IISS, a registered charity with offices in Washington, London, Manama and Singapore, is the world's leading authority on political–military conflict. It is the primary independent source of accurate, objective information on international strategic issues. Publications include *The Military Balance*, an annual reference work on each nation's defence capabilities; *Strategic Survey*, an annual review of world affairs; *Survival*, a bimonthly journal on international affairs; *Strategic Comments*, an online analysis of topical issues in international affairs; and the *Adelphi* series of books on issues of international security.

SUBMISSIONS

To submit an article, authors are advised to follow these guidelines:

- *Survival* articles are around 4,000–10,000 words long including endnotes. A word count should be included with a draft. Length is a consideration in the review process and shorter articles have an advantage.
- All text, including endnotes, should be double-spaced with wide margins.
- Any tables or artwork should be supplied in separate files, ideally not embedded in the document or linked to text around it.
- All *Survival* articles are expected to include endnote references. These should be complete and include first and last names of authors, titles of articles (even from newspapers), place of publication, publisher, exact publication dates, volume and issue number (if from a journal) and page numbers. Web sources should include complete URLs and DOIs if available.
- A summary of up to 150 words should be included with the article. The summary should state the main argument clearly and concisely, not simply say what the article is about.
- A short author's biography of one or two lines should also be included. This information will appear at the foot of the first page of the article.
- *Survival* has a strict policy of listing multiple authors in alphabetical order.

Submissions should be made by email, in Microsoft Word format, to the Managing Editor, Matthew Harries, survival@iiss.org. Alternatively, hard copies may be sent to *Survival*, IISS–US, 2121 K Street NW, Suite 801, Washington, DC 20037, USA. Please direct any queries to Matthew Harries.

The editorial review process can take up to three months. *Survival*'s acceptance rate for unsolicited manuscripts is less than 20%. *Survival* does not normally provide referees' comments in the event of rejection. Authors are permitted to submit simultaneously elsewhere so long as this is consistent with the policy of the other publication and the Editors of *Survival* are informed of the dual submission.

Readers are encouraged to comment on articles from the previous issue. Letters should be concise, no longer than 750 words and relate directly to the argument or points made in the original article.

ADVERTISING AND PERMISSIONS

For advertising rates and schedules

USA/Canada: The Advertising Manager, Taylor & Francis Inc., 530 Walnut Street, Suite 850, Philadelphia, PA 19106, USA Tel +1 (800) 354 1420 Fax +1 (215) 207 0050.

UK/Europe/Rest of World: The Advertising Manager, Routledge Journals, Taylor & Francis, 4 Park Square, Milton Park, Abingdon, Oxfordshire OX14 4RN, UK Tel +44 (0) 207 017 6000 Fax +44 (0) 207 017 6336.

SUBSCRIPTIONS

Survival is published bi-monthly in February, April, June, August, October and December by Routledge Journals, an imprint of Taylor & Francis, an Informa Business.

Annual Subscription 2016

Institution	$787	£449	€661
Individual	$216	£128	€175
Online only	$689	£393	€578

Taylor & Francis has a flexible approach to subscriptions, enabling us to match individual libraries' requirements. This journal is available via a traditional institutional subscription (either print with online access, or online only at a discount) or as part of our libraries, subject collections or archives. For more information on our sales packages please visit http://www.tandfonline.com/page/librarians.

All current institutional subscriptions include online access for any number of concurrent users across a local area network to the currently available backfile and articles posted online ahead of publication.

Subscriptions purchased at the personal rate are strictly for personal, non-commercial use only. The reselling of personal subscriptions is prohibited. Personal subscriptions must be purchased with a personal cheque or credit card. Proof of personal status may be requested.

Dollar rates apply to all subscribers outside Europe. Euro rates apply to all subscribers in Europe, except the UK and the Republic of Ireland where the pound sterling rate applies. If you are unsure which rate applies to you please contact Customer Services in the UK. All subscriptions are payable in advance and all rates include postage. Journals are sent by air to the USA, Canada, Mexico, India, Japan and Australasia. Subscriptions are entered on an annual basis, i.e. January to December. Payment may be made by sterling cheque, dollar cheque, euro cheque, international money order, National Giro or credit cards (Amex, Visa and Mastercard).

Survival (USPS 013095) is published bi-monthly (in Feb, Apr, Jun, Aug, Oct and Dec) by Routledge Journals, Taylor & Francis, 4 Park Square, Milton Park, Abingdon, OX14 4RN, United Kingdom.

The US annual subscription price is $787. Airfreight and mailing in the USA by agent named Air Business Ltd, c/o Worldnet Shipping Inc., 156-15, 146th Avenue, 2nd Floor, Jamaica, NY 11434, USA. Periodicals postage paid at Jamaica NY 11431.

US Postmaster: Send address changes to Survival, C/O Air Business Ltd / 156-15 146th Avenue, Jamaica, New York, NY11434.

Subscription records are maintained at Taylor & Francis Group, 4 Park Square, Milton Park, Abingdon, OX14 4RN, United Kingdom.

ORDERING INFORMATION

Please contact your local Customer Service Department to take out a subscription to the Journal: **USA, Canada:** Taylor & Francis, Inc., 530 Walnut Street, Suite 850, Philadelphia, PA 19106, USA. Tel: +1 800 354 1420; Fax: +1 215 207 0050. **UK/ Europe/Rest of World:** T&F Customer Services, Informa UK Ltd, Sheepen Place, Colchester, Essex, CO3 3LP, United Kingdom. Tel: +44 (0) 20 7017 5544; Fax: +44 (0) 20 7017 5198; Email: subscriptions@tandf.co.uk.

Back issues: Taylor & Francis retains a two-year back issue stock of journals. Older volumes are held by our official stockists: Periodicals Service Company, 351 Fairview Ave., Suite 300, Hudson, New York 12534, USA to whom all orders and enquiries should be addressed. *Tel* +1 518 537 4700 *Fax* +1 518 537 5899 *e-mail* psc@periodicals.com *web* http://www.periodicals.com/tandf.html.

The issue date is October–November 2016.

The print edition of this journal is printed on ANSI conforming acid free paper.

Able Archer 83: What Were the Soviets Thinking?

Gordon Barrass

Over the past 30 years, there has been much debate over how close the world came to nuclear war in 1983, as US–Soviet relations became increasingly fraught. Were we at the brink of Armageddon and, if so, why? Or was the so-called war scare part of a Soviet propaganda campaign to thwart the deployment of cruise and *Pershing* II missiles to Western Europe, throwing the NATO alliance into disarray? This haunting problem is part of a much bigger story – a story about the rivalry between NATO and the Warsaw Pact from the early 1970s to the late 1980s, as they each struggled to enhance their own security and boost their political clout by exploiting the revolution taking place in military technology.[1]

The debate over what happened in 1983 – in particular, the Soviet reaction to NATO's *Able Archer* exercise that year – received a new lease of life in October 2015 with the release of a top-secret review of the issue written in 1990 under the auspices of the President's Foreign Intelligence Advisory Board (PFIAB). The review concluded that 'we may have inadvertently placed our relations with the Soviet Union on a hair trigger', in response to which the Kremlin 'might have launched a pre-emptive strike against the US in response to a perceived but non-existent threat'.[2]

Several informed observers have expressed their reservations regarding this conclusion.[3] A principal reservation concerns how much the authors of

Gordon Barrass is Visiting Professor at LSE IDEAS, where he heads the Global Strategies @ LSE project. He had much to do with Soviet affairs during his years in the British Diplomatic Service and as a member of the Joint Intelligence Committee (1988–93). He interviewed Oleg Gordievsky on many occasions, both then and when he was writing his book, *The Great Cold War*, in the mid-2000s.

Survival | vol. 58 no. 6 | December 2016–January 2017 | pp. 7–30 DOI 10.1080/00396338.2016.1257176

the PFIAB report did *not* know at the time the report was written. Since the end of the Cold War, there has been a flood of new material: from Soviet and East European archives; from extensive interviews US officials conducted with Soviet military commanders, scientists and intelligence officials immediately after the end of the Cold War; and from British interviewers in 2005–06 preparing for a TV docudrama entitled *1983: The Brink of Apocalypse*. In addition, there are many memoirs by former Soviet leaders, officials and officers.[4]

This material makes it possible to take a fresh look at what really happened and reassesses how serious the risk of war had been in late 1983. Even so, the old rules of evidence still apply: we must give priority to what actors said at the time versus what they said later, when people often wish to portray themselves as having been more insightful or effective than they were; we must consider how well placed the source was to know about what was happening; and we must take into account the need of generals and heads of intelligence services to show their bosses that they have not missed a trick and are keeping their staff on their toes.

We also need to keep in mind that there was not one Soviet view; rather, there were several, reflecting the structure of the regime, the tight control over information and the persistent use of propaganda in the Soviet Union itself. In particular, we should remember the historic institutional rivalry between the KGB and the GRU, the Soviet military-intelligence service, with the former believing they could see things the GRU could not, and the GRU full of contempt for the KGB's ignorance of the realities of military matters.

What did Soviet leaders say in private?

The starting point for such an effort must be what Soviet leaders were saying to each other and to their close East European allies about president Ronald Reagan – the first American president to believe that the United States could end the Cold War by putting the Soviet Union under intense pressure on all fronts.[5]

Reagan's challenge was menacing because it came at a time when the Soviet leadership felt increasingly vulnerable. On the one hand, the Soviet economy was in trouble, Soviet forces were bogged down in Afghanistan, the declaration of martial law in Poland could not eliminate the threat from

Solidarity, and discontent was rising across the Soviet bloc. On the other, the Soviets' early-warning systems were unreliable; the Soviet Union could not match America's ability to harness IT to enhance the effectiveness of their weaponry and coordination of warfare; and NATO was preparing to deploy *Pershing* II ballistic missiles and *Gryphon* cruise missiles.[6]

One of the first signs of the depth of Soviet concern came, unsurprisingly, from the KGB. In a secret speech in February 1981, Vladimir Kryuchkov, the head of the KGB's foreign operations, exhorted KGB residencies to 'prevent the US and its allies from deciding to make a first-strike against the Soviet Union'.[7]

Almost immediately, the Soviet armed forces began the long process of heightening their readiness. Su-24 bombers, for instance, were deployed in East Germany, Poland and Hungary to boost the availability of nuclear-strike forces in the forward area. For the first time, nuclear-capable artillery was also deployed with Soviet forces on the NATO front line.[8]

In May 1981, the ailing president Leonid Brezhnev denounced Reagan's policies in a secret address to a major KGB conference in Moscow. The most dramatic speech, however, was given by Yuri Andropov, the chairman of the KGB and a leading member of the Politburo.[9] Andropov declared that the new American administration was actively preparing for nuclear war and that a nuclear first strike was possible. He then announced that, by a decision of the Politburo, the KGB and the GRU were for the first time to cooperate in a worldwide intelligence operation code-named RYAN (the Russian acronym for 'Nuclear Missile Attack').[10]

Since the end of the Second World War the chief task of the KGB had been 'to help frustrate the aggressive intentions of the American imperialists'.[11] Now, for the first time, the KGB was placing strategic military intelligence at the top of its collection priorities. The KGB's primary task was to provide advance warning of any decision by the US and its NATO allies to launch a nuclear attack. The underlying concept of RYAN, which had been developed by the KGB, was the belief that deviations from peacetime routines in a wide variety of spheres – military, political, economic, health administration, civil defence – could provide preliminary warning of Western preparations for a first strike.

'The slogan', General Oleg Kalugin of the KGB vividly remembered, was 'do not miss the moment when the West is about to launch war'.[12] The thrust of what Andropov said that day and later, however, was not that the Soviet Union needed enough warning to pre-empt a missile attack, but that it needed enough time to dissuade or deter the Americans from taking such a fatal step.

We know a lot about how the KGB went about this task from Colonel Oleg Gordievsky, who was working with the British Secret Intelligence Service (SIS) at the same time as being the number two in the KGB residency in London from 1982–85.[13] As always, the GRU's responsibility was to monitor NATO's capabilities and activities, and any signs that preparations were being made to attack the Warsaw Pact. Over the years they had collected a formidable amount of intelligence.[14]

In his speech to the KGB conference, Andropov had chosen his words carefully. Although he accused the United States of 'preparing' for war, he did not go so far as to accuse it of planning to initiate one. Two months later, Andropov spelt out his thinking to Erich Mielke, the member of the East German Politburo responsible for foreign and domestic intelligence:

> The US is preparing for war, but it is not willing to start a war. They are not building factories and palaces in order to destroy them. They are striving for military superiority in order to 'check' us and then declare 'checkmate' against us without starting a war. Maybe I am wrong.[15]

In December 1982, following Brezhnev's death, Andropov took over as general secretary. On 4 January 1983, he gave East European leaders in Prague an unemotional assessment of the shift that had taken place over the past four years. The *Pershing* IIs and *Gryphons* were the 'most serious challenge', he said, and 'the military situation was especially dangerous'. It was 'difficult to say', he continued, 'where the line lies between extortion and actual preparations to take a fateful step'. Despite American hostility, the Soviet Union was willing to 'go very far' to end the arms race. To that end, Andropov would try to get relations back on a better course and reopen a 'dialogue of equals' with Reagan.[16]

What was Andropov's objective?

Andropov's main aim was to prevent NATO deployment of *Pershing* II and *Gryphon* missiles. Moscow's most powerful tool for doing this was the massive peace movements that had sprung up in several NATO countries. While they reflected genuine concerns, some were secretly supported by Soviet funding, and all were bolstered by Soviet propaganda. To that end, Andropov hyped the threat these 'Euromissiles' posed to world peace, saying darkly that the prospect of 'nuclear war was overhanging mankind'.[17]

Much of this problem was of Moscow's own making. NATO's disarray in the early 1970s emboldened Moscow to undermine the confidence of the Western Europeans in America's ability to protect them in time of war, which would have required escalating to the first use of nuclear weapons to avoid defeat and restore deterrence. To this end, in the late 1970s, Moscow began deploying the SS-20, a new triple-warheaded missile with a range of some 4,500 kilometres. That made it possible to hold all of Western Europe at risk from deep within Soviet territory.

NATO's response was that, unless the Soviet Union massively cut its SS-20 force (which would eventually comprise some 400 missiles and launchers), NATO would deploy two new theatre weapons – the *Pershing* II and *Gryphon* missiles – at the end of 1983. When Reagan became president, the terms of this deal became tougher: the 'double zero' solution. NATO would not deploy its 108 *Pershing* IIs and 464 *Gryphons* if the Soviet Union eliminated all of its SS-20s.[18]

By the end of March 1983, soon after Reagan's announcement of the Strategic Defense Initiative, it became clear that the peace movement had failed and NATO's 'Euromissiles' would begin to be deployed on schedule in November. When the Politburo met on 31 May, Andropov asked its members whether American policymakers would use the Euromissiles without being provoked. Foreign minister Andrei Gromyko rightly replied: 'I think they wouldn't dare to use nuclear missiles without sufficient reason.'[19]

In Moscow on 4 May 1983, Andropov admitted to East German leader Erich Honecker that he did not really consider that *Pershing* II would change things much, as the Americans already had plenty of missiles with which to attack the Soviet Union and East Germany. The real reason for focusing on these missiles, he explained, was 'to raise the struggle against the whole course of militarisation onto a higher level'. 'Should the deployment take place', he explained, 'and everything indicates that it will, then the struggle against militarisation would nevertheless continue.'[20]

One way of continuing the 'struggle' would have been to provoke the West German peace movements into violence. That is probably why in early 1983 the KGB set about identifying places near US bases to conceal explosives that, when detonated, would have appeared to be a terrorist attack.[21] When, in October 1984, Honecker discussed with Gromyko the failure of the peace movement to prevent the deployment of the Euromissiles, Honecker said this was due to the fact that the protests had remained non-violent. It seems that as East–West relations became increasingly fraught in the following months, Moscow was not willing to take such a risk.

Soviet fear of nuclear war

Soviet leaders and generals had long threatened to 'launch on warning' if the Kremlin believed NATO was going to resort to the use of nuclear weapons in the context of a war between the Warsaw Pact and NATO. The military and the Strategic Rocket Forces regularly practised the deployment and use of their nuclear forces. There are, however, many first-hand accounts showing that Soviet leaders and generals alike were horrified by the prospect of nuclear war. Indeed, the Politburo adamantly refused to delegate the authority to launch nuclear missiles to military commanders.[22] When Vitalii Kataev, a former senior Central Committee defence adviser, was asked how the leadership would respond to a limited strike, he pondered silently for a while and then said 'I just don't know'.[23]

Despite the weaknesses of their early-warning systems, Soviet leaders had a high degree of confidence in nuclear deterrence. They believed that the Americans understood that, even if they opted for a surprise first strike, the Soviet Union would be able to launch enough land-based and submarine-based missiles to obliterate America's main cities and military facilities. This was a risk that American leaders would not take; and Soviet leaders themselves would not do so for precisely the same reason.

It was against this background that in the late 1970s to early 1980s a major shift took place in Soviet strategy: everything possible had to be done to prevent nuclear war. In practice, this meant that should conflict break out in Europe, 2,000 Soviet strike aircraft (carrying conventional weapons) would launch simultaneous attacks to destroy all NATO nuclear facilities there within 48 hours. By doing so, they hoped to be able to prevent NATO from resorting to theatre and tactical nuclear weapons, which they believed would inevitably escalate into global nuclear war.

A small number of Americans knew about this from tens of thousands of pages of documentary intelligence provided by Major-General Dmitry Polyakov of the GRU, and Colonel Ryszard Kuklinski, an officer on the Polish General Staff who was working with the Russians on the Warsaw Pact's command-and-control arrangements in time of war.[24] Kuklinski's contribution on the Warsaw Pact's operational concepts, command structure and exercises was of an unprecedented and unparalleled duration.[25]

American satellites had produced a lot of information about the new, deep command-and-control bunkers that were being built in the Moscow area for the Soviet leadership and the general staff.[26] In addition, Kuklinski had the details of the new bunker from which a war against NATO on the central front would be directed. And after Kuklinski's defection to the US in December 1981, Soviet leaders knew that the Americans knew about their bunkers and how they would fight a war in Europe.[27]

The nightmare of *Pershing* II

Soviet military experts believed *Pershing* IIs deployed in West Germany to be a greater danger than the ICBMs deployed in the United States.[28] These missiles would, after all, undermine Moscow's assumptions about deterrence – firstly, because of the capabilities of these missiles and, secondly, because if they were deployed it would show that NATO had achieved a new resilience, both politically and in terms of deterrence. According to the 1990 PFIAB report:

> The Pershing II missile 1800 km range would not have reached Moscow from planned deployment sites in West Germany. Warsaw Pact sources, however, attributed to this system a range of 2500 km, an accuracy of 30

> meters, and an earth-penetrating warhead. With a range of 2500 km the Soviets feared it would have been able to strike command and control targets in the Moscow area with little or no warning.[29]

The American figure of 1,800km was the publicly declared range for *Pershing* II, with a marginally shorter one for *Gryphon*. The figures claimed by the Soviets were the classified figures, which are now quoted on official American websites.[30]

Although the Soviet leadership judged that Reagan would not dare to launch a surprise nuclear strike, what might he do if he lost his sanity or believed that he had the capability to prevent Soviet retaliation? The possibility that made the most military sense to the Soviet strategists was for the US to use *Pershing* IIs to destroy Soviet command-and-control bunkers before the leadership could order a retaliatory strike, followed in short order by strikes from submarines and land-based missiles.[31]

The top intelligence priority

In these circumstances, the GRU's key intelligence requirement was to know whether *Pershing* IIs had arrived in Europe, whether enough of them were operational for an effective first strike, the state of their alert and whether political decisions had been taken to use them.

This was a task for which the GRU was well prepared. Over the years, the Soviet General Staff had acquired staggering amounts of documentary and other intelligence on NATO. The intelligence came not only from the GRU, but also from the KGB and the Soviet Union's Warsaw Pact allies, especially the East Germans. Markus Wolf, the former head of the East German foreign intelligence service, recalled that when, in the 1970s, he asked the commander of Soviet forces in East Germany what intelligence he needed, the commander replied 'Nothing, just the precise map co-ordinates of all NATO nuclear facilities.'[32]

The GRU had taken a keen interest in *Pershing* missiles since the mid-1960s, when 108 *Pershing* 1As were deployed by the US Army in West Germany, with a further 72 operated by the German Air Force, as part of SACEUR's nuclear force. The US Army had three battalions, each of which had four batteries of nine missiles. At all times one battalion was on Quick Reaction Alert. The 1As had a range of 740km and a nuclear warhead, with a blast yield between 60 and 400 kilotons. Their task was to strike at Warsaw Pact forces in Eastern Europe.

The *Pershing* II, however, was designed for attacks on the Soviet Union. The US and West Germany agreed that while the US *Pershing* force would be upgraded one-for-one, the West German Air Force would retain its ageing *Pershing* 1As.

Monitoring *Pershing* II

In 1979, NATO had announced that the deployment of the 108 *Pershing* II missiles to Germany would begin in late 1983. Following a vote the previous day by the West German Bundestag, deployment began on 23 November.[33]

There were plenty of indicators to help the GRU monitor the timing of the deployment and the operational readiness of these missiles. Knowing what was happening in Germany was relatively easy because the GRU had many different human and technical sources, plus intensive coverage by East German intelligence.

In the US, much of the GRU's attention would have been focused on the Martin Marietta production plant at Orlando, Florida, where the *Pershing* IIs were produced; nearby facilities on Cape Canaveral, where they were tested and crews were trained; and Patrick Air Force Base, from which the missiles would be transported to Germany.[34] Agent coverage of what was going on in the US was less good than in Germany, but the GRU did have intercept stations in Washington, New York and Los Angeles. In addition, some 2,500 staff based at Lourdes, Cuba, were well placed to monitor activities at Cape Canaveral, just over 600km away.[35]

An intensive programme of flight tests of the *Pershing* IIs began in July 1982. Prior to the deployment to Germany, three *Pershing* IIs were flight-tested at Cape Canaveral on 23 September 1983.[36] The missile, however, was never tested beyond its declared range of 1,800km.

In preparation for the arrival of the new *Pershing* IIs in Germany, some of the crews that were already there manning the *Pershing* 1As were sent back to Cape Canaveral for additional training; over the next two years some

1,500 personnel based in Germany were sent on this course, and new crew members were trained at Fort Sill in Oklahoma. As the erector transporters for the *Pershing* IIs were those used for the *Pershing* 1As that had been modified in Germany, the deployment of the *Pershing* IIs would not be a complicated task. The *Pershing* II missile itself was only 10.6 metres long by 1m wide. It comprised five sections, one of which was the approximately 2m-long warhead. This made it possible for the four sections to be transported by truck or helicopter, though never together with the warheads.

Pershing II missiles were brought by ground convoys to the training facility at Cape Canaveral and from there flown to Germany from the nearby Patrick Air Force Base. As the erector transporters were already in Germany, a battery of nine missiles could easily be transported on one C5a *Galaxy* aircraft. The warheads, the fifth section, were as always flown separately.

Rising tensions

The shoot-down by a Soviet pilot of Korean Air Lines Flight 007 on 1 September 1983 over the Sea of Japan, killing 269 passengers and crew, led to a spiral of vituperous exchanges between Washington and Moscow. A Tass article by Marshal Nikolai Ogarkov on 22 September reminded the Reagan administration that, even if it did launch a first strike, Soviet retaliation would impose 'unacceptable damage' on the US.[37] A week later, as relations deteriorated further, Andropov issued a blunt statement in *Pravda* on 29 September saying, in effect, that there was no hope of improving Soviet–US relations while Reagan remained president. The implication, however, was that, while waiting for him to go, the Soviet Union would need to be cautious.

Some of the top Soviet commanders had been reminded of this just three days earlier, when their recently established satellite early-warning centre showed that five American *Minuteman* missiles had been launched against the Soviet Union. The officer on duty decided this was a false alarm because, firstly, he did not believe the Americans would launch a surprise attack on such a small scale, and secondly, the ground-based radar was showing no signs of the missiles coming over the horizon.[38] As the system was unreliable, the leadership would have to be ultra-cautious.

Nevertheless, the Soviet military took the threat of a surprise nuclear attack seriously. In talking about these events in 2005, General Viktor Yesin of the Soviet Strategic Missile Forces explained that NATO's large-scale military exercises were 'fraught with possibilities that under the cover of such an exercise an unexpected nuclear missiles strike could be launched'.[39]

Thanks to Gordievsky we know what telegrams the KGB Centre was sending to their residencies in NATO capitals about RYAN.[40] These have often been cited for what they said about Moscow's increasing concern that the US would launch a first strike against the Soviet Union.

In February 1983, for example, the centre issued a permanent operating assignment to uncover NATO preparations for a nuclear-missile attack on the Soviet Union. This task was of 'growing urgency' given the expected arrival of the *Pershing* IIs and *Gryphon* cruise missiles towards the end of the year. In June, the Centre instructed residencies to step up their efforts. The accompanying briefing material showed the KGB's considerable knowledge of the different levels of NATO alerts.[41]

The dogs that didn't bark

Even more interesting, however, is what the telegrams from the Centre do not say. They are among 'the dogs that didn't bark', whose silence draws attention to other aspects of Soviet conduct and the thinking that lay behind it.

Despite RYAN, the centre did not put serious pressure on residencies to increase their efforts and vigilance, nor did it provide significant new briefing even as NATO prepared for its annual autumn exercises, stretching from Norway to Turkey, under the overarching title of *Autumn Forge*. In 1983, these involved approximately 100,000 troops, some 16,000 of which had, as always, been flown in from the United States.

The last in the series was *Able Archer*, the annual command-post (meaning no troops on the ground) exercise of NATO's Allied Command Europe, designed to practise command and staff procedures, with particular emphasis on the transition from conventional to nuclear weapons. The *Able Archer* exercise was always held around early November at the end of *Autumn Forge*. Although the dates were not widely known, Soviet intelligence could easily obtain them from its many sources in NATO. In 1983 it was to run from 2–11 November, with the transition to nuclear weapons usually taking place during the last five days.[42]

Each year the exercises were changed in minor ways. In parallel, according to the PFIAB report, there were some live mobilisation exercises of some US forces in Europe. Some US aircraft, for example, practised nuclear-warhead handling procedures, including taxiing out of hangars carrying realistic-looking dummy warheads.[43] Moscow would have learned about most of these changes from their intelligence sources and those of their allies.

The top Soviet intelligence priority, however, remained the question of whether the US had the capability to launch a 'decapitating' first strike. Given the GRU's close study of *Pershing* 1As over many years, the agency could be confident that the *Pershing* IIs were not yet in West Germany. What they needed to know was when the delivery got under way, how quick the build-up was, and how many of the missiles were operational. After all, 'decapitation' would require a lot of *Pershing* IIs.

It was three days after *Able Archer* began that the centre sent the London residency a bland telegram revealing, for the first time, the timetable of the (non-existent) Western plan for a first strike. 'It can be assumed', it stated, 'that the period of time from the moment when the preliminary decision for RYAN is taken up to the order to deliver the strike will be of very short duration, possibly 7 to 10 days.' The centre added a checklist of likely indicators that the countdown had begun.[44] Meanwhile, *Able Archer* rolled on.

On 8 or 9 November, when *Able Archer* was drawing to its nuclear close, out of the blue KGB residencies received a 'most urgent' telegram from the centre. The telegram claimed that American forces had been put on alert, when in fact the Americans had simply been tightening security at their overseas bases in response to the recent massacre of some 300 US and French troops in Beirut.

The most interesting feature of this telegram was that it was so pathetic. On the one hand, it listed several possible explanations for this so-called alert, one of which was that the countdown to a nuclear strike had begun under the cover of *Able Archer*. On the other, residencies were instructed to confirm the alert and evaluate the hypotheses.[45]

Similarly, the absence of panic in Moscow is attested to by Rainer Rupp, the star agent of East German intelligence at NATO headquarters. He was not contacted by East German intelligence about *Able Archer* until 9 November. In response to the simple question of whether NATO was preparing for war, his reply was that 'There was no indication that NATO was preparing for war at that time'. He was never contacted on this matter again.[46]

Had the Soviet leadership really feared war was likely, let alone imminent, all branches of Soviet intelligence would have been frantically active. The KGB certainly was not – but the GRU was.

Hedging bets

As usual, when NATO exercises were taking place the GRU assiduously monitored NATO communications from within Soviet embassies in Western Europe. Other GRU officers roamed around Western Europe in cars with listening devices to intercept any communications they could and, above all, to make sure that what was happening was still an exercise, not a guise for launching missiles.[47] Meanwhile, according to Werner Grossman, the deputy head of East German intelligence, he had 'around 500 very important sources in West Germany at that time and we knew the missile locations exactly'.[48] Soviet concerns were reflected in an unusually sharp increase in the volume and urgency of Warsaw Pact communications. Much of this was probably reporting from the GRU, which was providing situation reports on *Able Archer* every six to eight hours.[49]

Meanwhile, on the Western side, the US National Security Agency (NSA) and the UK Government Communications Headquarters (GCHQ) were constantly monitoring communications for signs of changes in the deployment and alert status of Soviet and Warsaw Pact forces. The information they obtained was not merely classified Top Secret, but also UMBRA, indicating that it came from highly sensitive intercept operations. Most of this information, especially that concerning the alert status for Soviet forces, has been redacted from the PFIAB report. Nevertheless, what remains does show that Soviet forces took a number of unusual actions during *Able Archer 83*, which they had not taken in earlier years. These began on 20 October and included:

- Air armies in East Germany and Poland were placed on alert;
- A suspension of all flight operations from 4–10 November, with the exception of intelligence flights, of which there were 35 (significantly more than in previous years);
- Increasing the number of Mig-23s on strip alert and fully armed (these fighter-interceptors were designed to track and shoot down the low-flying *Gryphon* cruise missiles with conventional armaments);
- Invoking a 30-minute, round-the-clock readiness time and assigning priority targets.

In addition, SU-24 nuclear-capable strike bombers had for the previous two years been deployed in East Germany and Hungary, greatly enhancing the availability of strike forces in the forward areas, and efforts had been made to speed up the loading of nuclear bombs onto aircraft and delivery units.[50]

At first glance, these steps may seem scary. But, as will become clear below, they were not taken in panic; rather, they were part of the continuing effort by Soviet military forces to show that they were alert and could respond effectively in a real crisis – and they were signalling to the US to be careful. Had the CIA been alerted to the closeness of the timing of *Able Archer* and the deployment of *Pershing* II, it would probably have expected to see something of this sort, and would have detected these signs earlier than it did.

Some 15 years after the PFIAB report was written, some tantalising information emerged, according to which, on the day that *Able Archer* began (2 November), Marshal Ogarkov moved to his wartime command bunker deep beneath Moscow. From there he ordered a 'heightened alert' for some of his forces in the greatest secrecy, so as not to generate a crisis he wished to avoid.

Although there is no collateral for this from Western sources, it seems highly likely that this happened, given other changes detected by the NSA and GCHQ. The main Soviet source was General Yesin, who in 1983 had been a senior operations officer for the SS-20 force. In a separate interview Captain Viktor Tkachenko also spoke of the heightened alert, during which he had been in charge of a unit of ten SS-19s.[51]

When he was interviewed by Flashback Television in 2005, Yesin said that part of the land-based Soviet strategic missile force went on heightened alert. This included 75 of the mobile SS-20s targeted to Western Europe, which had been moved out of their garrisons to well-camouflaged wartime firing positions, as well as an unknown number of SS-19s and an intercontinental ballistic missile with ten warheads, which remained hidden in their silos. As *Able Archer* reached its climax, commanders of the rocket forces spent all their time in their command centres and were on the most heightened state of alert waiting for orders.

On the morning of 8 November SACEUR requested initial use of nuclear weapons against fixed targets in the satellite countries of Orange (the hypothetical opponent). SACEUR's request was approved late that evening, and nuclear strikes were launched on the morning of 9 November. Fighting continued and SACEUR was authorised to use more nuclear weapons, which he did on the morning of 11 November, bringing the exercise to a close.[52]

Not only did the GRU not flinch, but by that day, the Soviet alert had been withdrawn and Soviet Air Force units in East Germany resumed flight training.[53] If the GRU had had any doubts about what was happening those flights would not have been resumed so quickly. On 14 November, three days after *Able Archer* had officially ended, Soviet Strategic Rocket Forces were 'brought back to their normal positions'.[54]

The aftermath

Shortly before the West German Bundestag approved the deployment of the *Pershing* IIs to US forces in Germany on 22 November, the first batch of nine missiles had already arrived at the US Rhein-Main Air Base, which was under exclusive US control. Missiles for a second battalion arrived on 24 November.[55]

Three days after the vote by the German Bundestag, *Pravda* and *Izvestia* published a statement in which Andropov lambasted Reagan, asserting that he was bent on 'world domination' and 'inventing new plans on how to unleash a nuclear war in the best way, with the hope of winning it'. It also listed the countermeasures that Moscow would take.[56]

It was not until 27 November that the *Pershing* IIs were taken approximately 100 miles to the 1st Battalion 41st Field Artillery Regiment. This unit was based at Mutlangen, near the main operational base of its headquarters group, the 56th Field Artillery Brigade, at Schwäbisch Gmünd. To avoid protesters trying to block the roads, convoys travelled in the middle of the night. The nuclear warheads were transported by *Chinook* helicopters to safe storage bunkers nearby. The personnel and equipment of the first battalion were certified combat-ready and assumed target coverage on 15 December.[57] One day earlier, Marshal Dmitry Ustinov, the Soviet defence minister, had given a speech in Moscow in which he said that, 'no matter how complicated the military and political situation, there is no point in dramatizing it', adding that the Soviet Union was not frightened by threats.[58]

In April 1984, two months after Andropov died and was replaced by Konstantin Chernyenko, the Soviet armed forces conducted the most comprehensive rehearsal of a nuclear war that the US has ever detected.[59] This was clearly to warn the US not to try to exploit its success in deploying Euromissiles. Over the next year tensions between the US and the Soviet Union began to ease and paved the way for the breakthroughs made by Mikhail Gorbachev, who was elevated to general secretary after Chernyenko's death in March 1985, with Reagan and UK prime minister Margaret Thatcher.

Looking back on the events of 1983, Yesin said:

> We knew that NATO was doing an exercise … although we couldn't fully eliminate the possibility that a nuclear strike might have been delivered … [We were] on heightened vigilance, not waiting for a strike to be delivered … I was in Cuba at the height of the 1962 missile crisis when we were expecting that any minute we would be given the order to launch missiles and we were waiting for the American attack to begin. In 1983, the atmosphere was so different.[60]

Learning lessons

The debate in Washington over the *Able Archer* 'war scare' began in early 1984, as the close study of signals intelligence revealed that there had been some unusual Soviet military activity in October–November 1983, and SIS also provided some indications, while remaining determined not to risk exposing that it had a Soviet source as well placed as Gordievsky.

In the somewhat calmer atmosphere of late April–early May 1984, Fritz Ermarth, then the national intelligence officer for the Soviet Union, and his team of senior analysts reviewed the events surrounding *Able Archer*. Their conclusion was the same as it had been in the latter part of 1983:

> We believe strongly that Soviet actions are not inspired by, and Soviet leaders do not perceive, a genuine danger of imminent conflict or confrontation with the United States.

Statements to the contrary, they believed, were 'propaganda'.[61] At the time, Ermarth had a high degree of confidence in the CIA's ability to detect that Soviet forces were being readied for war. The CIA had, he said, long been receiving 'an extraordinary range of intelligence on Soviet and Warsaw Pact military activities. This would show whether their forces had been put on a higher alert, were on the move or were readying for a major offensive.'[62]

After the Cold War was over, General Gelii Batenin, Marshal Ogarkov's deputy, expressed a similarly high degree of confidence in the Soviet ability to detect when NATO was preparing to launch nuclear weapons:

> We had confidence in our knowledge of when NATO was preparing to launch nuclear weapons. We would detect mating of warheads to missiles and uploading of nuclear bombs and artillery. We listened to the hourly circuit verification signal of your nuclear release communications systems and *we believed we would recognise* a release order. [63]

Despite their confidence, the two sides were both aware that their monitoring was not perfect. Each side needed to be particularly vigilant in looking for other indicators. That said, the above analysis, based on what we now know, demonstrates the soundness of the CIA's judgement. Even when General Yesin's information about Soviet missiles being put on a higher alert is taken into account, the events surrounding *Able Archer* were less frightening than many have claimed. But *Able Archer* was just one part of the long-running Soviet concerns over American intentions.

The *Able Archer* episode itself, however, does provide lessons on how to analyse and respond to situations of great tension, especially when the stakes are high. On this score, the PFIAB report made two sound recommendations. The first is to know what your own side has been doing. This is easier said than done. Much of the relevant information is highly classified, or politically sensitive, or both. It involves, for example, knowing what exercises your own military is conducting, and understanding its 'probing' exercises to see how the other side reacts or, more seriously, to undermine their confidence;[64] ensuring that your intelligence agencies are not feeding double agents with false information that may be detrimental to your own interests;[65] and being kept abreast of what is being said between leaders and what messages are being passed via back channels.

The PFIAB's other recommendation was that, when unusual things happen, one should consider a number of competing hypotheses and the assumptions that underpin them. This technique was already being adopted by the CIA at that time, and is now widely accepted by Western intelligence agencies. Making sure that this is done properly, however, is always a challenge, especially when many issues demand attention at the same time. The task is now made easier by computerised programmes that marshal the intelligence and information supporting different hypotheses. These programmes also help highlight the 'dogs that didn't bark', asking such questions as: Why don't we know anything about that issue? Why is it that the only information that we have relates to things that happened long ago?

Even more can be gained by getting inside the minds of others. Robert Gates, who was deputy director of intelligence at the CIA at the time of *Able Archer 83*, stressed that 'One of the things that kept the Cold War scary was the lack of understanding on each side of the mentality of the other'.[66] Another leading Soviet expert at the CIA phrased it more pithily: 'We didn't realise just how f***ing scared Soviet leaders were of us.'[67]

As Andrew Marshall, the head of the Office of Net Assessment at the Pentagon from 1973–2015, put it:

> To get inside the mind of another leadership you really have to start from scratch. It is not just a question of how their history and culture make them different from us, but the ways in which the structure of their regime affects the way they view the outside world and respond to developments … Valuable insights can be gained by observing what the other side does, but the real gains come from asking why they have done it. It may not seem reasonable to you, but it probably does to him. Rationality, after all, can come in many different forms.[68]

The PFIAB report confirms Gordievsky's contribution to alerting the US to broader Soviet fears that deterrence was breaking down and the risk of war was increasing. And that brings us to one of the paradoxes of intelligence: the extraordinary precautions that have to be taken to conceal the identity of an extraordinary source versus the dangers in withholding that information from the very people who need it. In each case, it is a judgement that even King Solomon would have had to think long and hard about.

It was not until SIS had smuggled Gordievsky out of the Soviet Union and his defection had been announced in London on 12 September 1985 that the CIA began to receive his detailed reports on *Able Archer*, the war scare and many other issues. Robert Gates graphically described Gordievsky's importance:

> Our sources in the Soviet Union tended to be those who provided us with information about their military and military R&D. What Gordievsky was giving us was information about the thinking of the leadership – and that kind of information was for us as scarce as hens' teeth.[69]

Ultimately, the war scare was a reflection of the wider Soviet concerns that would lie at the heart of the talks Reagan would be having with Gorbachev in Geneva in November 1985. As soon as Bill Casey, the director of central intelligence and a close friend of Reagan's, heard of the defection, he flew to Britain to debrief Gordievsky himself. Later, Reagan thanked Gordievsky at a meeting in the Oval Office, the first time a KGB officer had ever been there.

When powerful adversaries face each other but do not want war, good intelligence by both sides is vital to avoiding catastrophe. Equally important is the need to understand that one side's actions influence the other's perceptions. This is an interactive and dynamic process. One of the best pieces of advice that Gorbachev's foreign-policy adviser, Anatoly Chernyaev, ever gave him was that he had to understand how he was perceived by others, because everything he did – like it or not – sent a message.[70]

There are many things one could have disagreed about with Yuri Andropov, but he did understand that whereas it was vital not to underestimate the danger, overestimating could be disastrous.

Notes

1 This subject has been perceptively analysed by Diego A. Ruiz Palmer, NATO's expert on Soviet strategy. See Diego A. Ruiz Palmer, 'The NATO–Warsaw Pact Competition in the 1970s and 1980s: A Revolution in Military Affairs in the Making or the End of a Strategic Age?', *Cold War History*, vol. 4, 2014, pp. 533–73.

2 President's Foreign Intelligence Advisory Board, 'The Soviet "War Scare"' [hereafter 'PFIAB report'], 15 February 1990, p. xii, http://nsarchive.gwu.edu/nukevault/ebb533-The-Able-Archer-War-Scare-Declassified-PFIAB-Report-Released/2012-0238-MR.pdf.

3 Benjamin B. Fischer, 'Scolding Intelligence: The PFIAB Report on the Soviet War Scare', paper delivered to the International Studies Association in Atlanta, GA, 18 March 2016.

4 See, for example, John G. Hines, Ellis M. Mishulovich and John F. Shull, *Soviet Intentions 1965–1985*, Volume 2: *Soviet Post-Cold War Testimonial Evidence* (McLean, VA: BDM, 1995); broadcast and unbroadcast interviews for *1983: The Brink of Apocalypse*, Flashback Television, 2008, some of which are quoted in Gordon Barrass, *The Great Cold War* (Stanford, CA: Stanford University Press, 2009), pp. 285–310, and others held by Flashback Television; Dmitry Adamsky, 'The 1983 Nuclear Crisis – Lessons for Deterrence Theory and Practice', *Journal of Strategic Studies*, vol. 36, no. 1, 2013, pp. 4–41.

5 Ben B. Fischer, 'A Cold War Conundrum: The 1983 Soviet War Scare', CIA Center for the Study of Intelligence, 1997, https://www.cia.gov/library/center-for-the-study-of-intelligence/csi-publications/books-and-monographs/a-cold-war-conundrum/source.htm.

6 Barrass, *The Great Cold War*, pp. 243–76.

7 PFIAB report, p. 53.

8 *Ibid.*, p. 56.

9 Christopher Andrew and Oleg Gordievsky, *Comrade Kryuchkov's Instructions: Top Secret Files on KGB Foreign Operations, 1975–1985*

(Stanford, CA: Stanford University Press, 1991), pp. 67–90.

10 Later the term 'VRYAN' ('Surprise Nuclear Missile Attack') was also used.

11 Andrew and Gordievsky, *Comrade Kryuchkov's Instructions*, p. 91.

12 Oleg Kalugin, interviewed on *1983: The Brink of Apocalypse.*

13 See Andrew and Gordievsky, *Comrade Kryuchkov's Instructions*; and Oleg Gordievsky, *Next Stop Execution: The Autobiography of Oleg Gordievsky* (London: Macmillan, 1995), pp. 246–321.

14 Heinz Busch, *Die Militärspionage der DDR-Staatssicherheit* (Bonn: Europäische Sicherheit, 1993), pp. 130–1; 'East German Intelligence Assessment of NATO's Intelligence on the Warsaw Pact, 16 December 1985', in Vojtech Mastny and Malcolm Byrne (eds), *A Cardboard Castle? An Inside History of the Warsaw Pact, 1955–1991* (Budapest: Central European Press, 2005), pp. 514–15.

15 'Note About the Talks of Comrade Minister [Erich] Mielke with the Chairman of the KGB, Comrade [Yuri] Andropov on 11 July 1981 in Moscow', Office of the Federal Commissioner for the Stasi Records (BStU), MfS, ZAIG 5382, http://digitalarchive.wilsoncenter.org/document/115717.

16 Yuri Andropov, speech to the Political Consultative Committee of the Warsaw Pact, 4 January 1983, National Security Archive Electronic Briefing Book no. 14, document 19, http://nsarchive.gwu.edu/NSAEBB/NSAEBB14/doc19.htm.

17 'Secretary General Andropov's Address to the Central Committee, Moscow, 16 June 1983', *Pravda*, 17 June 1983.

18 NATO Communiqué, 12 December 1979.

19 *Ibid.*

20 Andropov quoted in Michael Ploetz, *Wie die Sowjetunion den Kalten Krieg verlor. Von der Nachrüstung zum Mauerfall* (Berlin and Munich: Propyläen Verlag, 2000), p. 274. See also Marian K. Leighton, 'Strange Bedfellows: The Stasi and the Terrorists', *International Journal of Intelligence and Counter-Intelligence*, vol. 4, 2014, pp. 647–65.

21 The Mitrokhin file, a collection of notes made by a former KGB archivist, reveals that in the 1980s, Yuri Andropov, first as head the KGB and then as Leonid Brezhnev's successor, authorised his service and its Warsaw Pact allies 'to use, or connive in the use of, terrorism against the United States and NATO targets'. Christopher Andrew and Vasili Mitrokhin, *The Mitrokhin Archive: The KGB in Europe and the West* (London: Penguin, 1999), p. 512.

22 Hines et al., *Soviet Intentions*, pp. 58–62, 145.

23 *Ibid.*, p. 101.

24 Sandra Grimes and Jeanne Vertefeuille, *Circle of Treason* (Annapolis, MD: Naval Institute Press, 2012). The authors were part of the CIA's Soviet and East European Division in the 1970s and 1980s.

25 Ruiz Palmer, 'The NATO–Warsaw Pact Competition in the 1970s and 1980s', p. 546.

26 Interview with A.S. Kalashnikov, former member of the Military-Technical Committee of the Soviet Ministry of Defence, in Hines et al.,

Soviet Intentions, pp. 89–90.

27 Benjamin Weiser, *Colonel Ryszard Kuklinski: A Secret Life* (New York: PublicAffairs, 2004), p. 245. Robert Gates, director of central intelligence 1991–93, described Kuklinski as 'one of the most important CIA sources of information on the Soviet military'. Robert Gates, *From the Shadows* (New York: Simon and Schuster, 1996), p. 238.

28 Aleksandr G. Savel'yev and Nikolay N. Detinov, *The Big Five: Arms Control Decision-Making in the Soviet Union* (Westport, CT: Praeger, 1995), p. 57.

29 PFIAB report, p. 39.

30 See 'The Pershing Missile: Peace Through Strength', Lockheed Martin, http://www.lockheedmartin.co.uk/us/100years/stories/pershing.html; and 'General Dynamics/McDonnell Douglas BGM-109G Gryphon', National Museum of the US Air Force, 29 May 2015, http://www.nationalmuseum.af.mil/Visit/MuseumExhibits/FactSheets/Display/tabid/509/Article/196000/general-dynamicsmcdonnell-douglas-bgm-109g-gryphon.aspx.

31 It was this concern that led the Soviet leadership to order work on 'Dead Hand', a system that could automatically launch a retaliatory strike if the leadership could no longer do so. Far into the future there was the daunting possibility that the Strategic Defense Initiative would become a reality and nullify even the revenge of the dead. See Barrass, *The Great Cold War*, p. 281; and David E. Hoffman, *The Dead Hand* (New York: Random House, 2009).

32 Author interview with Markus Wolf, Prenden, 26 August 2005.

33 The information in this section on *Pershing* II is drawn from Steven T. Burns, *The History of the Pershing Missile Systems* (print on demand, 2014). Burns served with *Pershing* 1A units in Germany and was closely involved in the deployment there of *Pershing* IIs. I am grateful to him for his comments on my draft. See also Department of the Army, 'Pershing II Weapon System Operators Manual', June 1986, http://pershingmissile.org/pershingdocuments/manuals/tm%20 9-1425-386-10-1.pdf.

34 Cliff Lethbridge, 'PERSHING II Fact Sheet', http://spaceline.org/rocketsum/pershing-II.html.

35 Jonathan Haslam, *Near and Distant Neighbours: A New History of Soviet Intelligence* (Oxford: Oxford University Press, 2015), p. 234.

36 Burns, *The History of the Pershing Missile Systems*, p. 329.

37 Bernard Gwertzman, 'Soviet Dismissal Now Being Laid to a Policy Split', *New York Times*, 13 September 1984, http://www.nytimes.com/1984/09/13/world/soviet-dismissal-now-being-laid-to-a-policy-split.html.

38 Permanent Mission of the Russian Federation to the United Nations, 'On Presentation of the World Citizens Award to Stanislav Petrov', press release, 19 January 2006.

39 Viktor Yesin, quoted on *1983: The Brink of Apocalypse*.

40 Andrew and Gordievsky, *Comrade Kryuchkov's Instructions*, pp. 67–90.

41 *Ibid.*, pp. 69–81.

42 Gregory Pedlow, SHAPE Historian, 'Exercise Able Archer 83: Information from SHAPE Historical Files', 28 March 2013, http://nsarchive.

gwu.edu/NSAEBB/NSAEBB427/docs/6.a.%20Exercise%20Able%20Archer%20SHAPE%20March%202013%20NATO.pdf.

43 PFIAB report, p. 35.

44 Andrew and Gordievsky, *Comrade Kryuchkov's Instructions*, pp. 86–7.

45 *Ibid.*, pp. 87–8.

46 Rainer Rupp, quoted on *1983: The Brink of Apocalypse.*

47 Ted Bliss (chief of nuclear operations, *Able Archer*), quoted on *1983: The Brink of Apocalypse.*

48 Werner Grossman, *ibid.*

49 Yesin, background interview for *1983: The Brink of Apocalypse.*

50 PFIAB report, pp. 56 and 71–3. (Note that many items have been redacted.)

51 Viktor Yesin and Viktor Tkachenko, background interviews for *1983: The Brink of Apocalypse*, quoted in Barrass, *The Great Cold War*, p. 300.

52 Pedlow, 'Exercise Able Archer 83: Information from SHAPE Historical Files', pp. 1–2.

53 PFIAB Report, p. 74.

54 Yesin, background interview for *1983: The Brink of Apocalypse.*

55 Correspondence with Steven T. Burns, member of the *Pershing* II force, September–November 2016.

56 *Pravda* and *Izvestia*, 25 November 1983, p. 1.

57 *Ibid.*

58 Dmitry Ustinov quoted in Don Oberdorfer, *From the Cold War to the New Era* (Baltimore, MD: Johns Hopkins University Press, 1997), p. 69.

59 PFIAB report, p. 83.

60 Yesin, background interview for *1983: The Brink of Apocalypse.*

61 Director of Central Intelligence, 'Implications of Recent Soviet Military-Political Activities', Special National Intelligence Estimate 11-10-84JX, 18 May 1984, p. iii, https://www.cia.gov/library/readingroom/docs/19840518.pdf.

62 Barrass, *The Great Cold War*, p. 300. The US, however, had not seen a force-wide Soviet alert since the Second World War. PFIAB report, p. 13.

63 Gelii Batenin, interview in Hines et al., *Soviet Intentions*, p. 8. Author's italics.

64 Fischer, *Cold War Conundrum*, pp. 6–9.

65 PFIAB report, p. 36.

66 Robert Gates, background interview for *1983: The Brink of Apocalypse*, quoted in Barrass, *The Great Cold War*, p. 379.

67 Milton Beardon, quoted in Barrass, *The Great Cold War*, p. 379.

68 Barrass, *The Great Cold War*, pp. 405–6.

69 Gates, background interview for *1983: The Brink of Apocalypse.*

70 Author interview with Anatoly Chernyaev, Moscow, 27 February 2006.

Britain's Dangerous New Politics

Matthew Harries

An irony may be Britain's undoing. The country was asked a clear question ('Should the United Kingdom remain a member of the European Union or leave the European Union?') and gave a clear answer ('Leave'), and yet has no clear idea of what to do next. The process of leaving a union with which British politics, law and society has been intertwined for some 40 years is deeply complex. For one thing, the jilted party, the EU, must agree to the terms of separation, and do so in the two years allotted by Article 50 of the Lisbon Treaty, which Prime Minister Theresa May intends to invoke in the first quarter of 2017. But first, Britain must work out what it wants, and doing so is proving to be a bitter and divisive process.

The problem with the EU referendum was that, in distilling so many issues into a single choice, it meant that people with different and sometimes contradictory interests could unite around the opposing poles.[1] This is a normal feature of democratic elections: not everyone supports a candidate or party for the same reasons. But in an election, candidates and parties produce policy statements and manifestos. For the referendum on Scottish independence, the Holyrood government published a 670-page White Paper on the shape of an independent Scotland, with the Scottish National Party speaking as the overwhelming favourite to govern that future country.[2] In Britain's EU referendum, there was no such guide to the meaning of a vote to leave.

Matthew Harries is Managing Editor of *Survival*, and Research Fellow for Transatlantic Affairs at the IISS.

Survival | vol. 58 no. 6 | December 2016–January 2017 | pp. 31–42 DOI 10.1080/00396338.2016.1257177

The UK Independence Party (UKIP), though influential in some ways, remained a fringe concern. The campaign organisation given official recognition from the electoral commission, Vote Leave, was not a party, and produced no manifesto for negotiating Brexit save for a brief memo published eight days before the vote.[3] Prior to that, Vote Leave had offered promises about the supposedly beneficial effects of leaving the EU, and the supposedly detrimental effects of remaining. At least one of each category – 'We will be able to save £350 million a week', and 'Turkey is one of five new countries joining the EU' – was false.[4] To make things more complicated, Vote Leave was joined by the noisier and more radical Leave.eu, which had unsuccessfully campaigned for the electoral-commission designation. The net effect was that the Leave campaign as a whole was free to use whatever collection of arguments were tactically useful in winning the vote, whether or not they added up to a coherent position.

It did so ruthlessly. When the economic case for leaving the European Union appeared to be unsupportable, the Leave campaign shifted to a focus on controlling immigration.[5] Even here, there was room for incoherence: Leave campaigners, including Michael Gove (then the education secretary) and Boris Johnson (now foreign secretary) called for the introduction of an Australian-style points-based immigration system, even though Australia's per capita net immigration is higher than that of the UK.[6] Regardless, much as Donald Trump's early and relentless focus on immigration served as a rallying point for his campaign for the Republican presidential nomination in the United States, this was an issue around which Leave voters could gather. Polling prior to the referendum campaign had shown that hostility to immigration was one of the best predictors of support for leaving the EU; 79% of those in favour of leaving agreed with the proposition that immigration is bad for the British economy, for example, compared with 21% of those in favour of remaining.[7] The Leave campaign combined this energy with what were essentially spoiling tactics on the economic front – confronted with a list of British allies and domestic and global institutions opposed to Brexit, for example, Gove responded that 'people in this country have had enough of experts'[8] – and won a narrow, shocking but decisive victory.

Immigration rules

A tactical combination of arguments was good enough to win the referendum, but it will not work in negotiating its implementation. Restricting free movement of people from the EU will come at the cost of membership of the single market. There may be options for compromise – perhaps around individual sectors, such as financial services, or trading degrees of market access for degrees of limitations on immigration – but they will be partial, difficult to negotiate and messy to implement. This was recognised implicitly by various Leave figures in their mooting of various post-Brexit options – including arrangements similar to those of Norway, or alternatively the western Balkans – but no specific option was on the ballot paper. Choosing between these models is largely a matter of what other EU countries will tolerate, but it is also a matter of the UK government determining which among the public's competing priorities it considers most important.

It is likely that Theresa May will follow the model of the Leave campaign, and rank controlling immigration at the top of that list. Evidence of May's personal inclinations can be found in her speech to the 2015 Conservative Party conference – a notable break with the centrist tone struck at that conference by then-prime minister David Cameron and chancellor George Osbourne. May, home secretary from 2010 until becoming prime minister in 2016, claimed that immigration was depressing wages in low-paid jobs and forcing people out of work; asserted that, 'when immigration is too high, when the pace of change is too fast, it's impossible to build a cohesive society'; and concluded that 'there is no case, in the national interest, for immigration of the scale we have experienced over the last decade'.[9]

In 2013, a pilot project initiated by May's Home Office sent vans to seven London boroughs, all of which had large non-white populations, to drive around with billboards reading 'In the UK illegally? Go home or face arrest'. Even May's colleagues on the Conservative benches blanched at the spectacle. After considerable criticism (and a report that the vans had been responsible for only one self-deportation, as if the problem was merely one of efficiency), May conceded that they had been 'too blunt an instrument'.[10] Then, the vans were dismissed as crass, a co-option of the language of the far-right fringe. That might not be true today. In the days after the

Brexit vote, 'Go home' was sprayed onto the front of a Polish cultural centre in Hammersmith, and 'Pack your bags' was seen painted onto a shed in Newington Green.[11] A flood of anecdotes such as these was supported by data: in the following month, reported hate crimes in London rose by more than 50%.[12] Country-wide, reported hate crimes rose by 58% in the week after the vote, compared to the equivalent week the previous year, and remained 14% higher two months later.[13]

A change in national mood is hard to define. But Brexit certainly changed something. When UKIP leader Nigel Farage toasted the vote as a victory 'for ordinary people, a victory for decent people', it was not difficult to identify whom he meant. Immigration, Farage has previously said, has turned parts of Britain into something resembling 'a foreign land'. Any 'normal' person, he has asserted, 'would have a perfect right to be concerned if a group of Romanian people suddenly moved in next door'.[14] Four months after Farage's 'victory', the home secretary was proposing that companies declare how many foreigners they had hired; the international trade secretary was describing the legal status of EU residents in Britain as 'one of our main cards' in the negotiations to come; and the *Sun*, Britain's best-selling newspaper, was calling for child refugees to have their teeth examined to make sure they were really children (or, as the headline shouted, 'TELL US THE TOOTH').[15]

Newspaper headlines are not government policy. Nevertheless, in an increasingly hostile climate, the government is likely to make the imposition of limits on immigration a non-negotiable demand. In her first major speech on Brexit after becoming prime minister, May told the Conservative Party conference that, although talks with the EU would involve some give and take, 'we are not leaving the European Union only to give up control of immigration again'.[16] The opposition Labour Party, which even before the referendum was at risk of losing white working-class votes over the issue of immigration, may struggle to challenge this bottom line. Senior Labour figures, including those who campaigned strongly for the UK to remain in the EU, have already signalled their agreement with the emerging conventional wisdom: that the vote for Brexit was a vote to limit freedom of movement.[17]

Brexit and its discontents

If, by virtue of this conventional wisdom, full membership of the single market is unlikely, negotiating Brexit will be a complex task of determining the next best economic option. This may in itself be more than the civil service can cope with, and will have a knock-on effect on the rest of government. As a recent academic study put it, 'whether a machinery … focused on Brexit-related matters will be sufficiently agile to develop comprehensive policies to address purely domestic agendas is questionable'.[18] Brexit will dominate not just the workings of the bureaucracy, but likely much of British strategic thought, for several years to come. The economic and fiscal effects of leaving (or mostly leaving) the single market could yet be severe, and the conditions are ripe for a surge in public discontent. In these circumstances, an argument over whom to blame for Britain's struggles cannot be far away.

Luckily for the government, there is a natural candidate: the section of the population who voted to Remain, and who have expressed dismay at what has happened since. Because 2016 is the year of tedious portmanteaus, they are now the 'Bremoaners'.

On 6 October, the day after Theresa May's closing speech to the party conference, sterling hit a 31-year low against the dollar.[19] It fell further the following week, after a leak of Treasury documents predicting £66 billion in lost tax revenue from a hard Brexit.[20] Sterling's weakness was interpreted by financial reporters as a vote of no confidence in the government's plans, spurred by indications that the UK would be leaving the single market.[21] The focus of Brexit-supporting newspapers, however, lay elsewhere. 'Damn the unpatriotic Bremoaners and their plot to subvert the will of the British people', cried the cover of the *Daily Mail*, the UK's second-biggest daily newspaper.[22] 'TIME TO SILENCE EU EXIT WHINGERS', declared the *Daily Express*.[23] The gist of the critique was that pressure on the government to seek a soft Brexit, or to make the final deal subject to a second referendum, amounted to subversion of the popular mandate to leave the EU – and that the instigators of this pressure were threatening to wreck the success that Brexit would otherwise be. This argument would soon get sharper.

On 3 November, the High Court ruled that, as a matter of constitutional law, the government could not give notice of the UK's intention to leave the EU, under Article 50 of the Lisbon Treaty, without parliamentary approval.[24] It was not immediately clear what form a bill in Parliament on triggering Article 50 would have to take, nor was it clear whether MPs and Lords would risk angering Brexit supporters by preventing Article 50 from being triggered. If they were not willing to do so, their negotiating leverage in demanding concessions from the government – for example in seeking assurances related to the single market or the status of EU nationals in the UK – would be limited. Moreover, the government quickly announced that it would appeal the decision, and it is quite possible that the Supreme Court will overturn it.[25]

Yet if the practical implications of the decision were rather murky, its effects on British political discourse were immediate and troubling. The *Sun* put a picture of Gina Miller, the (Guyana-born and non-white) claimant in the Article 50 case, next to the subtitle 'Loaded foreign elite defy will of British voters'. The *Daily Mail* printed full-face photos of the three High Court judges above the headline 'ENEMIES OF THE PEOPLE'. The *Daily Telegraph*, Britain's best-selling broadsheet, did the same, with the line 'The judges versus the people'.[26] As *Times* journalist Matt Chorley put it, these were the kind of headlines 'usually reserved for terrorists, paedophiles and Tony Blair'.[27] Less amusingly, this language echoed the terrible nadir of the referendum campaign: the killing of MP Jo Cox by a man who, when charged with murder five days before the Brexit vote, gave his name as 'death to traitors, freedom for Britain'.[28]

Dismissing this reaction as mere tabloid rabble-rousing would be a mistake. For one thing, as journalist Andy Beckett has pointed out, newspapers, and especially tabloids, still help set the political agenda in an era of broadcast news: party leaders must ingratiate themselves with editors; politicians and issues are framed in phrases the length of a headline; and television journalists with airtime to fill are grateful, in the evening, for the chance to review the next day's papers. At the 2015 general election, newspaper readership provided a better indicator of party support than any other factor, and the effect is especially intense on the political right.[29] Moreover, it was neither just the press nor only fringe politicians who took this line on the verdict. Cabinet minister Sajid Javid said it was 'an attempt to frustrate the will of the British people and it is unacceptable', while former Conservative Party leader Iain Duncan Smith asserted that it was 'not the position of the courts to tell parliament or the Government how that process should work', and warned of a 'constitutional crisis'.[30]

The danger in such a climate lies in what politicians may choose to do with the public anger – spontaneous or otherwise – that is likely to develop as the difficult mechanics of Brexit proceed. The British constitution is unwritten, dependent on convention and not terribly well understood by its subjects. The UK Supreme Court, which will hear the government's Article 50 appeal, is only seven years old, and even among the politically informed, few Britons can name its members. As the practicalities of implementing the referendum result unfold, and a seemingly simple popular mandate confronts tricky legal and technocratic obstacles, politicians with a desire to further undermine trust in the political establishment have a golden opportunity to do so. Nigel Farage, for his part, has threatened to lead a 100,000-strong march on the Supreme Court at the start of the appeal hearing.[31]

The government's response to the press coverage of the Article 50 case amounted to a bland statement released two days after the verdict, and was received with widespread dismay. As Conservative MP and former attorney general Dominic Grieve put it, 'Irrespective of [the government's] own view on the decision of the court, it was its positive duty to support the judiciary in its work and the right of the applicants to obtain legal redress in the Queen's courts'.[32] Conservative MP (and barrister) Stephen Phillips resigned from Parliament, citing the government's 'failure to appreciate the constitutional necessity of properly consulting Parliament with regard to leaving the European Union'.[33] Yet if the reaction of May's government to the verdict shows a willingness to harness the power of anti-establishment resentment, that should not come as a great surprise. The prime minister has said that 'people in positions of power behave as though they have more in common with international elites than with the people down the road', and told the public that politicians and commentators 'find your patriotism distasteful, your concerns about immigration parochial'.[34]

What comes next? In conditions of such uncertainty, it is difficult to say. But there is now a somewhat greater incentive for May to call an early general election.[35] Her parliamentary majority is small, and her opponents are weak. Even without the Brexit challenge, Labour would have been in a perilous position. It has been wiped out in Scotland, it has a historically unpopular leader and it sits 16 points behind the Conservatives in the polls.[36] The party's situation is made worse by the fact that several pro-Remain Labour MPs represent constituencies that were strongly pro-Leave. May might wish to make them face an angry electorate, and seek an expanded majority in Parliament. With such a majority secured, May's task in gaining parliamentary approval for her negotiating strategy – should she legally require it – without making major concessions could become easier.

Whether May calls an election or not, the challenges she will face in negotiating with the EU will remain daunting. And Donald Trump's victory in the US presidential election makes the toxic climate in Britain especially dangerous. Neither the UK nor the rest of the EU can afford to waste time on an acrimonious divorce at a time of such strategic uncertainty. With a less reliable American partner, the major European states may have to take on more of the burden of protecting the liberal international order. This will require pragmatism and, crucially, a restored sense of European solidarity. It does not bode well that Britain's post-referendum politics have been so ugly, polarised and volatile.

Notes

1 On the implications of referendums for democratic decision-making, see Erik Jones, 'Brexit's Lessons for Democracy', *Survival*, vol. 58, no. 3, June–July 2016, pp. 41–9.

2 Scottish Government, 'Scotland's Future: Your Guide to an Independent Scotland', November 2013, http://www.gov.scot/resource/0043/00439021.pdf.

3 See http://www.voteleavetakecontrol.org/a_framework_for_taking_back_control_and_establishing_a_new_uk_eu_deal_after_23_june.html. The memo stated that 'Flexibility will be vital. There is no need to rush the process. The precise details and the exact timing of the final settlement will only be clear when the Prime Minister's new negotiating team engages and negotiations begin.'

4 For the Leave campaign's promises, see http://www.voteleavetakecontrol.org/why_vote_leave.html. The £350m-per-week figure did not include the EU's budget rebate to the UK, let alone considerations of reduced tax revenues in a Brexit-hit

economy. Meanwhile, Turkey is a candidate to join the EU, but it is a long way from meeting the criteria for membership (and as its membership would require approval by the European Council, European Parliament and national parliaments, it could not be achieved against the UK's wishes).

5 Nicholas Watt, 'EU Referendum: Vote Leave Focuses on Immigration', BBC News, 25 May 2016, http://www.bbc.co.uk/news/uk-politics-eu-referendum-36375492.

6 See Jonathan Lindsell, 'The Australian Points System Would Boost UK Migration', Civitas, 3 February 2015, http://civitas.org.uk/2015/02/03/the-australian-points-system-would-boost-uk-migration/; and Alan Travis, 'Brexiters Are Missing the Point of Australian-Style Immigration', *Guardian*, 1 June 2016, https://www.theguardian.com/uk-news/2016/jun/01/brexiters-missing-point-australian-style-immigration-conservatives.

7 Matthew Goodwin and Caitlin Milazzo, 'Britain, the European Union and the Referendum: What Drives Euroscepticism?', Chatham House, December 2015, p. 6, https://www.cer.org.uk/sites/default/files/bulletin_105_st_article1.pdf. See also Simon Tilford, 'Britain, Immigration and Brexit', CER Bulletin, no. 105, December 2015–January 2016, https://www.cer.org.uk/sites/default/files/bulletin_105_st_article1.pdf; and Matthew Harries, 'Brexit and Political Malpractice', *Survival*, vol. 58, no. 3, June–July 2016, p. 36.

8 Henry Mance, 'Britain Has Had Enough of Experts, Says Gove', *Financial Times*, 3 June 2016, https://www.ft.com/content/3be49734-29cb-11e6-83e4-abc22d5d108c.

9 Theresa May, speech to Conservative Party conference, 6 October 2015, http://www.independent.co.uk/news/uk/politics/theresa-may-s-speech-to-the-conservative-party-conference-in-full-a6681901.html.

10 Andrew Grice, 'Theresa May to Axe "Go Home" Vans After Pilot Scheme Deemed a Failure', *Independent*, 22 October 2013, http://www.independent.co.uk/news/uk/politics/theresa-may-to-axe-go-home-vans-after-pilot-scheme-deemed-a-failure-8896717.html.

11 Richard Watts and Kaya Comer-Schwartz, 'Islington Council Says "No to Hate Crime" in Emergency Motion', *Islington Gazette*, 1 July 2016, http://www.islingtongazette.co.uk/news/crime-court/islington_council_says_no_to_hate_crime_in_emergency_motion_1_4599670.

12 Hannah al-Othman, 'Brexit Hate Crimes: Reports Rise by More Than 50 Per Cent Since the EU Referendum', *Evening Standard*, 5 July 2016, http://www.standard.co.uk/news/crime/brexit-hate-crimes-reports-rise-by-more-than-50-per-cent-since-the-eu-referendum-a3288681.html.

13 Caroline Mortimer, 'Brexit Caused Lasting Rise in Hate Crime, New Figures Show', *Independent*, 8 September 2016, http://www.independent.co.uk/news/uk/crime/brexit-hate-crime-racism-eu-referendum-poland-islam-more-in-common-a7231836.html.

14 See Matthew Harries, 'Nigel Farage Hits the Trump Trail',

Politics and Strategy, 25 August 2016, http://www.iiss.org/en/politics%20and%20strategy/blogsections/2016-d1f9/august-bc9b/nigel-farage-hits-the-trump-trail-8cc5.

15 See Richard Ford, 'Firms Must List Foreign Workers', *Times*, 5 October 2016, http://www.thetimes.co.uk/article/firms-must-list-foreign-workers-gw20ndp5x; 'EU Nationals in UK "One of Our Main Cards" in Brexit Deal – Liam Fox', Sky News, 4 October 2016, http://news.sky.com/story/eu-nationals-in-uk-one-of-our-main-cards-in-brexit-deal-liam-fox-10605533; and Jack Royston and James Mills, 'TELL US THE TOOTH: MPs Demand Dental Tests of "Child" Migrants as Concerns Grow Over Ages of Asylum Kids Arriving in Britain Who Look Closer to 40', *Sun*, 18 October 2016, https://www.thesun.co.uk/news/2003927/mps-demand-dental-tests-of-child-migrants-as-concerns-grow-over-ages-of-asylum-kids-arriving-in-britain-who-look-closer-to-40/.

16 Theresa May, speech to Conservative Party conference, 2 October 2016, http://press.conservatives.com/post/151239411635/prime-minister-britain-after-brexit-a-vision-of.

17 See, for example, Olivia Bailey (ed.), 'Facing The Unknown: Building a Progressive Response to Brexit', Fabian Policy Report, September 2016, http://www.fabians.org.uk/wp-content/uploads/2016/09/FABJ4808_Europe_Report_130916_WEB_2.pdf.

18 The UK in a Changing Europe for Political Studies Association of the UK, 'Brexit and Beyond: How the United Kingdom Might Leave the European Union', November 2016, p. 19, http://ukandeu.ac.uk/wp-content/uploads/2016/11/Brexit-and-Beyond-how-the-UK-might-leave-the-EU.pdf. See also Lawrence Freedman, 'Brexit and the Law of Unintended Consequences', *Survival*, vol. 58, no. 3, p. 10.

19 Roger Blitz and Elaine Moore, 'Pound Hits 31-Year Low and Yields Rise on "Hard Brexit" Talk', *Financial Times*, 6 October 2016, https://www.ft.com/content/d13d3966-8bba-11e6-8aa5-f79f5696c731.

20 Sam Coates and Oliver Wright, 'Hard Brexit Could Cost £66bn a Year', *Times*, 11 October 2016, http://www.thetimes.co.uk/article/hard-brexit-could-cost-66bn-a-year-phpmh6fcd.

21 See, for example, Masayuki Kitano and Lisa Twaronite, 'Sterling Shaky After Diving to 31-Year Low on "Hard" Brexit Fears', Reuters, 7 October 2016, http://uk.reuters.com/article/global-forex-idUKL3N1CD0TP.

22 'Whingeing. Contemptuous. Unpatriotic. Damn the Bremoaners and Their Plot to Subvert the Will of the British People', *Daily Mail*, 12 October 2016, http://www.daily-mail.co.uk/debate/article-3833496/DAILY-MAIL-COMMENT-Whingeing-Contemptuous-Unpatriotic-Damn-Bremoaners-plot-subvert-British-people.html. The print edition's front page carried the headline described here, referring to the opinion piece which ran on an inside page.

23 David Maddox, 'Time to Silence EU Exit Whingers', *Daily Express*, 12 October 2016, p. 1.

24 For the full judgement, see *R*

(Miller) v. Secretary of State for Exiting the European Union, EWHC 2768 (Admin), 3 November 2016, https://www.judiciary.gov.uk/wp-content/uploads/2016/11/judgment-r-miller-v-secretary-of-state-for-exiting-the-eu-20161103.pdf.

25 For a strong critique of the government's approach to arguing the case, implying that a better approach at the Supreme Court could be successful, see John Finnis, 'Terminating Treaty-based UK Rights', Judicial Power Project, 26 October 2016, http://judicialpowerproject.org.uk/john-finnis-terminating-treaty-based-uk-rights/; and John Finnis, 'Terminating Treaty-based UK Rights: A Supplementary Note', UK Constitutional Law Association, 2 November 2016, https://ukconstitutionallaw.org/2016/11/02/john-finnis-terminating-treaty-based-uk-rights-a-supplementary-note/.

26 See Claire Phipps, 'British Newspapers React to Judges' Brexit Ruling: "Enemies of the People"', *Guardian*, 4 November 2016, https://www.theguardian.com/politics/2016/nov/04/enemies-of-the-people-british-newspapers-react-judges-brexit-ruling.

27 Matt Chorley, 'Remainers' Plotting Could Trigger a Decisive Mandate for May', *Times*, 4 November 2016, http://www.thetimes.co.uk/edition/news/remainers-plotting-could-trigger-a-decisive-mandate-for-may-62ssmkgrk.

28 'Jo Cox MP Death: Thomas Mair in Court on Murder Charge', BBC News, 18 June 2016, http://www.bbc.co.uk/news/uk-36567005.

29 Andy Beckett, 'Revenge of the Tabloids', *Guardian*, 27 October 2016, https://www.theguardian.com/media/2016/oct/27/revenge-of-the-tabloids-brexit-dacre-murdoch.

30 See 'Brexit Case "Attempt to Block Will of People" Says Sajid Javid', BBC News, 4 November 2016, http://www.bbc.co.uk/news/uk-politics-37866411; and Laura Hughes, 'Prospect of Early General Election Increases After High Court Rules Government Cannot Trigger Article 50 Without Parliamentary Approval', *Telegraph*, 3 November 2016, http://www.telegraph.co.uk/news/2016/11/03/high-court-to-rule-on-brexit-legal-battle-and-theresa-mays-decis/.

31 Christopher Hope, 'Farage to Lead 100,000-Strong March on Supreme Court on Day of Historic Brexit Court Hearing', *Telegraph*, 6 November 2016, http://www.telegraph.co.uk/news/2016/11/06/nigel-farage-to-lead-100000-strong-march-on-supreme-court-on-day/.

32 Dominic Grieve, 'On the Brexit Court Ruling, Our Government Fuels the View That Politicians Act Without Principle', *New Statesman*, 7 November 2016, http://www.newstatesman.com/politics/staggers/2016/11/brexit-court-ruling-our-government-fuels-view-politicians-act-without.

33 'Stephen Phillips: I Can't Live With Being Called a Conservative', Guido Fawkes, 4 November 2016, http://order-order.com/2016/11/04/stephen-phillips-cant-live-called-conservative/.

34 Theresa May, speech to Conservative Party conference, 5 October 2016, http://www.telegraph.co.uk/news/2016/10/05/theresa-mays-conference-speech-in-full/.

35 Assuming she is able to do so – another subject of constitutional dispute after the passage of the 2010 Fixed-Term Parliaments Act. See 'Reality Check: Could Theresa May Call an Early Election?', BBC News, 4 November 2016, http://www.bbc.co.uk/news/uk-politics-37876851.

36 ICM–Guardian poll, October 2016, https://www.icmunlimited.com/wp-content/uploads/2016/11/2016_oct2_guardian.pdf.

Clinton, Trump and the Catholic Church

Massimo Franco

The 2016 US presidential election was uncomfortable for the Vatican and the American bishops. The Holy See has seldom faced two candidates for the White House who were both, in different ways, so at odds with its values and geopolitical vision.

The problems with each candidate had little to do with their ostensible religious affiliations (Donald Trump is a Presbyterian, Hillary Clinton a Methodist). The Catholic vote, once viewed as a homogeneous bloc, no longer exists as such in the United States or elsewhere. Since 1972, a majority of US Catholics have voted for the winning candidate, and anti-Catholicism is largely a thing of the past.

Rather, Clinton is viewed by the Pope's inner circle, and by almost all American bishops, as a 'beacon of secular culture and ideology', as one influential cardinal put it.[1] She represents a long cultural battle between the Democratic Party and the Catholic hierarchy on abortion, gay rights and the role of women. Disputes between Vatican representatives and Hillary Clinton at conferences in Cairo in 1994 and in Beijing in 1995, the first on population and development, the second on the role of women, permanently scarred their relationship. Furthermore, during the Pope's September 2015 visit to the US, the papal entourage noticed that Hillary failed to show up for so much as a quick hello. That episode was viewed as confirmation of a cold relationship.

Massimo Franco is a political columnist for the Italian leading daily *Corriere della Sera* and an expert on Italian politics and Vatican foreign policy. He recently released an updated edition of his book *Imperi Paralleli* (Il Saggiatore, 2016), published in English under the title *Parallel Empires: The Vatican and the United States – Two Centuries of Alliance and Conflict*.

Survival | vol. 58 no. 6 | December 2016–January 2017 | pp. 43–47 DOI 10.1080/00396338.2016.1257178

Adding to the awkwardness was the treatment received by Clinton's Democratic rival, Bernie Sanders. Not only was Sanders invited to speak at a conference in the Vatican City organised by the Pontifical Academy of Social Sciences, but he also had an ostensibly accidental meeting with Pope Francis at 6am in front of Casa Santa Marta, the papal residence inside the Vatican, while Francis was heading to the airport. Although the Pope himself explained that he had bumped into Sanders by chance, the meeting was a political and diplomatic gaffe that could only serve to strain relations between the Holy See and the Clintons.[2] 'They'll make us pay a price for that. We don't know how and when, but it will happen', a Vatican official very close to the Pope admitted afterwards.[3]

I refer to the Clintons, plural, since the relationship between Hillary's husband Bill Clinton and the Vatican has also been marred by a long history of tensions and misunderstandings, dating back to his presidency. The former president's struggle with Pope John Paul II on issues such as abortion played out in public. More recently, Bill Clinton twice attempted, in the last 18 months or so, to get a private meeting with Pope Francis at Casa Santa Marta, and twice received a courteous but firm refusal. He could only be admitted, the Vatican explained, to the kiss-the-hand ceremony in St Peter's Square, along with other dignitaries.[4] Apparently, Vatican protocol does not allow for any other procedure.

Another Clinton in the White House will be problematic for the Church. Certainly, it will be problematic for US bishops, who fear the passage of more laws promoting a secular vision of American society after a long struggle with outgoing president Barack Obama over the Obamacare mandate for contraceptive care. The fact that Hillary is considered a hawk on foreign policy and believed to favour an assertive approach to issues such as Syria and Russia could make things worse, causing tensions with Vatican diplomats and the Latin American pontiff himself. For Francis, the Russian Federation and President Vladimir Putin personally are effectively allies in the struggle to defend Christian minorities from persecution at the hands of the Islamic State in places like Syria. Furthermore, Putin – who does nothing to hide his influence over Patriarch Kirill in Moscow – is key to a dialogue between the Vatican and the Orthodox Church.

The Pope is well aware of the limitations of this Russian connection. When I asked him whether there had been a kind of strategic convergence with Russia on the Middle East, Francis interrupted me and stressed that, although they have some goals in common, Russia's agenda is different from the Holy See's. He added that, when dealing with Moscow, one must never forget that Russian blood always carries with it drops of its past empire. He was referring, I believe, not to the Soviet Union but to tsarism.[5]

A vision of unity

The differences between the Vatican and Republican presidential candidate Donald Trump were starker, of course. These became public in February 2016, when Trump accused Francis of being an agent of the Mexican government regarding immigration. Trump's evidence was a trip by Francis to the border between Mexico and the United States, where he had celebrated a Mass on Mexican territory and repeated that bridges, not walls, should be built to unite rather than divide people. 'Whoever thinks that walls and not bridges are to be built is not a Christian', he said.[6] As an Italian cardinal observed afterwards, 'nobody knows what remained in Trump's soul after those words, so unusual for Vatican diplomacy'.[7]

The Pope's remarks in Mexico reflected his broader fear that Trump might become the champion of a kind of xenophobic Internationale – a beacon of racism, white supremacy and an exclusive version of Christianity that could attract many conservative Catholics as well. Such a phenomenon is already on the rise throughout Europe, where populist forces are gaining strength. The peculiarity of the present situation lies not in a growing number of racists, but rather that demagogues such as Trump are extending their reach beyond their natural bases, finding a sympathetic ear among disillusioned people who are neither racist nor anti-Islamic. The prospect that the United States might elect a president who is openly against immigration, particularly from Latin America, and who conflates Islam and jihadist terror, was a nightmare for an Argentinian pontiff struggling to improve relations between North and South America, and who has sought to convince conservative Catholics that Islam and terrorism are two different things.

A cultural battle is being fought which may appear to be focused on Trump but which was already well under way inside the Catholic world. An alliance between European populism and Trump's racism might prove devastating. That is why, even with the US election decided, the Holy See is concerned about the potential long-term effects of the campaign: an America bitterly divided over its fundamental values, with xenophobic and secular positions having both been radicalised.

The problem is made worse by the Pope's inclusive, and intermittently disorienting, interpretation of Catholic doctrine on issues such as gay rights and the status of divorced people within the Church. In many Western dioceses, his words have been met with confusion, and in some cases have been quietly disputed or even rejected. His recent selection of 17 cardinals of whom only five, clearly selected for the symbolic value of their profiles, were from Europe has confirmed suspicions about his enduring lack of confidence in European leadership. It is a cultural divide: to a Latin American Francis, the old continent is past its prime, secular and out of step with his idea of a Catholic Church rooted in the peripheries of the world. Western hegemony does not figure in his vision of the future.[8]

Instead, the Pope is the major proponent of what has been called the 'diplomacy of mercy'. He envisions a foreign policy for the Holy See that aims at 'direct and fluid relationships with superpowers, without joining a preordained network of alliances and influence'. There is a refusal 'to divide the world between victims and executioners'.[9]

It is easy to see the difficulties involved in selling such an approach to portions of the Western world that are frightened and horrified by the murderous terrorism of groups such as ISIS, and to Catholics who view economic instability, immigration and terrorism as threats to be defended against. Francis is still hugely popular, but he is swimming against the tide. That tide might be strongest in the United States.

In March 2013, the United States, along with much of the world, was startled by the conclave that transformed Jorge Mario Bergoglio into Pope Francis. Now, it is the Vatican's turn to determine what the contest between Clinton and Trump means to the Holy See, and to the world.

Notes

1 Quoted in Massimo Franco, *Imperi Paralleli* [Parallel Empires] (Milan: Il Saggiatore, 2016), p. 309.

2 Nicole Gaudiano and Jayne O'Donnell, 'Pope Francis Calls Sanders Meeting "Polite", Not Politics', *USA Today*, 20 April 2016, http://www.usatoday.com/story/news/world/2016/04/16/bernie-sanders-met-pope-francis/83118290/.

3 Franco, *Imperi Paralleli*, p. 308.

4 Massimo Franco, 'La laica Hillary o Trump l'estremo? Francesco è per il male minore' [Secular Hillary or Trump the Extremist? Francis Is for the Lesser Evil], *Corriere della Sera*, 6 March 2016, http://www.corriere.it/esteri/16_marzo_07/vaticano-laica-hillary-o-trump-l-estremo-francesco-il-male-minore-034c9f58-e3de-11e5-aa1e-c06fd7dc1288.shtml.

5 Massimo Franco, 'Il mio abbraccio ai fratelli ortodossi' [I Embrace My Orthodox Brothers – Conversation with Pope Francis], *Corriere della Sera*, 8 February 2016, pp. 1–3.

6 Stefania Falasca, 'Il Papa: alzare muri non è da cristiani' [Building Walls Up is Not Christian], *Avvenire*, 19 February 2016, pp. 1–5.

7 Confidential conversation with the author, 1 July 2016.

8 See Massimo Franco, 'A Latin American Pope in the United States', *Survival*, vol. 57, no. 6, December 2015–January 2016, pp. 69–75.

9 Antonio Spadaro, 'La misericordia come processo politico' [Mercy as a Political Process], *La Civiltà cattolica*, 13 February 2016, pp. 209–26.

Noteworthy

510 million
Total population of the EU single market

3.5 million
Population of the Belgian region of Wallonia, which was able to delay a trade deal between the EU and Canada[1]

Korean drama

'Ms Choi effectively told the president to do this and do that. There was nothing the president could decide alone.'

Lee Seong-han, a former employee of Choi Soon-sil, the long-time friend of South Korean President Park Geun-hye who has been accused of abusing her ties to the president, told a local newspaper that Choi called Park 'sister' and had her own team of advisers to assist with government decisions. Choi's father, Choi Tae-min, a cult-like religious-group leader often compared to Rasputin, is said to have had considerable influence over Park as a young politician, a role many say his daughter assumed following his death in 1994.[2]

'Please forgive me. I committed a sin that deserves death.'

Choi Soon-sil makes a ritualised apology at the Seoul prosecutor's building.[3]

A lot to talk about

'I believe we now have a glorious opportunity: we can pass our laws and set our taxes entirely according to the needs of the UK economy.'

British Foreign Minister Boris Johnson assesses the future of a post-Brexit UK.[4]

'I've committed to Theresa [May] that we will consult closely with her as she and her government move forward on Brexit negotiations to make sure we don't see adverse effects in our trading and commercial relationship … But first things first. The first task is figuring out what Brexit means with respect to Europe.'

President Barack Obama comments on US priorities in relation to the UK and Europe post-Brexit.[5]

'The V4 countries will be uncompromising. Unless we feel a guarantee that these people [living and working in Britain] are equal, we will veto any agreement between the EU and Britain.'

Robert Fico, Slovakia's prime minister, speaks on behalf of the V4, or Visegrad group – Hungary, Poland, the Czech Republic and Slovakia – the day after an informal EU leaders' meeting in Bratislava.[6]

'I want a mature, co-operative relationship with our European partners. I recognise the scale of the challenge ahead. I am sure there will be difficult moments. It will require some give and take.'

British Prime Minister Theresa May comments on her first EU summit, at which EU leaders gave her limited time to speak about Brexit.[7]

'It is going to be rough going … but what she said is OK. It's a good foundation on which to continue to work with Great Britain.'

German Chancellor Angela Merkel comments on May's speech in Brussels.[8]

Survival | vol. 58 no. 6 | December 2016–January 2017 | pp. 48–50 DOI 10.1080/00396338.2016.1257179

Wishful thinking?

'There is a sense that modern conflict is ordained to be only as small and as short term as we want to afford.'

Richard Barrons, who retired in April 2016 as commander of Britain's joint forces command, outlines his concerns about the readiness of the UK military in a memo addressed to Defence Secretary Michael Fallon.[9]

Tragedy in Aleppo

'There are only three parties that fly in Syria: the coalition, the Russians, and the Syrian regime. It was not the coalition.'

Pentagon spokesman Capt. Jeff Davis denies any coalition involvement in an airstrike that destroyed a UN aid convoy in Syria on 19 September 2016.[10]

'We are considering, with resentment and indignation, attempts by some foreign curators of rebel units and terrorists in Syria to put the blame for the incident on the Russian and Syrian air forces.'

The Russian Foreign Ministry denies reports that the aid convoy was hit by a Russian airstrike.[11]

'Aleppo is to Syria what Sarajevo was to Bosnia, or what Guernica was to the Spanish war.'

François Delattre, French ambassador to the UN, condemns the bombing of Aleppo during an emergency session of the Security Council on 25 September 2016.[12]

'All of the tombs are filled.'

Mr Shekho, an aid worker with the White Helmets in Syria, notes that residents of opposition-held territory in Aleppo, Syria are running out of places to bury their dead.[13]

Unfinished business

'This is the first day of the state of Israel without Shimon Peres.'

Israeli Prime Minister Benjamin Netanyahu opens a special cabinet meeting on 28 September 2016.[14]

'Sometimes people ask me, "What is the greatest achievement you have reached in your lifetime or that you will reach in the future?" So I reply that there was a great painter named Mordecai Ardon, who was asked which picture was the most beautiful he had ever painted. Ardon replied, "The picture I will paint tomorrow." That is also my answer.'

Shimon Peres, speaking in 2011.[15]

12

Number of political parties that contested Iceland's October 2016 parliamentary elections

260,000

Size of Iceland's electorate[16]

Picture this

'I don't know any jihadis. My customers are the Alderley Edge crowd, footballers' wives and those sort of people.'

British flower seller Stephen Leyland reacts to the discovery that his picture had appeared in Rumiyah *magazine, which is published by the Islamic State, alongside a call to commit violence against ordinary British citizens.*[17]

Sources

1 Jennifer Rankin, 'EU–Canada Trade Deal in Crisis as Canadian Minister Walks Out', *Guardian*, 22 October 2016, https://www.theguardian.com/world/2016/oct/21/eu-canada-ceta-trade-deal-meltdown-canadian-minister-walks-out.

2 Choe Sang-hun, 'A Presidential Friendship Has Many South Koreans Crying Foul', *New York Times*, 27 October 2016, http://www.nytimes.com/2016/10/28/world/asia/south-korea-choi-soon-sil.html.

3 'Woman at Centre of South Korean Row Says She "Deserves Death"', Associated Press, 31 October 2016, https://www.theguardian.com/world/2016/oct/31/south-korean-scandal-choi-soon-sil-pleads-for-forgiveness.

4 'Brexit: Boris Johnson Says UK Not "Turning Its Back" on Europe', BBC, 24 June 2016, http://www.bbc.co.uk/news/uk-politics-eu-referendum-36618734.

5 Rowena Mason, 'Theresa May Refuses to Commit to Brexit Pledges on Immigration and NHS', *Guardian*, 5 September 2016, http://www.theguardian.com/politics/2016/sep/04/theresa-may-refuses-to-guarantee-brexit-pledges-on-immigration-and-nhs.

6 Jon Henley, 'EU States Set to Veto Any Brexit Deal Threatening Free Movement', *Guardian*, 17 September 2016, https://www.theguardian.com/politics/2016/sep/17/eastern-bloc-countries-will-uphold-citizens-rights-to-live-in-uk.

7 Theresa May, 'European Council October 2016: Prime Minister's Press Statement', Brussels, 21 October 2016, https://www.gov.uk/government/speeches/european-council-october-2016-prime-ministers-press-statement.

8 Joe Murphy, 'Theresa May Sidelined at EU Summit as PM Faces Brexit Snub and Silence', *Evening Standard*, 21 October 2016, http://www.standard.co.uk/news/politics/theresa-may-sidelined-at-eu-summit-as-pm-faces-brexit-snub-and-silence-a3375446.html.

9 Jamie Grierson, 'UK Armed Forces "Could Not Withstand Attack by Major Power Like Russia"', *Guardian*, 17 September 2016, https://www.theguardian.com/uk-news/2016/sep/17/uk-armed-forces-could-not-withstand-attack-by-major-power-like-russia.

10 Julian Borger and Spencer Ackerman, 'Ban Ki-moon Condemns "Apparently Deliberate" Syria Aid Convoy Attack', *Guardian*, 20 September 2016, https://www.theguardian.com/world/2016/sep/20/un-suspends-all-aid-convoy-movements-in-syria-after-airstrike.

11 'Moscow Says Attempts to Accuse Russia of Aid Convoy Attack are "Outrageous"', Tass, 20 September 2016, http://tass.com/politics/901114.

12 Julian Borger and Kareem Shaheen, 'Russia Accused of War Crimes in Syria at UN Security Council Session', *Guardian*, 26 September 2016, https://www.theguardian.com/world/2016/sep/25/russia-accused-war-crimes-syria-un-security-council-aleppo.

13 Megan Specia and Yara Bishara, 'A Bomb Shatters an Aleppo Building, and Videos Capture the Rescue Minute by Minute', *New York Times*, 28 September 2016, http://www.nytimes.com/2016/09/29/world/middleeast/aleppo-syria-airstrike-rescuers.html.

14 Peter Baker and Isabel Kershner, 'Obama and Bill Clinton to Travel to Honor Shimon Peres', *New York Times*, 28 September 2016, http://www.nytimes.com/2016/09/28/world/middleeast/world-leaders-react-to-shimon-peres.html.

15 'Shimon Peres's Reflections on War, Peace and Life', *New York Times*, 27 September 2016, http://www.nytimes.com/interactive/2016/09/28/world/middleeast/shimon-peres-quotes.html.

16 Kimiko de Freytas-Tamura, 'Iceland's Prime Minister Resigns, After Pirate Party Makes Strong Gains', *New York Times*, 30 October 2016, http://www.nytimes.com/2016/10/31/world/europe/icelands-prime-minister-resigns-after-pirate-party-makes-strong-gains.html.

17 David Brown et al., 'Death to Cheshire Florist, Declares ISIS Magazine', *Times*, 7 September 2016, http://www.thetimes.co.uk/edition/news/death-to-cheshire-florist-declares-isis-magazine-5xvh6w53t.

A Strong and Balanced Approach to Russia

Ash Carter

There were many symbolic ends to the Cold War. The most obvious was when the Berlin Wall was opened and East and West Germany reunified. But for many, the Cold War ended on more personal terms: a divided family reunited; a young student free to study abroad; citizens casting their first vote in a truly democratic election.

My career began in the Cold War, working on missile defence, space weapons, nuclear command, control, communications and intelligence, and MX missile basing (the last of which is now long forgotten, thankfully). For me, the Cold War ended when the last nuclear weapon rolled out of Ukraine. I was there in Pervomaysk that summer day in 1996 when sunflowers were planted where a Soviet missile silo once stood. As someone who dedicated the early part of his career to understanding – only in theoretical terms, happily – the technical capabilities and terrible nature of nuclear weapons, this moment demonstrated that, despite humanity's need for security, a country could choose to give up nuclear weapons.

That moment also demonstrated that the world could change: standing in Pervomaysk with US secretary of defense Bill Perry and Ukrainian minister of defence Valeriy Shmarov was their Russian counterpart, defence minister Pavel Grachev. The denuclearisation of Ukraine, after all, was the result of multilateral diplomacy carried out by far-sighted American, NATO, Ukrainian and, of course, Russian statesmen, dedicated to overcoming old geopolitical divisions and making a better world together. For those

Ash Carter is United States Secretary of Defense.

Survival | vol. 58 no. 6 | December 2016–January 2017 | pp. 51–62 DOI 10.1080/00396338.2016.1257180

of us who had laboured throughout those decades of confrontation, this cooperation was a tangible demonstration of the benefits of the Cold War's quiet end and the new world's promise.

In the years following the end of the Cold War, the United States, Russia and many other nations often came together to contribute to a principled international order. States worked together to address pressing international security challenges, including the threat of loose nuclear material in the former Soviet Union and the horrors of ethnic cleansing in the Balkans. Although our relationship with Russia was never perfect, it was broadly constructive. Our two countries contributed meaningfully and consistently to the peace and stability of the post-Cold War world.

But in recent years, unfortunately, Russia's behaviour has changed. Rather than working to support the international order, Russia appears intent on spoiling decades of progress. Russia's aggression in Ukraine and Georgia, its contributions to the tragedy in Syria, its attacks in cyberspace, its violation of arms-control treaties and other international agreements, and, above all, its nuclear sabre-rattling, are not what the world expects of a responsible power in the twenty-first century. Rather, these actions undermine global security and erode an international order that has been of mutual benefit.

Russia and the international order

Given Russia's aggressive and provocative behaviour in recent years, it can be easy to forget that it was not always so. Russia's contributions to the post-Cold War world did not end with sunflowers in Pervomaysk; in fact, the United States, Russia, NATO and other elements of the international community often worked together in the years after the Cold War in pursuit of a principled international order characterised by security cooperation, the peaceful resolution of disputes and the right of nations to make their own security and political choices, free from coercion and intimidation.

At the end of the Cold War, the United States and its allies and partners deliberately sought a productive relationship with Russia. Rather than isolate Russia or treat it like a defeated power, we supported the Russian people and their institutions during the difficult days of transition following the collapse of the Soviet Union, and worked consistently to integrate Russia into the international community.

This included bringing Russia into important international institutions such as the World Trade Organization (WTO), the Group of Eight (G8) and the Asia-Pacific Economic Cooperation (APEC) forum, and establishing the NATO–Russia Council. The United States cooperated with institutions such as the International Monetary Fund (IMF) to encourage economic liberalisation in Russia, and to shore up Russia's economy amid the difficult transition from communism. And we sought Russian cooperation and support in meeting the pressing international issues of the day, in the belief that the international order would be stronger, and our actions would be more effective, if we worked together.

Russia was in large part a willing partner. In 1995, Russia joined the United States and NATO allies to bring peace to war-torn Bosnia and to end the ethnic cleansing of vulnerable populations there. Under the Cooperative Threat Reduction programme, the United States and Russia cooperated to dismantle thousands of missiles and deactivate thousands of nuclear warheads, all to mitigate the danger that nuclear components might fall into the wrong hands. Russia also constructively participated in the denuclearisation of Ukraine, Belarus and Kazakhstan, and together with the United States reduced the nuclear threat through arms-control agreements such as START I, the 2002 Moscow Treaty and New START. In addition, Russia worked with the United States and the international community to address the challenges posed by North Korea's nuclear and missile provocations, Iran's nuclear programme and other threats to global security.

It was no surprise that Russia, with its proven capabilities, unique and proud history, and dynamic people, should have been a leading voice and dedicated contributor to the post-Cold War international system. And yet, despite the progress we made together in the aftermath of the Cold War, Russia's recent actions have sought to undo the principled order that it supported, helped solidify and benefited from.

In Europe, Russia is behaving in a manner reminiscent of the nineteenth century, rather than one befitting a responsible member of the modern international community. Russia has used its political, economic and military power to undermine the sovereignty and territorial integrity of Georgia and Ukraine, flouting accepted international principles such as non-aggression as well as violating international agreements to which Russia is a party, such as the UN Charter, the Helsinki Accords, the NATO–Russia Founding Act and others. It has sought to intimidate Sweden, Finland and the Baltic states, as well as other countries along Russia's periphery, and used an array of tactics, including disinformation campaigns, in an effort to foster division in Europe and undermine institutions such as NATO and the European Union.

Russian actors have also violated important international principles in other areas, notably in cyberspace. As Director of National Intelligence James Clapper and Secretary of Homeland Security Jeh Johnson recently stated, the United States Intelligence Community is confident that the Russian government directed the recent hacking of emails from American political organisations, including the Democratic National Committee. With these hacks and subsequent disclosures, Russia evidently intends to interfere with the US electoral process – the essence of our democracy – and attempt to undermine Americans' faith in our own political process and institutions. This is not a unique occurrence: Russia has repeatedly used similar tactics across Europe.

Russia has made the situation in Syria more dangerous

Meanwhile, in Syria, Russia has been throwing gasoline on an already devastating fire, prolonging a civil war that fuels the very extremism Russia claims to oppose. Russia entered the Syrian tragedy saying it wanted to counter the Islamic State (also known as ISIS or ISIL) and end the civil war, which is the source of so much suffering, through a political transition. So far, Russia, with its support for the regime of Bashar al-Assad, has made the situation in Syria more dangerous, violent and intractable, prolonging the conflict and increasing loss of life. Russia has pursued a military campaign that has further isolated it from the international community, and employed tactics with unspeakable civilian costs. Russia is responsible for the humanitarian catastrophe it has helped fuel, and it must decide if it wants to influence the Syrian regime towards a political transition that ends the civil war, or continue to inflict suffering on the Syrian people, with untold consequences. Despite our differences, the Defense Department de-conflicts its coalition operations in Syria with Russia through a professional military-to-military channel, which is active every day.

Alongside this troubling behaviour, Russia has also been aggressively modernising its warfighting doctrine, as well as its military capabilities, and is using those capabilities in provocative and destabilising ways. Russia has carried out major military exercises on the borders of its neighbours, reintroducing large-scale no-notice or snap exercises. These actions appear designed to sow fear and intimidation among the countries on Russia's periphery, and to evade existing transparency requirements, pursuant to the Vienna Document, for what constitute the largest exercises in Europe in over 20 years. Its aircraft have repeatedly and consistently violated the airspace of countries around the periphery of Europe. Its personnel have conducted unwarranted and unsafe intercepts of US and NATO ships and aircraft operating in international waters and international airspace, violating principles of due regard. And, through the new Russian approach to warfare, often referred to as 'hybrid warfare', it is conducting information-warfare campaigns with military and non-military means to destabilise a number of countries and to infringe upon their sovereignty.

Finally, and most disturbing of all, Russia is behaving irresponsibly and aggressively with respect to nuclear weapons. Russia has long been a nuclear power, but Moscow's recent sabre-rattling, combined with its building of new nuclear-weapons systems, raises serious questions about its leaders' commitment to strategic stability, their regard for the long-established abhorrence of brandishing nuclear weapons as tools of intimidation, and whether they respect the profound caution that Cold War-era leaders showed with respect to using nuclear weapons. We see this in Russian leaders' dangerous statements about using nuclear weapons in a potential war to deter or prevent us from coming to the aid of our European allies.[1] We saw it when Russia recently pulled out of a nuclear agreement, the Plutonium Management and Disposition Agreement, without warning, and when it undermines long-standing nuclear accords, including the Intermediate-Range Nuclear Forces (INF) Treaty, where it remains in violation of its obligations not to possess, produce or flight-test a ground-launched cruise missile with a range capability of 500 to 5,000 kilometres, or to possess or produce launchers of such missiles.[2]

As it does all of this, Russia appears driven by misguided ambitions and misplaced fear. Russia wants to be considered, understandably, as the important power it is. Russia's history is indeed rich, and one of which its people should be proud. But in recent years, some in Moscow and the Kremlin have reinterpreted that history and used it to fuel grandiose visions rather than the power and prestige they deserve. Unfortunately, Russia's tendency is to pursue the sense of international respect its leaders believe it is owed by undercutting the work and contributions of others, rather than by creating or making any positive contributions of its own. It sows instability rather than cultivating stability. It lashes out, alleging that it fears for its own safety and future, even though no nation – neither the United States nor any other state – seeks to defeat it or constrain its potential. Just the opposite; the United States and many in the international community have expressed an interest in working more closely with Russia.

The Pentagon's new playbook

In the face of Russia's aggressive behaviour, the United States will ensure that Russia cannot drag the US and the international community back to a darker past, while seeking to preserve the possibility that we can move forward again together into a brighter and more cooperative future.

The United States does not seek a new cold war with Russia, let alone a hot war. We do not seek an enemy in Russia; rather, we have long sought a peaceful relationship. But no one – neither in Moscow nor anywhere else – should forget that the United States will defend its allies, the principled international order and the positive future that order affords all of us. We will counter attempts to undermine our collective security. And we will not ignore attempts to interfere with our democratic processes.

In response to Russia's behaviour, the United States is taking a strong and balanced approach to address its actions and deter its aggression. We will take the steps required to protect and to strengthen ourselves, our allies and partners, and the principled international order against Russia's aggression and coercion, while also preserving bilateral cooperation where interests align.

America's initial response to Russia's recent behaviour has included economic, diplomatic and military steps. Economically, the United States and our European partners have used modern, targeted sanctions in response to Russia's aggression in Ukraine and illegal attempted annexation of Crimea. The United States and its partners have taken a number of diplomatic measures as well, including temporarily removing Russia from the G8 group of nations. This sent the message that Russian behaviour is unacceptable, and we have rallied a broad coalition of nations in support.

The Department of Defense has been taking steps in military terms as well. The DoD is not simply reprising the twentieth-century playbook used to contain Soviet ambitions during the Cold War, because that playbook is an imperfect match for the Russian challenge of today. Rather, we are responding to new threats by leveraging America's unique strengths, along with those of its allies and partners, in new and creative ways. We are adapting and innovating to meet new challenges such as cyber threats and hybrid warfare, to integrate our conventional and nuclear deterrence, and to adjust our military posture and presence in Europe to be more agile and quicker in responding to the threats that Russia poses.

Following this initial response, the United States is preparing for a longer-term situation of tension and military competition with Russia. Since the end of the Cold War, the transatlantic community has not had to prioritise deterrence against Russia. Unfortunately, we do now. As a result, the United States is adapting its deterrence posture in Europe, emphasising higher-impact approaches such as rotating forces into Europe, the prepositioning of armour and large-scale exercises throughout the Alliance. Our defence budget for fiscal year 2017 includes $3.4 billion for our European Reassurance Initiative, more than quadruple what we allocated this last year.[3] That will allow us to rotate an armoured-brigade combat team into Europe on a persistent basis, and to preposition another armoured brigade's equipment to be used by American troops flown into Europe, in addition to the two brigades the United States already has stationed in Europe.

The United States continues to invest in military exercises with allies and partners to demonstrate resolve and build resilience, while enhancing inter-operability. In 2016 alone, for example, the United States will have conducted or participated in at least 175 exercises and events in the Baltic states, including 139 US events (15 in Estonia, 79 in Latvia and 45 in Lithuania) and 36 NATO, national and multinational exercises, events or activities.[4] We expect this frequency to continue in 2017. One example demonstrates the size and scope of this effort: the US military participated this spring in *Exercise Anakonda 16*, a joint exercise in Poland that included more than 20 countries and more than 25,000 participants, to deepen US and NATO habits of cooperation with allies and partners.

In the face of Russia's recent actions, the Defense Department is also updating and refining its contingency and operational plans, including ways to overcome emerging threats, such as cyber attacks, anti-satellite weapons and anti-access/area-denial systems. The Defense Department also continues to embark on a force-wide, all-service transition from an era focused on counter-insurgency operations to an era focused on the full spectrum of military operations. To do so, we are reinvigorating our training across the services to return to full-spectrum readiness, building in modularity, thinking more about simultaneity, and injecting agility and flexibility into our processes.

Innovative concepts and innovative capabilities go hand in hand. This year's Defense Department budget funds important new technologies that, when coupled with revised operational concepts, will ensure the United States can deter, and if necessary win, a high-end conventional fight in an anti-access/area-denial environment across all domains and warfighting areas, not just sea and air and land, but also in cyber, electronic warfare and in space. We are investing in the technologies that are most relevant to countering Russia, including new unmanned systems, enhanced ground-based air and missile defences, new long-range anti-ship weapons, the long-range strike bomber, and also innovation in technologies such as the electromagnetic railgun, lasers and new systems for electronic warfare, space and cyberspace.

The United States is also investing to modernise its nuclear deterrent, which is critical in light of Russia's nuclear sabre-rattling. Nuclear weapons play a key role in reinforcing deterrence, ensuring strategic stability and limiting escalation should conflict occur. Accordingly, the United States plans to invest $108bn over the next five years to sustain and recapitalise the nuclear force and associated strategic command, control, communications and intelligence systems, ranging from increased funding for manpower, equipment, vehicles and maintenance to technological efforts that will help sustain our nuclear forces, and more.[5] Additionally, our budget also fully funds the first stages of our plans to ensure that the capabilities required to sustain nuclear deterrence do not become obsolete. This includes building replacements for the *Ohio*-class ballistic-missile submarines; keeping strategic bombers effective in the face of more advanced air-defence systems, in part by replacing ageing air-launched cruise missiles with a more effective long-range stand-off weapon; replacing old intercontinental ballistic missiles (ICBMs) with new ones that will be less expensive to maintain; and replacing F-16s in the dual-capable aircraft fleet with stealthy F-35s and the B61-12 gravity bomb. And, in the face of a renewed nuclear challenge from Russia, the department will take the steps necessary to ensure that America's nuclear deterrent remains safe, secure and reliable.

Investing in and adapting the NATO Alliance

The United States is not alone in this effort. For more than 67 years, NATO has been the quintessential example of nations working together to respond to security challenges. And as it was during the Cold War, NATO will be critical to the security of the transatlantic community in the face of new and renewed threats. Some thought NATO would grow irrelevant after the Cold War. But it proved useful in many ways in the following decades, including by shaping the militaries of new democracies, including Kosovo and Afghanistan.

Today, the transatlantic community faces challenges very different from those of past decades. In the east, Russia is acting aggressively and advancing new forms of hybrid warfare. On the southern flank, the continuing refugee crisis is pressuring domestic institutions, and returning foreign fighters present real security threats. And further abroad, the transatlantic community faces threats in Afghanistan and with ISIL and other terror groups.

The Defense Department is helping NATO grow stronger, more agile and more adaptive so it can meet and overcome these new challenges, and nowhere are these efforts more important than in meeting the threat posed by Russia. Given increased Russian submarine activity in the North Atlantic, we are working with our allies to build towards a continuous arc of highly capable maritime-patrol aircraft operating over the Greenland–Iceland–United Kingdom gap. We are making delivery of Europe's first stealthy F-35 Joint Strike Fighter aircraft to the UK. And given Russia's use of hybrid warfare – exemplified by the so-called 'little green men' in Ukraine – we are investing in additional rotational presence of US Special Operations Forces, which are particularly well equipped to help allies respond to such activities.

The United States is also encouraging its NATO allies to do more, and to use a new playbook as well. We are enhancing our capability to respond to crises wherever they occur. The Very High Readiness Joint Task Force can deploy Alliance forces on 48 hours' notice from multiple locations in Europe to any crisis on NATO territory. This is a real innovation, involving commitments from many members of the Alliance to respond to crises involving Russia or any other challenge.

The Alliance is also coming together to strengthen deterrence. At the July 2016 NATO Summit in Warsaw, four NATO countries, including the United States, announced that they will each deploy a battalion to one of the three Baltic nations and to Poland. The United States will lead the battalion in Poland, the United Kingdom will do so in Estonia, Canada will lead one in Latvia and Germany will do the same in Lithuania.

Meanwhile, NATO and its members are also providing support to partners such as Ukraine and Georgia, both of which have seen their sovereignty and territorial integrity violated by Russia. We are helping them to strengthen their capabilities for national defence, improve their ability to work with NATO and reform their defence institutions. These efforts took major steps forward in Warsaw, when NATO endorsed a Comprehensive Assistance Package for Ukraine and a substantial assistance package for Georgia, and with the signing of the US–Ukraine Partner Concept in September 2016 and the Memorandum on Deepening the Defense and Security Partnership with Georgia in July 2016.

Through all of these measures, we are building stronger networked security, enhancing our collective deterrence and defence posture, and demonstrating that Russia's behaviour does not undermine our alliances and partnerships but rather drives us closer together. Together with NATO allies and partners, the United States is helping stand up for the international principles and norms Russia has been violating.

To ensure NATO continues to do so, all NATO countries must accept their fair share of security responsibility to each other; and as allies we all must choose to invest in, develop and field new capabilities. NATO countries have made some progress on spending: since the 2%-of-GDP pledge made at the 2014 Wales summit, the vast majority of allies have stopped making cuts, and most allies have also committed to at least small increases in defence budgets; but there is still more to do. No country can retrench and escape responsibility for confronting the threats that face us all. NATO has to be more capable – and able, if necessary, to meet two or more challenges at once.

Holding the door open

Given significant disagreements, the prospects for deep US–Russia cooperation are limited at present. But Russia is simply too big, too powerful and potentially too dangerous to be ignored or fully isolated. Accordingly, even as we take the steps outlined above, and even as we prepare for longer-term competition with Russia, we will work to preserve cooperation on issues where our interests align, and hold the door open to renewed partnership in the future.

The United States will continue to cooperate with Russia when it is willing and when its interests coincide with the interests of the international community. We have seen what good we can do when we work together, whether in producing the Joint Comprehensive Plan of Action on Iran's nuclear programme, which has effectively cut off Iran's pathways to the fissile material for a nuclear bomb, or responding to North Korea's nuclear and missile provocations. The United States will continue to hold out the possibility that Russia will assume the role of respected partner, not one that is isolated and going backwards, as it is today. People in the United States and Europe, and indeed in Russia, all benefited from our past collaboration. But it is up to the Kremlin to decide which path to take.

After all, we do not desire a hostile relationship with Russia; we want Russia to again become the partner with which we cooperated so fruitfully during the years after the Cold War. I remember that time personally. As the United States and Russia, and our policymakers, were blinking in the bright light of peaceful possibilities, we chose to work with common purpose. At Pervomaysk 21 years ago, in countering nuclear proliferation, when bringing peace to the Balkans, and more, we stood together and helped build a better world and a stronger international order. Our collaboration demonstrates that the United States and Russia can work together for the benefit of both our countries and the rest of the international community. Someday I hope to see that spirit rekindled.

Notes

1 See, for example, Tom Parfitt, 'Vladimir Putin Issues New "Large Nuclear Power" Warning to West', *Telegraph*, 16 October 2014, http://www.telegraph.co.uk/news/worldnews/vladimir-putin/11167192/Vladimir-Putin-issues-new-large-nuclear-power-warning-to-West.html; and 'Russia Threatens to Aim Nuclear Missiles at Denmark Ships If It Joins NATO Shield', Reuters, 22 March 2015, http://www.reuters.com/article/us-denmark-russia-idUSKBN0MI0ML20150322.

2 US Department of State, 'Adherence to and Compliance with Arms Control, Nonproliferation, and Disarmament Agreements and Commitments', July 2014, p. 8, http://www.state.gov/documents/organization/230108.pdf.

3 Secretary of Defense Ash Carter, '2017 Defense Posture Statement: Taking the Long View, Investing for the Future', US Department of Defense, February 2016, p. 18, http://www.defense.gov/Portals/1/Documents/pubs/2017DODPOSTURE_FINAL_MAR17UpdatePage4_WEB.PDF.

4 General Curtis M. Scaparrotti, remarks at the 2016 US Strategic Command Deterrence Symposium, La Vista, NE, 7 July 2016, https://www.stratcom.mil/speeches/2016/178/2016_Deterrence_Symposium.

5 Carter, '2017 Defense Posture Statement', p. 39.

America, Europe and the Necessary Geopolitics of Trade

Jennifer M. Harris

As America begins to look past a bruising two-year presidential election, one thing all sides agree on is the need for a starkly different approach to trade. Donald Trump became the first Republican nominee in nearly a century to embrace higher tariffs as a general defence against low-cost imports. None of the leading contenders for the nomination of either major party – neither Ted Cruz nor Donald Trump, nor Hillary Clinton nor Bernie Sanders – supported President Barack Obama's signature trade pact, the Trans-Pacific Partnership (TPP).

Polling data indicates that Americans' overall support for foreign trade is higher than it has been for more than 20 years – a trend that has been evident since 2008.[1] This sentiment does not extend to TPP, however: polls tend to show more Americans opposing TPP than supporting it, with evidence that the gap widens the more voters learn about the deal.[2] US congressional leaders, perhaps sensing the electorate's mood, have indicated they will not put TPP to a vote in the remaining weeks of the current legislative session.[3]

This suggests that trade is not dead – but it does need some basic rethinking. Recent debates over TPP highlight just how far the work of trade liberalisation has sprawled beyond tariff reduction – indeed, much of the work of eliminating tariffs was accomplished in the 1990s – toward a far larger set of economic variables (including regulation, tax, anti-trust and more) affecting a country's overall economic health and competitiveness. Yet, despite this shift

Jennifer M. Harris is Senior Fellow at the Council on Foreign Relations in New York, and co-author, with Robert D. Blackwill, of *War by Other Means: Geoeconomics and Statecraft* (Harvard University Press, 2016), from which a portion of this article is derived.

Survival | vol. 58 no. 6 | December 2016–January 2017 | pp. 63–92 DOI 10.1080/00396338.2016.1257181

in purpose and ever-expanding scope, the US playbook for trade liberalisation, enshrined in TPP and other recent 'gold standard' agreements, remains little changed. Trade agreements today may be longer, but the design choices and the processes behind them remain largely as they were in the North American Free Trade Agreement (NAFTA), concluded in 1994.[4]

Even as the widespread revolt against TPP creates near-term headwinds for the deal's passage, it has also opened up space to step back and reconsider the basic aims of US trade agreements, and how best to achieve them. There are hints that this more foundational debate may be ripening: Hillary Clinton has called for 'a fundamental rethink of how we approach trade deals going forward'.[5]

Thus far, attention remains fixed solely on the economic dimensions of this rebuilding. Exactly how US foreign-policy interests will or should figure into any new trade blueprint has been largely overlooked (the primary exception perhaps being Clinton herself, who has said that future US trade agreements must 'create … jobs, raise wages and advance [US] national security').[6]

This oversight is not especially new. It stems from a broader discomfort in Washington with using trade as a tool of foreign policy. Certainly, few US policymakers would deny that trade carries important geopolitical consequences. And leaders are quick to invoke foreign-policy arguments to sell trade deals domestically. President Obama has consistently framed TPP as a referendum on US leadership in Asia, just as General Colin Powell, then-chairman of the joint chiefs of staff, told Congress in 1990 that NAFTA was 'essential for the security of the long U.S. border with Mexico'.[7] Yet, they rarely prioritise foreign-policy considerations when actually designing and negotiating these agreements. In fact, quite the opposite: to quote international-relations theorist Robert Gilpin:

> this separation of international economics and politics (that is, of diplomacy and the market) … has correctly remained a goal of American foreign policy … The American goal of depoliticized and non-discriminatory trade not only fostered an unprecedented era of world commerce but it greatly reinforced the harmony of interest among the United States and its allies.[8]

Hardly unique to trade, this push to purge geopolitics from international economic institutions more broadly has been a fixture of US foreign policy throughout the post-Cold War period. It is borne of what Walter Russell Mead once lamented as a 'habitual American tendency to approach international politics through some combination of moral and legal ideas', as if geopolitics were not a present and driving force.[9] Ironically, it is precisely America's hyper-dominance since the Cold War that has fed this tendency. The lack of any credible geopolitical rival has liberated American, and to some degree European, policymakers to construct a reality in which moral and legal questions trump geopolitical ones.[10]

They may have only managed to convince themselves. Rising powers such as Russia and China appear less, not more, convinced than they were a decade ago. Meanwhile, after decades defending these institutions as neutral and politics-free, Western leaders have painted a picture that is not terribly attractive to their own domestic publics. Growing proportions of Americans and Europeans no longer believe these institutions to be consistent with national interests.[11] In fact, the US-led global economic order – from 1945 to the present – has always been far more dependent on a certain constellation of geopolitical circumstances than Western leaders prefer to acknowledge. The efforts of US and EU policymakers to rid the global economic order of geopolitics appear to be failing abroad and backfiring at home, undermining the very structures they aim to protect.

It is worth considering a course correction. Returning trade policy to a more overt foreign-policy exercise could generate two kinds of benefits. Most obviously, it could advance important US foreign-policy interests – and because foreign-policy concerns often resonate as high priorities for the electorate, including them within negotiations could potentially make for more saleable agreements.

Equally important, reintroducing geopolitics could also help restore the political legitimacy of the entire project of trade liberalisation and the multilateral trading system. The rising backlash to globalisation seen in America and Europe pits nationalism and national interests against multilateralism and international institutions. The Brexit debate, populist surges of far-right parties across the EU, and similar strands of left- and right-leaning populism re-emerging in the US all share a sense that international rules are in tension with sovereignty and national interests, and a push to liberate national interests accordingly. From Front National leader Marine Le Pen's assertions that 'the European Union has become a prison of peoples', to Trump's pledge that, with his ascension to the White House, 'the era of economic surrender will finally be over', multilateralism and economic globalisation are cast as the problem against which national interests must take aim.[12]

Restoring the legitimacy of the trading system is a long-term project that goes well beyond the scope of this article. Certainly, much of the backlash is rooted in economic grievances – a warranted scepticism that the trading system, with its steady diet of continued globalisation and liberalisation, is still delivering economically for the US and Europe.[13] But economic interests are only one component of national interests. Geopolitical interests matter, too. And in a world where major trading partners are no longer also geopolitical allies, whatever benefits the US or EU in economic terms can no longer be assumed to do so in geopolitical terms as well. Both kinds of benefits will need to be proven. Indeed, history teaches us that attempts at liberalisation divorced from a geopolitical logic are unlikely to succeed.

If Washington or Brussels were inclined toward such a course correction, neither would need to look far. The current negotiations on the Transatlantic Trade and Investment Partnership (TTIP), launched by the US and EU in 2013, offer as good an opportunity as either side could hope to find. Because TTIP is still under active negotiation, it remains malleable (more so than TPP, which was finalised in October 2015). It also appears increasingly untenable in its current form: anti-trade sentiment blowing across the United States and Europe, together with the UK's decision to exit the EU, insert existential doubts over the deal's fate. In effect, if TTIP is to succeed, it will not do so without extensive changes. Some of these will be straightforward. Hillary Clinton has staked out clear opposition to investor–state dispute settlement (a system through which individual companies can sue countries for alleged discriminatory practices), suggesting that Washington and Brussels could find themselves debating simply how best to jettison the provision. Other adjustments will be less straightforward, as American and

European publics – and, increasingly, leaders – seem clear in their desire to rewrite not just the rules but the very aims of trade. And while this will, and should, be a largely economic exercise, both sides could seize the opportunity of a reimagined TTIP to advance shared strategic interests.

TTIP may or may not pass – and not all policymakers will agree on how best to include foreign-policy aims, or indeed whether to include them at all. Still, both TTIP and the possibility of including various foreign-policy objectives are ultimately vehicles for thinking differently about trade. Only by interrogating the boundaries of what is considered plausible and reasonable to include within a trade agreement can we hope to begin shifting those boundaries to better reflect national interests.

The historical exceptionalism of Bretton Woods

Nation-states, no less than individuals, are prone to editing history to suit their desired self-images.[14] For the United States, a prime example is trade policy since the Cold War, where successive generations of policymakers have approached the task of liberalising trade just as Robert Gilpin described: as a legal, rules-based endeavour, to be pursued in its own right and justified by a near-moral belief in the intrinsic superiority of liberal–capitalist values and free markets. The problem with this account is not merely that it is a historical fiction, but that it is an increasingly dangerous one.

For all of their efforts to distance trade policy from geopolitical considerations, US trade negotiators are working in a realm that, from its foundations on up, reflects American power. Harvard economist Dani Rodrik once put it this way: imagine it was Bangladesh or Mozambique that designed our global trading system. What are the chances that this system would look like the one in effect today?[15] It is precisely because the system works to America's advantage that US policymakers have all the more incentive to hold up as neutral the disciplines of trade, investment and finance that together comprise this rules-based order, vesting them with the authority of Rawlsian impartiality, blind to the national interests of any one country over any other.

This internal logic, though, only goes so far. However fiercely the United States (or any country) sees fit to bind itself to this rules-based order, and however much international authority and logic such a system might assume, there is no escaping that the WTO's authority and legitimacy, or that of any trade arrangement, still ultimately remains derivative – loaned to it by member states, and therefore subject to the same underlying geopolitical realities governing how these states interact in other realms.

This is precisely why genuinely multilateral trading arrangements like the current one – global, open trading and investment regimes, where geopolitics are kept at bay – are historically few and short-lived.[16] The 1786 Anglo-French commercial treaty, arguably the first such effort, lasted until the French Revolution. The Anti-Corn Law League (1838–46) freed the United Kingdom, secure in its considerable lead over competitors, to pursue liberalisation for a few decades, until the rise of Germany and the United States forced a British retreat to an imperial-preference scheme. It was only with the post-war General Agreement on Tariffs and Trade (GATT) that a broad, rules-based system for trade liberalisation was born. The GATT succeeded where previous attempts failed precisely because it rested on, and reinforced, a grand geopolitical alignment between the US and Western Europe. This is what Yale Law Professor David Singh Grewal has called 'the enormous convenience' of the twentieth century – namely that America's leading trading partners were also military allies.[17]

Put differently, the modern rules-based trading system took root during the Cold War, at a time when the neoclassical logic of economic liberalisation largely aligned with the United States' geopolitical interests. In that conflict, America faced an adversary (in the Soviet Union) that was opposed to free trade, which meant that any gain for free trade anywhere was a gain for the Western world.[18] With the prescriptions of economic liberalisation and US geopolitical needs so closely aligned, the disciplinary tensions between neoclassical economics and foreign policy were momentarily resolved. 'Ah, how easy it must have been to do grand strategy in those days!', as Grewal has put it.[19]

As the Cold War wound down, Western neoclassical economic orthodoxy persisted, as did the resulting divides between foreign-policy strategists, still concerned with relative gains, and neoclassical economists, who focused on absolute gains and continued to favour globalisation and liberalisation. Beginning in the 1970s, and accelerating after the Cold War, US policymakers came to view freer trade and liberalised markets as ends to be pursued on their own terms and according to purely economic logic; markets were to be kept free of geopolitics.

For a time, it mattered little. America faced no serious strategic challenge that required re-evaluating the alignment between neoclassical ideas and US foreign-policy needs. Certainly, the globalisation and liberalisation of this period exposed America to serious economic competition – from Japan in the 1980s, for instance, or via NAFTA in the 1990s – yet, fierce as these economic contests were, they played out under the US security umbrella.

Today, when so much liberalisation and deepening of economic ties involves countries, such as China and Russia, which are not US allies, tensions between neoclassical economics and foreign policy are returning, newly sharpened. The US and Europe now face states, many of them rising powers, which have little problem using economics as an instrument of national power. The results sit uncomfortably with the tenets of neoclassical economics, which has difficulty accounting for the geopolitical aims of adversaries' economic policies.

Tensions between neoclassical economics and foreign policy are returning

What makes for good neoclassical economics, in other words, no longer necessarily makes for good geopolitics. Washington's approach to trade since the Cold War still assumes a convergence of economic and geopolitical interests, which, while true for the latter half of the twentieth century, can hardly be taken for granted today. It was Adam Smith, after all, who observed that simply because an action is beneficial for countries in economic terms, hardly makes it so from a geopolitical standpoint. According to Smith, 'the wealth of a neighbouring country' might be 'dangerous in war and politics' even though 'certainly advantageous in trade'.[20]

None of this is to imply that the US ought to abandon the current rules-based order. But it is to recall the advice of Adam Smith and other early liberal economists, as well as Keynes and his neoclassical contemporaries, who, in fashioning Bretton Woods, clearly saw themselves as situated within – indeed, guided by – prevailing realities of state power in all its aspects, and who saw dangers in illusions to the contrary. Advancing a vision of trade that is more overtly responsive to US national interests, both economic and strategic, implies a willingness to deepen trade and market ties with allies, because they are allies. It urges renewed attention to relative (not merely absolute) gains, especially in a period where the bulk of economic liberalisation is occurring between the US and Europe, on the one hand, and countries adversarial to the US and Europe, on the other. It suggests modesty about what can be achieved in genuinely multilateral, open forums, like the WTO, where geopolitics are kept at bay. And it argues for a renewed willingness to design trade agreements to advance foreign-policy and economic interests.

TTIP as a more robust foreign-policy tool

Many were hopeful that TTIP would serve as the ideal canvas for this kind of experimentation: an agreement, different in kind from previous agreements, designed to address economic and strategic issues alike. In launching negotiations in 2012, both sides indicated their desire to see TTIP do exactly this. The negotiating mandate explicitly instructed negotiators to use TTIP to address common challenges that reach beyond the traditional ambit of trade or investment.[21]

In part, leaders touted these differences as a way of managing expectations; prior to TTIP, neither side had attempted free-trade negotiations with a relative peer. Still, the initial appeal was geopolitics, as much as anything. Washington saw in TTIP a chance to lend centripetal force to the European idea – an important counterweight to the financial, refugee and terrorism-related crises threatening to pull the union apart. For Brussels, TTIP offered reassurance – a means of comforting European leaders that any US 'pivot' to Asia would not dampen transatlantic relations.

But conceding geopolitical motivations for TTIP does not amount to a concession that geopolitical considerations should shape the negotiations, or that the deal should be designed in order to serve geopolitical objectives. This distinction came into sharp relief in late 2012, when then-secretary of state Clinton argued the strategic case for launching TTIP, calling it a much-needed 'economic counterpart to what NATO represents on the security side'.[22] US trade officials voiced private disgruntlement at the time, complaining that couching trade policy in such naked state-power terms risked unduly politicising it.[23] Yet 18 months later, when Russian bullying in Ukraine and Eastern Europe became a rallying point for US and EU trade officials, leaders on both sides publicly championed TTIP with calls for, of all things, an 'economic NATO'.[24]

This sort of packaging often succeeds in garnering political support. Despite the fact that geopolitical considerations are not a guiding factor in TTIP negotiations, they nonetheless are frequently the lens through which Congress sees the deal. 'From a standpoint of national security, this agreement is important', one US senator explained, adding that he had opposed previous trade deals, but supported TTIP. 'The geopolitical concerns are what really put this over the edge for many of us.'[25] But invoking geopolitics to market a deal is one thing; incorporating specific geopolitical objectives into TTIP is another.

What would doing so actually entail? Take climate change, for instance. If climate change is indeed 'an urgent and growing threat to [US] national security', as the Obama administration warns,[26] one could imagine using TTIP to negotiate a set of climate provisions that not only outline a set of minimum standards (as with the environmental chapters of trade deals), but establish affirmative measures to help transition America and Europe to post-carbon economies. Or one could imagine using TTIP to develop explicit understandings around sanctions cooperation, perhaps avoiding the sort of protracted back-and-forth around European military sales to Russia that occurred during the Ukraine conflict.

Here, I consider three issue areas that, while not currently included within TTIP, could significantly advance US and EU foreign-policy interests if brought into the negotiations: curbing cyber attacks against private companies; strengthening European and global energy security; and increasing economic stability in the Middle East and North Africa. These examples are merely illustrative of the kinds of issues that could be addressed in TTIP.

Cyber

As the cyber sphere has evolved into a realm of full-blown geopolitical contest between states, the task of policing it – of articulating cyber norms for state behaviour, and imposing international legal and governance structures – has become one of Washington's most urgent and vexing foreign-policy challenges. Cyber intrusions cost America at least $100 billion annually (and likely more), inflicting what US officials have called 'material' damage to the country's economic health and consistently ranking among its top national-security concerns.[27] Beyond massive theft of intellectual property, cyber attacks provide foreign governments the means to bring down individual companies, erode entire economic sectors and compromise basic infrastructure, from electrical grids to banking systems and ballot boxes. Over time, all of this not only wears on bilateral relationships – such frictions are seen in Washington's relations with Moscow and Beijing, both frequently accused of state-sponsored cyber attacks against US targets – but it also undermines popular support for the open, integrated international economic order.[28]

Bilateral dealings with China have yielded some progress. Following the September 2015 US–China cyber accord, available evidence suggests that Chinese cyber attacks against private US targets have decreased in volume, but increased in sophistication.[29] Recourse via the WTO is similarly limited.[30] While the US and EU have pledged deeper coordination, launching the US–EU Cyber Dialogue in 2015, thus far these efforts remain limited to information sharing.

Unsurprisingly, some cyber experts are beginning to look to trade agreements, including TTIP, as potentially promising options.[31] Admittedly, for much of Washington's cyber agenda, the path to progress may not run through either Brussels or TTIP. Sharp differences between US and European approaches to data privacy make certain issues – information sharing between governments and IT companies, for instance – off-limits (although, after recent terror attacks in Europe, EU data-privacy views are beginning to shift closer to US views).[32] It will be necessary to confine cooperation to areas where both sides share similar legal and regulatory approaches. Cyber provisions in TTIP would also need to be flexible enough to keep pace with one of the world's fastest-changing policy landscapes – especially difficult over the longer time horizons inherent to trade agreements.

But at least one important area where the EU could prove a natural ally, and TTIP a natural fit, is in developing new defences against cyber attacks on private companies. Both sides are duly incentivised. Not only do the costs of cyber-enabled theft fall disproportionately on American and European firms, as the leading suppliers of technology-intensive goods and services, but such cooperation would also carry outsized benefits. Coordinated cyber measures between the US and EU could mitigate the first-mover penalties sometimes associated with remedies to cyber theft, as well as the whack-a-mole quality these remedies can assume (where exclusion from one market simply adjusts to other markets).

The costs of cyber theft fall on American and European firms

The most promising areas for cooperation fall into three broad categories. The first is updating existing trade legislation. While the US and EU both have laws to exclude pirated goods from their respective markets, US lawmakers last updated these laws decades ago, long before the internet existed. As part of modernising these statutes to better address cyber-enabled piracy, negotiators might consider granting mutual recognition so that any US or EU exclusion order (or any order involving cyber theft) would apply to both markets.[33]

The same logic extends to the pursuit of coordinated remedies for cyber attacks against US or EU firms. The US has long maintained a 'Special 301 Watch List' to identify countries with inadequate intellectual property regimes. Prepared annually by the United States trade representative, the watch list gives US officials enhanced powers to monitor intellectual-property infringements, authorising unilateral sanctions (also known as countervailing duties) where countries are found to violate a trade agreement or otherwise engage in unfair trade practices. A similar designation process for countries that fail to police cyber attacks against private US or EU targets – a Cyber 301 Watch List of sorts, administered jointly by

US and EU officials – could force governments to either shut down cyber attackers operating within their borders, or risk internalising the costs of these attacks.

Secondly, TTIP negotiators might consider creating new private rights of action that would better enable US or EU firms harmed by cyber attacks to bring claims against firms benefiting from the stolen data. In the US, lawmakers could amend the Economic Espionage Act (EEA) to provide a federal private right of action for trade-secrets theft – a proposal that cyber experts have urged for years.[34] A new EU directive on trade-secrets theft, unanimously adopted in 2016, provides EU officials with a similar basis for cooperation.[35] Remedies could range from coordinated penalties for purchasers of stolen intellectual property, to new requirements on US and EU companies to police supply chains, to measures limiting the contracting powers of foreign companies found to have committed (or routinely benefited from) cyber attacks against other companies. Where, for example, a company suffers a cyber attack that materially contributes to bankruptcy filings, the US and EU could agree to new provisions better enabling creditors to recover from any entity found to have directly benefited from the cyber attacks.

Finally, officials might also consider new sanctions measures within TTIP. Compared to potential trade-related and private remedies for cyber attacks (where cases could take years before any final judgment), coordinated sanctions could allow for swifter penalties against private companies knowingly benefiting from cyber attacks and governments sponsoring (or at least materially encouraging) them. New US–EU sanctions could, for example, target the ability of such companies to contract, thereby increasing their borrowing costs. The concept, loosely modelled on international-law principles of odious debt,[36] might work as follows: where any US or EU company suffers material economic damage from a competing firm arising from a cyber attack, parallel US–EU sanctions could designate future contracts of the offending company as unenforceable in US and EU courts.[37] Forced to lend to the offending company without legal protections, investors would demand higher premiums for any financing they provide, thereby increasing that company's borrowing costs.

Energy security

Although EU leaders have made little secret of their desire to see energy security included in TTIP – one EU commissioner suggested he could 'scarcely imagine TTIP without an energy chapter' – thus far, the idea has been mostly a cause looking for substance.[38] Brussels has yet to offer a clear picture of what such a chapter might include. Although it is so far not formally opposed, the US has expressed scepticism, insisting that, because the general provisions of an agreement would generally cover energy unless otherwise specified, an energy chapter would be redundant.[39] (Washington forgets, perhaps, that it has insisted on separate energy chapters in free-trade agreements with countries that are large oil exporters to the US.)

From Iranian nuclear ambitions, to climate change and Russian assertiveness, many of the United States' and EU's toughest foreign-policy challenges trace back to European and global energy-security needs. TTIP could help in at least three ways. Firstly, European leaders could use TTIP to clarify US export commitments, thereby solidifying US supply as a reliable fallback to Russian energy. For EU leaders, recourse to US liquefied natural gas (LNG) serves as part insurance policy, part negotiating clout in their dealings with Moscow; even the mere spectre of US LNG has already provided some EU states with important leverage. Take Lithuania, which recently used a proposal for a floating LNG import terminal to win a 25% discount from Russia's Gazprom.[40] Certain European countries, notably the Baltic states and Poland, appear increasingly willing to pay a premium for US LNG in order to lessen dependence on Russia. It was only in December 2015, however, that US lawmakers lifted a 40-year-old US crude-oil export ban. Mindful that what Congress lifts, it can just as easily reinstate, EU officials are eager to codify access to US crude exports not just as a matter of US domestic law, but of international obligation. The same is true for US natural gas. While current US law automatically grants export authorisation for LNG to any free-trade-agreement partner of the United States, EU officials would rather not rely on the whims of US law, preferring instead a legal requirement in TTIP guaranteeing EU access to US LNG supplies.

For the most part, these trades are not yet commercially viable. But what is commercially viable can quickly change, especially in energy markets.

Pessimism that energy provisions in TTIP could alter real-world energy patterns largely rests on doubts that Europe could ever compete with Asia on gas prices. These doubts are not warranted even in the near term – let alone over the longer horizons that free-trade agreements should prioritise. A glut of global supply between 2014 and 2016 has collapsed gas prices everywhere, shrinking the price premium that has long characterised Asian markets. Further, as East Asian countries source a growing share of their gas from Russia, the Middle East and Australia, the US could well become an increasingly natural supplier to Europe.[41]

Energy provisions in TTIP could also give US entities standing to oblige the EU to enforce its own rules. A main reason why the EU punches below its weight in its energy dealings with Russia is a failure to enforce those rules. So long as the EU remains a big, balkanised market, individual states will remain overly dependent on Russia for natural gas, all but guaranteeing Moscow's continued ability to wage pipeline politics in Europe. Enacted in 2011, the latest round of EU energy legislation sought to improve the functioning of the internal energy market, ostensibly obliging member states to grant third-party access to pipelines, eliminate destination clauses for gas supplies (ensuring unrestricted re-selling of gas on international markets), and unbundle certain large state-backed monopolies (in effect, separating energy supply and generation from the operation of transmission networks) – all measures that Gazprom and Russia fiercely oppose. Yet, EU implementation and enforcement of these laws has been lacklustre, with widespread non-compliance by several countries – including France and Germany – some five years on.[42]

Perhaps the strongest argument for including energy provisions in TTIP, however, is the opportunity to lay down global norms governing energy-security cooperation. These challenges are hardly new: the US has been fighting energy and commodities nationalisation globally since the formation of OPEC (often with Europe at the centre of this fight). But they are newly pressing, as China's interest in global energy governance grows. Because any chapter covering energy would presumably also cover natural resources, TTIP could include measures designed to limit the ability of countries to use commodity exports as a geopolitical weapon, as with

China's 2010 embargo on rare-earth exports to Japan amid rising tensions in the East China Sea. This could take a number of different forms, ranging from simply cultivating an explicit norm against geopolitically motivated commodity-export embargoes, to potentially specifying a process for levelling counter-sanctions. (Given the downstream havoc that Chinese commodity bans could wreak on US and EU supply chains, coordinated countervailing-duties measures may be one option worth exploring.)

Management of strategic oil reserves is another area where global cooperation lags well behind changing energy patterns. Comforted by the magnitude of US stocks, EU countries have long failed to maintain adequate reserves of their own. Yet as America's exposure to supply disruptions diminishes, so too should its interest in shouldering the burden of maintaining the bulk of global reserves. The time is ripe: Washington, just beginning efforts to overhaul (and likely downsize) the US strategic petroleum reserve, could use this as leverage to pressure Europe to increase the overall size and effectiveness of its own reserves (beyond size concerns, energy experts have long urged changes to the management and composition of EU reserves).[43]

Any progress between Washington and Brussels on strategic reserves could then form the basis for modernising the International Energy Agency (IEA). With the world's largest oil consumers now outside of the IEA framework, the IEA can no longer claim to speak for the world's leading consumer nations. Already the world's second-largest oil consumer, China recently surpassed Japan to become the world's second-largest holder of emergency oil stocks, behind the US.[44] With OECD countries now comprising less than 50% of global oil demand (down from 75% in the 1970s), IEA stocks no longer afford the global cover they once did.[45] If the IEA is to remain relevant, it will need to bring India and China into its membership ranks, and return its global coverage (that is, IEA-controlled stocks benchmarked to global oil consumption) back to historical baselines.

Economic stability in the Middle East and North Africa

In the weeks following the Arab Spring, Washington and Brussels each pledged ambitious trade and investment initiatives with the Middle East and North Africa (MENA) region, also promising to coordinate these efforts.[46]

Yet, six years on, underwhelming as progress has been on the United States' and EU's respective initiatives, coordination between them has fared even worse. Economic conditions in the MENA region, meanwhile, have only deteriorated further, compounding the region's security challenges.

The United States' decision to prioritise the economic roots of these uprisings was, in part, a diplomatic one. But it also made sense on the merits: with the average MENA country exporting at 30% of its potential, US officials knew that the region would likely not create the necessary jobs or GDP growth without substantially improving export performance (especially non-oil exports) and deepening integration into global supply chains.[47] They also knew the EU, as the leading destination for MENA non-oil exports, would be more central to any new trade vision for the region than would the United States.[48] But privately, these officials hesitated linking US plans too closely with those of the EU, concerned that Brussels would not move swiftly enough.[49] Even if this concern was warranted at the time, the United States' own lack of progress in the years since would seem to refute it.

Differences in rules of origin generate a web of compliance costs

For all of the EU's ongoing internal difficulties, Brussels is arguably a more capable, motivated partner on issues of MENA economic stability than at any point since the initial 2011 uprisings. While still facing a long recovery, the eurozone has cleared the most trying phases of financial crisis. And as against a current baseline of millions of refugees and migrants crossing into Europe, EU leaders may now look more favourably on ambitious proposals to stabilise the economies of MENA countries, especially if Brussels could convince the United States to share in the fiscal and political burdens.

Cooperation within TTIP could take a few different forms. The goal could be simply to rationalise as much of the EU's Euro–Mediterranean Partnership and the US MENA Trade and Investment Partnership (MENA-TIP) as possible. More ambitiously, both sides could use TTIP to negotiate a single model trade-and-investment agreement, tendered jointly by the US and EU, open to all comers in the MENA region which meet the criteria. In either scenario, the US and EU would begin by weaving together their respective bilateral free-trade agreements with MENA countries, harmonising these separate agreements wherever possible into a single, updated set of terms, which could then serve as the basis for negotiations between Washington, Brussels and participating MENA states.[50] Differences in the rules of origin across these various free-trade agreements generate a dizzying web of rules and added compliance costs for exporters, ultimately limiting intra- and inter-regional trade. Harmonising these diverging rules, even just across the deals involving the US and EU, would help integrate supply chains in MENA countries, a central requirement for increasing the region's overall competitiveness and non-oil exports.

Any joint US–EU trade vision for the region would need to overcome at least three kinds of challenges. The first is membership. Should US and EU officials seek to do more than harmonise existing efforts, embarking upon new liberalisation could raise delicate questions of delineating membership. One option could be an open-platform model, whereby the US and EU would promulgate a voluntary, region-wide framework open to any MENA country that meets certain standards (akin to TPP involving some, but not all, members of the Asia-Pacific Economic Cooperation forum).

Secondly, rather than pursuing trade liberalisation as an end in itself, negotiators would need to train their sights on a different kind of deal, motivated more by development and economic-integration aims. Especially for the US, the notion of tailoring the country's traditional, gold-standard free-trade-agreement template to goals other than the narrow removal of trade barriers would mark a significant policy shift, likely requiring at least modest institutional and bureaucratic changes to Washington's typical negotiating structure.

Finally, the arrangement would need to prove attractive to MENA governments. To incentivise participation, the US and EU could attach new designated lines of economic and technical assistance to help participating MENA countries achieve their own stated reform commitments (in areas such as infrastructure, trade-capacity-building, small-and-medium-sized-enterprise financing and governance, among others). Helpfully, a blueprint already exists. Developed by the Obama administration and pitched to Congress in 2013, the 'MENA incentive fund' proposed $770 million in new financing, a mixture of grants and loans, to support 'countries that are moving to undertake the democratic and economic reforms necessary to address citizens' demands and provide lasting stability in the region'.[51] Its timing, though, proved lousy. The $770m request came just as Congress became gridlocked in the worst budget fights in decades. And even had Congress obliged, this is a relatively small figure – certainly by Saudi or Emirati standards – and too modest, sceptics have argued, to incentivise meaningful reforms.[52] Still, with some adaptation (including increased funding), the concept offers a promising starting point for how the US and EU might incentivise MENA countries to join regional trade-harmonisation efforts.

It is not for lack of trying that the region has no real trade vision or architecture of its own. US and EU leaders have tried and failed independently for roughly five decades. But given the utter dearth of progress on a long-term economic vision for the MENA region, the US and EU also have little to lose in trying again (and especially in trying jointly, which would mark a first for both sides). Increasing MENA non-oil exports and intra-regional trade will require discrete intermediate steps and, most likely, a separable timeline from other portions of TTIP. As with options for cyber or energy-security negotiations, TTIP could simply incubate cooperation, which could eventually proceed independently. Negotiators might use TTIP simply to agree on a single set of rules of origin to govern existing US and EU trade deals in the MENA region, such that this template could serve as the basis for subsequent negotiations, spun off from TTIP, with MENA countries.

Challenges to using TTIP for foreign policy

To suggest that TTIP could become a more explicit – indeed, potentially quite valuable – foreign-policy tool is not to imply it would be easy or cost-free. Many of the thorniest questions would be issue-specific: how cyber provisions within TTIP might be insulated from data-privacy debates, for example, or whether there are any energy provisions within TTIP that would be both agreeable to Washington and desirable to Brussels. But beyond these challenges, the basic notion of prioritising foreign-policy aims raises three broad sets of concerns.

One worry is that fashioning trade deals into more explicit tools of foreign policy will make these deals trickier to negotiate. Introducing new objectives into TTIP would clearly add to the overall number of issues open for negotiation. But whether a larger set of negotiating objectives would make it more difficult to conclude agreements is a complicated empirical question. Game theory teaches that expanding the number of issues under consideration can often expedite negotiations, by enabling more issue linkage and widening the possible outcome sets that are satisfactory to all parties.[53]

A related objection is the slippery-slope argument: if foreign-policy interests become legitimate negotiating objectives, what is to prevent other widely recognised interests – the promotion of disability rights, wildlife conservation or the fight against global organised crime – from also becoming the subject of demands for inclusion? At what point does the purpose of a trade deal become so diluted as to lose all coherence? Presumably, the impetus for including these varied interests in trade negotiations is that trade deals are believed to be among the most enforceable and least dysfunctional species of international agreements. But if trade deals become a Christmas tree from which to hang all manner of issues, then wouldn't policymakers run the risk of making them as dysfunctional as other kinds of international agreements?

This is a non-trivial objection, but it proves too much, as it could just as easily apply to US trade deals in their present form. Trade agreements already run the gamut from intellectual property and regulatory harmonisation to environmental protection and labour rights. In addition, as the case studies above illustrate, we can use trade deals to advance foreign-policy *objectives* without significantly broadening the types of *topics* at the table. For example, adding a provision to TTIP that restricts Russia's use of geopolitically motivated tariffs would serve a foreign-policy objective while still focusing on a traditional trade-negotiation topic.

Another concern is forcing new trade-offs between economic and security objectives. Prioritising foreign-policy interests certainly could, in some cases, come at cost to US economic objectives. However, this is less true in the case of TTIP and deals like it, where the US is negotiating with a close ally which shares many of the same foreign-policy interests. Including foreign-policy aims as part of trade negotiations with geopolitical allies makes sense both because the upsides are greater (there is a greater likelihood of progress when negotiating foreign-policy issues with an ally as opposed to a non-ally) *and* because the downsides are lower (assuming the foreign-policy objective is one that both sides support, the risk of one side using it to force concessions diminishes – granting, of course, that intensity of preferences still matters, creating leverage for whichever side cares least).

Negotiating foreign-policy objectives with allies certainly helps, in other words. But even with non- or lukewarm allies, prioritising foreign-policy objectives in trade agreements can, at least in some cases, also support US economic interests. In the case of TPP, greater US emphasis on certain strategic interests – disciplining currency manipulation and state-owned enterprises (SOEs) as two examples – could have paid economic dividends as well.

TPP as a true geopolitical endeavour would have included currency disciplines and stronger SOE provisions. China routinely deploys its SOEs and its foreign-exchange reserves to win allies, punish adversaries and coerce those in between. Beyond their geopolitical value, currency and stronger SOE disciplines in TPP should interest Washington at least as much for economic reasons. A growing body of economic evidence finds steeper US economic losses (especially in manufacturing) from exposure to Chinese imports than previously realised, much of it attributable to Chinese currency manipulation and illegal subsidies benefiting Chinese SOEs.[54] Yet US officials resisted introducing currency disciplines in TPP, and settled for SOE standards in some respects weaker than those achieved in previous deals.[55]

Other, more principled objections involve a concern about unduly politicising the realm of trade. Perhaps for the United States, all things considered, upholding a neutral rules-based economic system – complete with maintaining a patina of geopolitics-free trade policy – remains the best strategy for maximising present US geopolitical objectives.[56] After all, the United States still supplies far more global public goods than any other country, including policing of the global commons. The rules-based system is in many ways meant to ease the cost of those tasks, and so the United States has more to lose if that system collapses on itself.

In practice, however, this argument suffers from two problems. The first is that it tends to imagine that the system's early benefits have continued unchanged and undiminished down to the present. This is not the case. However well this system performed as a US geopolitical asset in the decades following the Second World War, it is delivering less in the way of strategic returns as rising powers (often through naked geopolitical attempts of their own) undercut it.[57] China has already set up more than a dozen parallel structures designed to systematically realign the international economic order away from the United States and toward Beijing.[58]

This argument also suffers from a revealed-preferences problem. If indeed US policymakers were reluctant to introduce foreign-policy objectives into trade negotiations out of deliberate concern for the rules-based international economic system and the geopolitical value it holds, then one would expect to see US foreign policy expending duly significant political weight and energy maintaining that system. Not only is there no evidence of this sort of undertaking, but there is plenty of evidence of the converse: the US lagged in its contributions to the IMF for years, and Washington proved unwilling to spend even a fraction of the diplomatic muscle it routinely expends on security crises in the Middle East toward curbing China's plans for a multilateral alternative to the World Bank.

If anything, such categorical attempts to insulate the global trading system from geopolitics may do it more harm than good. Like all laws and institutions, the international economic order and the institutions charged with administering it must have some permeability to politics in order to evolve and adapt. In insulating them from the tactical impulses and demands of US geopolitical interests, the defenders of these institutions risk relegating them to irrelevance.

* * *

What, then, constitutes an acceptable foreign-policy use of trade? Five factors can help in deciding. The first is whether countries are bargaining among friends, as in TTIP. Introducing foreign-policy objectives into trade negotiations is likely to yield greater net value when negotiating with geopolitical allies. Secondly, when it comes to identifying acceptable foreign-policy uses of trade, Western policymakers will likely still pledge strict fidelity, warranted or not, to the current rules-based trading order. This means that any foreign-policy use of trade may need to appear at least neutral in its impacts on the multilateral trading system (and on US economic interests). Even working within this exacting standard, this leaves plenty more that trade deals, including TTIP, could do. Of the earlier cyber, MENA and energy-related proposals outlined here, all could arguably be structured to satisfy these parameters.

Third are the roles of public and policymaker perceptions. Measures such as cyber defences or currency manipulation could be worth including in US trade deals because they are seen as addressing problems that Americans rank as high concerns. Including these issues not only helps the democratic function of trade, it improves popular support for trade and trade deals. Similarly, policymaker perceptions of benefits can matter as much as or more than the benefits themselves. Recall the EU's insistence on an energy chapter within TTIP: even though the actual market benefits of enshrining EU access to US energy supplies within the deal may be negligible, the fact that EU policymakers believe it to be valuable could prove a moderately useful bargaining tool for US negotiators.

Next, for many policymakers, the fact that trade deals already cover all manner of issues is hardly grounds to worsen the problem. Using a trade negotiation to address a foreign-policy aim is likely to be less disruptive where policymakers can use established trade practices and concepts to fashion remedies.

Finally, it is worth considering what institutional changes all of this would require of the US government, after decades of deliberately purging geopolitics from trade. Even where it is conceptually possible for a trade deal to advance foreign-policy interests, the larger challenge may be in overcoming bureaucratic neglect and resistance. This touches on a problem that extends well beyond foreign policy. Modern US trade policy began with the relatively modest aim of liberalising tariffs, a goal it had largely accomplished by the late 1990s. One option would have been simply to declare victory. US trade policy has instead evolved into a far more sprawling, ambitious project aimed at levelling playing fields. This shift in basic purpose, though, produced no corresponding shift in tools or approach; since the 1990s, US trade negotiators have simply taken on an ever-expanding list of economic issues and traits, all quite different from tariffs – labour and environmental standards, direct and indirect subsidies, regulations of various kinds, and so on – using the same basic tools and approaches initially designed to reduce tariff schedules.

Trade deals, TTIP included, have by now grown so sprawling as to lie well beyond the expertise and remit of the United States' current trade agencies. Changes to the US government's bureaucratic and institutional footing on trade policy are long overdue. That these changes might improve America's ability to advance foreign-policy interests through trade is but one of several worthwhile grounds for undertaking them, sooner rather than later.

Notes

1 See Dylan Matthews, '21 Maps and Charts that Will Change How You Think about the Election', *Vox*, 24 October 2016, http://www.vox.com/policy-and-politics/2016/10/24/13273622/21-maps-charts-election; and Max Ehrenfreud, 'What Americans Really Think about Free Trade', *Washington Post*, 25 March 2016, https://www.washingtonpost.com/news/wonk/wp/2016/03/25/what-americans-really-think-about-free-trade.

2 A September 2016 Harvard poll showed that, of voters who had familiarity with TPP, 63% opposed the deal. See Doug Palmer, 'POLITICO–Harvard Poll: Americans Say "TPP Who?"', *Politico*, 23 September 2016, http://www.politico.com/story/2016/09/americans-say-tpp-who-228598. A March 2016 Morning Consult poll showed 29% of Americans opposing TPP and 26% supporting it. Ryan Rainey, 'As Trade Plays in Campaigns, Most Americans Don't Know What TPP Is – Morning Consult', Morning Consult, 21 April 2016, https://morningconsult.com/2016/04/21/trade-talk-may-play-trail-americans-dont-know-tpp/. A separate poll conducted by Caddell & Associates, also in March 2016, showed 15% supporting the deal and 22% opposing (with the remainder as 'don't know'/'no view'); after hearing arguments for and against the deal, 22% supported the deal, while 53% said they opposed it. Caddell & Associates, 'The Trans-Pacific Partnership Trade Deal: Public Opinion on TPP and TTIP – Ballotpedia', 10 March 2016, https://ballotpedia.org/The_Trans-Pacific_

Partnership_trade_deal:_Public_opinion_on_TPP_and_TTIP.

3 William Mauldin, 'Obama Makes a Long-Shot Bid for TPP Trade Deal', *Wall Street Journal*, 1 November 2016, http://www.wsj.com/articles/obama-makes-a-long-shot-bid-for-tpp-trade-deal-1478014457.

4 Contemporary trade agreements 'use a similar model, from the general structure of the text to the language', to NAFTA. Alexander Gauthier and Pascal Tremblay, '21st Century Trade Agreements: From NAFTA to the TPP', HillNotes, 1 February 2016, https://hillnotes.wordpress.com/2016/02/01/21st-century-trade-agreements-from-nafta-to-the-tpp/.

5 David Nakamura, 'Clinton Does Not Back Obama Trade Vote in Post-Election Congressional Season', 5 May 2016, https://www.washingtonpost.com/politics/clinton-does-not-back-obama-trade-vote-in-post-election-congressional-session/2016/05/05/ce94f76e-12d7-11e6-8967-7ac733c56f12_story.html.

6 Dan Merica and Eric Bradner, 'Hillary Clinton Comes Out Against TPP', CNN, 7 October 2015, http://www.cnn.com/2015/10/07/politics/hillary-clinton-opposes-tpp/.

7 See Dave Boyer, 'Obama to Try to Save Trans-Pacific Partnership Trade Deal While in China', *Washington Times*, 29 August 2016, http://www.washingtontimes.com/news/2016/aug/29/obama-to-try-to-save-asia-trade-deal-in-china; and C.L. Lim, Deborah K. Elms and Patrick Low (eds), *The Trans-Pacific Partnership: A Quest for a Twenty-first Century Trade Agreement* (Cambridge: Cambridge University Press, 2012), p. 49.

8 Quoted in David A. Baldwin, *Economic Statecraft* (Princeton, NJ: Princeton University Press, 1985), p. 209.

9 Walter Russell Mead, 'The End of History Ends', *American Interest*, 2 December 2013, http://www.the-american-interest.com/2013/12/02/2013-the-end-of-history-ends-2/.

10 *Ibid.*

11 See, for example, 'U.S. Polling Shows Strong Opposition to More of the Same U.S. Trade Deals from Independents, Republicans and Democrats Alike', Public Citizen, July 2015, p. 7, https://www.citizen.org/documents/polling-memo.pdf; and 'Americans Are of Two Minds on Trade', Pew Research Center, 9 November 2010, http://www.pewresearch.org/2010/11/09/americans-are-of-two-minds-on-trade/.

12 See Marine Le Pen, 'After Brexit, the People's Spring Is Inevitable', *New York Times*, 28 June 2016, http://www.nytimes.com/2016/06/28/opinion/marine-le-pen-after-brexit-the-peoples-spring-is-inevitable.html?_r=0; and Thomas Edsall, 'Global Trade War, Trump Edition', *New York Times*, 6 October 2016, http://www.nytimes.com/2016/10/06/opinion/campaign-stops/global-trade-war-trump-edition.html.

13 This is true, certainly, for those individuals falling within what economist Branco Milanovic describes as the 'decile of discontent', or the 10% of people globally – largely concentrated in the bottom income levels of developed economies – who have not seen their incomes rise in the current era of

technology-enabled globalisation. But the point stretches beyond these structural features, to inculpate recent US trade deals themselves. The US–Korea deal, for example, has significantly underperformed (compared to initial US International Trade Commission estimates) since it took effect in 2012. See Branco Milanovic, *Global Inequality* (Cambridge, MA: Harvard University Press, 2016); and US International Trade Commission Interactive Trade Data Web, August 2016, https://dataweb.usitc.gov.

14 This section draws and elaborates upon themes initially outlined in Jennifer Harris and Robert D. Blackwill, *War by Other Means: Geoeconomics and Statecraft* (Cambridge, MA: Harvard University Press, 2016).

15 Dani Rodrik, 'The Global Governance of Trade as if Development Really Mattered', submitted to the United Nations Development Programme, July 2001, http://www.giszpenc.com/globalciv/rodrik1.pdf. See also Dani Rodrik, 'How to Make the Trade Regime Work for Development', working paper, Kennedy School, Harvard University, 2004; and David Singh Grewal, *Network Power: The Social Dynamics of Globalization* (New Haven, CT: Yale University Press, 2008), pp. 240–6.

16 'The Transatlantic Trade Investment Partnership as a Foreign Policy Tool: Insights from a Council on Foreign Relations Workshop', Council on Foreign Relations, 28 April 2016, http://i.cfr.org/content/publications/attachments/Workshop_Report_CGS_TTIP_OR.pdf.

17 Grewal, cited in Blackwill and Harris, *War by Other Means*, p. 177. Grewal explores these tensions (between the logic of globalisation, which favours economic liberalisation, and the logic of geopolitics) in Grewal, *Network Power*, pp. 235–7.

18 Blackwill and Harris, *War by Other Means*, footnote 5.

19 David Singh Grewal, email message to author, 22 August 2015.

20 Adam Smith, *An Inquiry into the Nature and Causes of the Wealth of Nations*, cited in Baldwin, *Economic Statecraft*, p. 80.

21 The final report of the US–EU High Level Working Group (HLWG), which formed the basis for TTIP negotiations, called on both sides to include 'enhanced cooperation for the development of rules and principles on global issues of common concern' as an explicit part of the negotiations. Moreover, in translating the HLWG findings into negotiating instructions, the EU Commission directed that 'the strategic importance of the EU–US economic relationship should be reaffirmed and deepened' through TTIP, and that 'the EU and the US should design common approaches to global trade, investment and trade-related issues such as standards, norms and regulations, *in order to develop a broader transatlantic vision and a common set of strategic goals*' [emphasis added]. European Council President Donald Tusk, reporting a December 2014 conversation with US President Barack Obama, insisted that TTIP 'is not just about free trade; it is an expression of our geopolitical partnership. We

agreed to step up our efforts towards reaching agreement.' See European Union High Level Working Group, final report, 11 February 2013, http://trade.ec.europa.eu/doclib/docs/2013/february/tradoc_150519.pdf; European Parliament, 'Resolution on EU Trade and Investment Negotiations with the United States of America', 2013/2558(RSP), 23 May 2013, http://www.europarl.europa.eu/sides/getDoc.do?pubRef=-//EP//TEXT+TA+P7-TA-2013-0227+0+DOC+XML+V0//EN; and Donald Tusk, press statement, 1 December 2014, http://www.euintheus.org/press-media/statement-by-european-council-president-donald-tusk-after-his-telephone-call-with-u-s-president-barack-obama-1-december-2014.

22 Hillary Clinton, remarks at Transformational Trends Forum, Washington DC, 30 November 2012, http://foreignpolicy.com/2012/11/30/hillary-clintons-remarks-at-fps-transformational-trends-forum/. See also Hillary Clinton, 'The Transatlantic Partnership: A Statesman's Forum with Secretary of State Hillary Clinton', remarks at Brookings Institution, Washington DC, 29 November 2012, https://www.brookings.edu/wp-content/uploads/2012/11/20121129_transatlantic_clinton.pdf.

23 Author's experiences while serving in the US Department of State, 2012–14.

24 Adam Beshudi, 'Froman: U.S.–EU Trade Deal Should Be as Strong as NATO', *Politico*, 21 March 2014, http://www.politico.com/story/2014/03/michael-froman-us-eu-trade-deal-should-be-as-strong-as-nato-104895. Then-secretary-general of NATO Anders Fogh Rasmussen said: 'The transatlantic trade and investment partnership that is now under discussion is sometimes described as an "economic NATO". I think that's a good comparison.' Anders Fogh Rasmussen, 'A New Era for EU–US Trade', speech to Confederation of Danish Industry, Copenhagen, 7 October 2013, http://www.nato.int/cps/en/natolive/opinions_103863.htm.

25 William Mauldin, 'U.S., U.K. Politicians Eye Strategic Aims of Trans-Atlantic Trade Talks', *Wall Street Journal*, 25 September 2013, http://blogs.wsj.com/washwire/2013/09/25/u-s-u-k-politicians-eye-strategic-aims-of-trans-atlantic-trade-talks/.

26 US Department of Defense, 'National Security Implications of Climate-Related Risks and a Changing Climate', 23 July 2015, p. 3, http://archive.defense.gov/pubs/150724-congressional-report-on-national-implications-of-climate-change.pdf?source=govdelivery.

27 Catherine Lotrionte, 'Countering State-Sponsored Cyber Economic Espionage Under International Law', *North Carolina Journal of International Law*, no. 40, 2016, p. 453, footnote 30. See also Justin McCarthy, 'Americans Cite Cyberterrorism Among Top Three Threats to U.S.', Gallup, 10 February 2016, http://www.gallup.com/poll/189161/americans-cite-cyber-terrorism-among-top-three-threats.aspx.

28 For views on cyber attacks and international economics, see Richard Wike, 'Americans' Concerns about

China: Economics, Cyberattacks, Human Rights Top the List', Pew Research Center Global Attitudes Project, 9 September 2015, http://www.pewglobal.org/2015/09/09/americans-concerns-about-china-economics-cyberattacks-human-rights-top-the-list/; and Margaret Vice, 'Views on National Economies Mixed as Many Countries Continue to Struggle', Pew Research Center Global Attitudes Project, 9 August 2016, http://www.pewglobal.org/2016/08/09/views-on-national-economies-mixed-as-many-countries-continue-to-struggle/.

29 'One Internet', report of the Global Commission on Internet Governance, June 2016, p. 115, https://www.chathamhouse.org/sites/files/chathamhouse/publications/research/2016-06-21-global-commission-internet-governance.pdf.

30 The WTO's nullification and impairment clause is not currently available for the Trade-Related Aspects of Intellectual Property Rights (TRIPs) agreement, and the Chinese government argues that, because the trade-secrecy provisions of TRIPs do not mention espionage, TRIPs does not cover espionage. Lotrionte, 'Countering State-Sponsored Cyber Economic Espionage under International Law', p. 453.

31 See, for example, John Mallery et al., 'Defending Our Economic Future against Cyber Threats to Innovation', IDA Occasional Paper, July 2016; and Lotrionte, 'Countering State-Sponsored Cyber Economic Espionage under International Law'.

32 Sam Jones et al., 'EU Spymasters Lobby for Change in Encryption Law', *Financial Times*, 22 August 2016, http://www.ft.com/cms/s/0/08fe566e-679e-11e6-ae5b-a7cc5dd5a28c.html#axzz4Lefq59xO.

33 As proposed by the intellectual-property commission chaired by Dennis Blair. See 'Report of the Commission on the Theft of American Intellectual Property', National Bureau of Asian Research, May 2013. For the US, see Section 337 of the 1930 Trade Act; for the EU, see EU Council Regulation No. 608/2013, adopted in 2014.

34 Daren Orzechowski, 'Amendments to the Economic Espionage Act Broaden Trade Secret Protection', *White & Case Technology Newsflash*, 15 January 2013, http://www.whitecase.com/publications/article/amendments-economic-espionage-act-broaden-trade-secret-protection.

35 EU Directive 2016/943, 8 June 2016, http://eur-lex.europa.eu/legal-content/EN/TXT/PDF/?uri=CELEX:32016L0943&from=EN.

36 Odious debt works as a loan embargo. The concept stipulates that sovereign debt incurred by a regime for purposes that do not serve the interests of the nation should not be enforceable.

37 The scope of affected contracts could be narrowly tied to any deal involving stolen intellectual property, or, more aggressively, could extend to any future contracts entered into by the offending firm.

38 Benjamin Fox, 'EU Repeats Demand for Energy Chapter in US Trade Treaty', *Euobserver*, 10 September 2014, https://euobserver.com/news/125544.

39 *Ibid.*

40 'Cheniere Offers Gas Price 25% Lower than Gazprom, Lithuania Says', *Bloomberg Business Week*, 27 May 2011, http://www.bloomberg.com/news/articles/2011-05-27/cheniere-offers-gas-price-25-lower-than-gazprom-lithuania-says.

41 Charlie Wells, 'How Exporting U.S. Liquefied Natural Gas Will Transform the Politics of Global Energy', *Wall Street Journal*, 17 November 2015, http://blogs.wsj.com/experts/2015/11/17/how-exporting-u-s-liquefied-natural-gas-will-transform-the-politics-of-global-energy/?cb=logged0.21172881281301792. I am grateful to an anonymous reviewer, who notes that, because both Russia and North Africa have the reserves to increase gas supply to Asia without cutting deliveries to Europe, it is difficult to predict how such shifts will alter the competitiveness of US gas exports to Europe.

42 See, for example, Ladka Mortkowitz Bauerova and Radoslav Tomek, 'Russia–Germany Gas Link Polarizes Europe, EU Energy Chief Says', Bloomberg, 20 April 2016, http://www.bloomberg.com/news/articles/2016-04-20/russia-germany-gas-link-polarizes-europe-eu-energy-chief-says; and William Powell, 'EC Warns France to Implement Third Package', *Natural Gas World*, 22 July 2016, http://www.naturalgasworld.com/ec-warns-france-to-implement-third-package-30725.

43 See, for example, David Goldwyn and Cory Gill, 'Chapter 20 Update: Managing Strategic Reserves', Wilson Center, December 2015, https://www.wilsoncenter.org/publication/chapter-20-update-managing-strategic-reserves#_edn12. Goldwyn and Gill note that EU government reserves cover only 56 days of net imports, well below the IEA guideline of 90 days. See also Blake Clayton, 'Lessons Learned from the 2011 Strategic Petroleum Reserve Release', Council on Foreign Relations, September 2012, http://i.cfr.org/content/publications/attachments/CFR_WorkingPaper14_Clayton.pdf. Clayton notes shortcomings in the composition and overall management of EU oil reserves during the 2011 disruptions that occurred as a result of violence in Libya.

44 See 'How Much Oil Is Being Stockpiled around the World? No One Really Knows, but Here's Our Best Guess', *Oil Sands Magazine*, 12 August 2016, http://www.oilsandsmagazine.com/news/2016/8/12/total-global-oil-petroleum-stockpiles-estimated-at-8-billion-barrel; and 'China Oil & Gas', J.P. Morgan Asia-Pacific Equity Research, 29 June 2016, https://markets.jpmorgan.com/research/email/-88aek3d/zMlZlTkJLz73jNK2RMX_OA/GPS-2060581-0.

45 See, generally, US Energy Information Administration, 'Short-Term Energy and Winter Fuels Outlook: Global Petroleum and Liquid Fuels', 13 October 2016, https://www.eia.gov/forecasts/steo/report/global_oil.cfm. OECD countries consume 46.5 million barrels of oil per day, compared to non-OECD countries, which consume 48.8m barrels per day. This is a striking shift from 1970, when OECD countries comprised 75% of global oil

demand. See also Mark Finley, 'The Oil Market to 2030 – Implications for Investment and Policy', *Economics of Energy and Environmental Policy*, vol. 1, no. 1, 2012, pp. 25–36. IEA publicly held stocks are currently around 1.4 billion barrels (with another 2.6bn in privately held reserves). With IEA estimates placing global oil consumption at roughly 95m barrels per day, these publicly held stocks would cover roughly 13 days of global oil consumption. Goldwyn and Gill make a similar point, noting that 'while [IEA] government and industry stocks provided nearly 60 days of import cover in 1990, this figure has been progressively declining and IEA forecasts they will provide around only 40 days of import cover by 2035'. Goldwyn and Gill, 'Chapter 20 Update: Managing Strategic Reserves'.

46 Launched by the US government in 2011, the Middle East North African Trade and Investment Partnership (MENA-TIP) sought to increase trade and investment across the MENA region. In 2011 and 2012, the EU announced new trade- and investment-related funding for Arab Spring countries and committed to negotiate 'deep and comprehensive free trade agreements' (DCFTAs) with interested Arab Spring countries (except Libya).

47 The average MENA country exports at roughly 30% of its potential (the entire region, with a population close to 320m, has less non-oil exports than Finland or Hungary). Yet, firms that export or import supply more than half of wage-paying jobs in many MENA countries. See Mélise Jaud and Caroline Freund, 'Champions Wanted: Promoting Exports in the Middle East and North Africa', *Directions in Development*, April 2015; World Bank, 'From Privilege to Competition: Unlocking Private-Led Growth in the Middle East and North Africa', 2009, http://siteresources.worldbank.org/INTMENA/Resources/Privilege_complete_final.pdf; World Bank, 'Jobs or Privileges: Unleashing the Employment Potential of the Middle East and North Africa', 2014, http://elibrary.worldbank.org/doi/pdf/10.1596/978-1-4648-0405-2; and Caroline Freund and Aloberto Portugal-Perez, 'Assessing MENA's Trade Agreements', in Michael Gasiorek (ed.), *The Arab Spring: Implications for Economic Integration* (London: Centre for Economic Policy Research, 2013).

48 Elena Ianchovichina, 'MENA's Non-Oil Export Performance in the Last Decade', World Bank, April 2011, p. 3.

49 Author's observations during her time in the US State Department.

50 Morocco, Tunisia, Egypt, Lebanon and Jordan have signed bilateral association agreements with the EU, while Morocco, Jordan and Lebanon have signed bilateral free-trade agreements with the US.

51 US Department of State, 'Executive Budget Summary: Function 150 & Other International Programs', fiscal year 2014, p. 97, http://www.state.gov/documents/organization/207305.pdf.

52 Shadi Hamid and Peter Mandaville, 'Bringing the United States Back into the Middle East', *Washington Quarterly*, vol. 36, no. 4, 2013, p. 99.

53 Paul Poast, 'Does Issue Linkage

Work? Evidence from European Alliance Negotiations, 1860 to 1945', *International Organization*, vol. 66, no. 2, 2012, p. 305.

54 David H. Autor, David Dorn and Gordon H. Hanson, 'The China Syndrome: Local Labor Market Effects of Import Competition in the United States', *American Economic Review*, 2013, p. 2125.

55 Tsuyoshi Kawase, 'The Trans-Pacific Partnership as a Set of International Economic Rules', E15 Initiative, May 2016. Kawase argues that 'the SOE chapter is still less ambitious in that it adopted a narrow definition of SOE and failed to mandate a gradual reduction in government ownership and involvement in SOEs'. Compared to the US–Singapore free-trade agreement, for example, TPP employs a narrower definition of SOE and also adopts a higher revenue threshold, below which SOEs are exempted from coverage. See Ben Hancock, 'Reach of TPP's SOE Disciplines Limited by Definition, Scope, Exceptions', 7 November 2015, http://www.bilaterals.org/?reach-of-tpp-s-soe-disciplines.

56 See, for example, Ashley Tellis, 'The Geopolitics of the TTIP and the TPP', in Sanjaya Baru and Suvi Dogra (eds), *Power Shifts and New Blocs in the Global Trading System* (Abingdon: Routledge for the IISS, 2015), pp. 93–120.

57 The Heritage Foundation's James Roberts summed it up well: 'The Bretton Woods institutions serve a purpose, but not on such a grand scale as in previous decades.' Quoted in Ian Talley, 'In Democrats' Eyes, Republicans Are Helping Foster Chinese Power', *Wall Street Journal*, 27 March 2015, http://blogs.wsj.com/economics/2015/03/27/in-democrats-eyes-republicans-are-helping-foster-chinese-power/.

58 Sebastian Heilmann, founding president of the Mercator Institute for China Studies in Berlin, and colleagues argue that 'while current crises in the Ukraine, Syria, Iraq and West Africa have moved to the centre of global attention, China is advancing with a restructuring of the international order. While Beijing remains an active player within existing international institutions, it is simultaneously promoting and financing new parallel structures. Some of these parallel structures ... may also come to compete directly with existing institutions.' Sebastian Heilmann et al., 'China's Shadow Foreign Policy: Parallel Structures Challenge the Established International Order', *China Monitor*, no. 18, 28 October 2014. See also Andrew Higgins and David E. Sanger, '3 European Powers Say They Will Join China-Led Bank', *New York Times*, 17 March 2015. Higgins and Sanger characterise China as 'an alternative to the creaking international structures shaped by the U.S. in the postwar period'.

Stress-Testing American Grand Strategy

Hal Brands and Peter Feaver

The 2016 presidential campaign, and its ultimate outcome, raised sharper questions about the fundamental nature and purpose of the United States' grand strategy than at any time in a generation. In doing so, the campaign also served as a reminder of the critical role of assumptions in shaping US statecraft. In the grand-strategic context, assumptions are the ingrained, overarching ideas that US officials have about how the world works, and about America's role within the global arena. Simply put, such assumptions represent the intellectual foundation upon which American statecraft rests. If the foundation is solid, then American strategy has a decent chance of success. If the foundation is shaky, American strategy is likely in for a world of trouble.

Yet because assumptions are, by their very nature, often implicit rather than explicit, and because the most fundamental assumptions underlying American grand strategy do not frequently surface in the course of day-to-day policy debates, these assumptions are rarely scrutinised or even made explicit to the degree they ought to be. This is dangerous. If assumptions are not identified and stress-tested, how will policymakers know, other than by pure intuition, when those assumptions are no longer valid and the conceptual foundation of strategy has begun to crack?

Hal Brands is the Henry A. Kissinger Distinguished Professor of Global Affairs at Johns Hopkins University's School of Advanced International Studies. His most recent book is *Making the Unipolar Moment: U.S. Foreign Policy and the Rise of the Post-Cold War Order* (Cornell University Press, 2016). **Peter Feaver** is Professor of Political Science and Public Policy at Duke University, where he directs the American Grand Strategy Program and the Triangle Institute for Security Studies.

Survival | vol. 58 no. 6 | December 2016–January 2017 | pp. 93–120 DOI 10.1080/00396338.2016.1257199

Today, the need to critically examine the core assumptions of American grand strategy is becoming ever more pressing. Since the Cold War's end, the United States has pursued a grand strategy centred on maintaining America's global primacy, deepening and extending the liberal international order, and heading off major threats to the generally happy state of the post-Cold War world. That grand strategy has rested upon a set of bedrock assumptions that have also stayed largely constant over time – assumptions about the nature and sustainability of American dominance, the direction in which the world is moving geopolitically and ideologically, the ways in which Washington can best prevent or address emerging threats, and so on. Assumptions about specific policy issues have evolved over time, of course, but the core intellectual premises of American strategy have not been extensively revised for nearly a quarter-century. Collectively, those assumptions have added up to a broadly optimistic view of global affairs – a view that the United States enjoys essentially uncontested supremacy in most key aspects of international relations; that the dominant ideological, geopolitical and economic currents are running Washington's way; and that, with properly vigilant and enlightened American policy, this comparatively benign situation need not be fundamentally disrupted by resurgent great-power conflict or other throwbacks to an earlier and less hopeful age.[1]

Yet today, roughly 25 years into the post-Cold War period, some of the essential assumptions of American grand strategy are either coming under real strain, or are increasingly likely to do so in the next 10–20 years.[2] This is not to say that all of these core assumptions have been fully or even largely invalidated, because their residual strength does vary, and because their erosion has not yet, for the most part, reached a critical stage. Moreover, we should remember that critics have prematurely proclaimed the inevitable demise of America's post-Cold War 'unipolar moment' before.[3] Yet these disclaimers aside, there is little question that the validity of these core assumptions is more contested now than at any other time during the post-Cold War era, and that this validity will only become more contested over the next decade or two if current trends hold. As this happens, look out: American officials will have to get used to operating in a world in which they can take less for granted, in which the international environment is significantly more contested and challenging, and in which it will become steadily harder to sustain the grand strategy – and international order – that the country has pursued since the end of the Cold War.

The assumptions of US post-Cold War grand strategy

Since the end of the Cold War, the US has pursued an ambitious and fairly consistent grand strategy aimed at shaping the international system.[4] The particulars of that approach have shifted from year to year, administration to administration, but from the early 1990s onward, many of the core goals and initiatives of American statecraft have remained largely the same. Every president since George H.W. Bush has committed the United States to maintaining American global primacy, and to deepening and expanding the liberal international order that took hold after the Second World War. Every president has likewise committed to proactively meeting any emerging or resurgent threat that might disrupt this favourable world order in the near term, while also hedging against deeper challenges that could threaten that order over the longer term. And notwithstanding important variations, every president has done all this via initiatives that have also been replicated across administrations: by preserving America's unequalled military capabilities; by maintaining and even extending US alliances and overseas military deployments as sources of stability and influence in key regions; by supporting the spread of democracy, free trade and globalisation; and by being willing to use tools including military force to address major threats to the international system and to US interests, ranging from aggressive regional powers such as Saddam Hussein's Iraq in the early 1990s, to terrorist groups with global reach today.[5]

One reason that American grand strategy has remained fairly stable during the post-Cold War period is that the core assumptions underlying it have also remained fairly stable. Assumptions, concisely defined, are the intellectual premises on which policy rests. They may be, for example, the core beliefs that policymakers hold about the nature and direction of the international system, their baseline views on a country's particular role within that system, or their unstated theories about how some type of action will lead to some desired geopolitical result. Assumptions can be big or small: they can deal with the most overarching questions of international order (for example, 'states will remain the primary actors in international politics'), or with specific issues or regions ('there is no viable alternative to a US partnership with Saudi Arabia'). They can be old, dating back generations or even centuries ('America is an exceptional nation'), and they can be newer, relating to issues that have arisen more recently ('a North Korean nuclear capability is a troubling but manageable problem').

And crucially, although assumptions may sometimes be stated explicitly, they more often remain in the background, creating the implicit intellectual guidelines within which policy debates occur. Indeed, precisely because assumptions are, by definition, things that are assumed, they are generally those ideas that are commonly accepted in policy circles *without* having to be explicitly or systematically proven. Assumptions are the received wisdom among the policymaking elite, not the controversial new theses that must be systematically substantiated before they can be accepted.

The core assumptions that have undergirded recent American grand strategy have taken shape over varying lengths of time. Yet many emerged most fully in the wake of the Cold War. The collapse of the Soviet Union and America's rise to unrivalled international primacy represent the most recent structural transformation of the international system.[6] It is therefore logical that the post-Cold War environment shaped many guiding assumptions of US policy.

To be clear, not all of the important assumptions underpinning American policy have remained stable across the post-Cold War era. The 9/11 attacks caused US policymakers to radically reformulate assumptions about the costs of action versus inaction in confronting terrorist groups and rogue regimes thought to possess weapons of mass destruction, for instance, while the unsatisfying course of the wars that followed led to a further reformulation of these and other assumptions.[7] Yet looking across the post-Cold War era, one can identify a set of assumptions that have been widely shared by US policymakers, and that have remained broadly constant during most or all of this period. One can also discern that a number of these core assumptions are now coming under greater strain.

Accordingly, this article critically examines seven vital assumptions that are either becoming more contested today, or are likely to become so over the next 10–20 years. For analytical purposes, these assumptions can be divided into two groups. The first group (assumptions 1 through 4) addresses the fundamental geopolitical structure of the post-Cold War world – the idea that the United States and its allies enjoy a massive and essentially unchallenged preponderance of global power, and that this situation is unlikely to be disturbed by the emergence of a hostile great-power challenger or the resurgence of great-power war. The second group (assumptions 5 through 7) addresses the more amorphous, but no less important, conviction that the United States is on the right side of history – that the deeper ideological, economic and technological trends shaping the international system all favour America, and that those trends are likely to continue indefinitely.[8] The fact that both groups of assumptions are now becoming more contested indicates that the international system is changing in ways that will pose significant challenges for US strategy in years to come.

Assumption 1: The United States enjoys and will continue to enjoy uncontested military primacy, not just globally, but in all key strategic theatres

Perhaps the primary geopolitical effect of the Cold War's end was to kill off the only country that was anything like a military peer to the United States. The subsequent years have thus been defined by unrivalled American military primacy. This primacy has been clearly evident at the global level, at which Washington has enjoyed uncontested leads in overall military might, crucial power-projection capabilities and the ability to control the global commons. It has also been evident in virtually every key strategic theatre around the globe, where the US could deploy combat power superior to anything a potential challenger could amass even within its own regional backyard.[9]

For a quarter-century, this asymmetry has been a fundamental enabler of America's post-Cold War strategy. It has underwritten the country's overseas presence and security guarantees in key regions, numerous military interventions to confront challenges to America's preferred concept of international order, and the general overbalance of power that has so greatly favoured Washington and its allies during this period. To be sure, every post-Cold War administration recognised that the United States might one day confront a new rival for military primacy, at least in key regions, and yet every administration saw that prospect as a far-off challenge on the distant horizon. The idea that American military primacy should and will persist for the foreseeable future has thus been a fixture of virtually every post-Cold War strategy document.[10]

So what is the state of US military primacy today? At the global level, the United States continues to possess impressive advantages in key power-projection capabilities – from aircraft carriers and airborne warning and control systems to nuclear-powered submarines and fifth-generation tactical aircraft – that will not be equalled for decades.[11] Yet the assumption of uncontested primacy is nonetheless coming in for greater challenge, particularly as key regional balances have shifted against the United States.

Russia's military modernisation has allowed it to achieve local overmatch

A two-decade military build-up in China, for instance, is rapidly changing the military balance in East Asia, threatening US access to the area within the first island chain (and perhaps eventually beyond it), and complicating America's ability to intervene in contingencies involving Taiwan and perhaps other allies and partners. 'Over the next five to 15 years, if US and PLA forces remain on roughly current trajectories, Asia will witness a progressively receding frontier of US dominance', one RAND Corporation report concludes.[12] In Eastern Europe, a major Russian military-modernisation programme has allowed Moscow to achieve local overmatch along NATO's eastern frontier, and to contest the United States' ability to intervene on behalf of its allies should conflict break out.[13] Looking beyond Russia and China, the broader proliferation of precision-strike capabilities, integrated air-defence systems and other advanced capabilities are threatening, or at least decreasing, US superiority. Add in the fact that Washington is now facing a larger number of significant regional challenges than at any other time in decades – in the Middle East, Eastern Europe and East Asia simultaneously – and the stresses on US military primacy in each of these areas come into even sharper relief.

To understand how significantly the testing of American regional primacy might affect US strategy, consider just one aspect of that phenomenon: the waning of American air supremacy in key theatres. Air supremacy, defined as 'that degree of air superiority wherein the opposing force is incapable of effective interference within the operational area using air and missile threats', is the highest level of advantage recognised by Air Force doctrine.[14] Since the end of the Cold War, the United States has enjoyed virtually unchallenged air supremacy in every shooting conflict in which it has been engaged. In other words, US ground forces have never faced a serious threat from the air in any military operation they have conducted for the past 25 years. Yet that supremacy is now being severely challenged. In East Asia, and particularly near China's coastline, the combination of adverse geography and vastly improved Chinese air-defence and air-superiority capabilities is confronting American planners with the prospect of a much more contested aerial environment. In Eastern Europe and the Baltics, the tyranny of distance and Russia's modernisation of its own air-defence and air-superiority capabilities is creating similar problems.[15]

This means that, in some of the most likely contingencies in these regions (a NATO-led defence of the Baltic allies, or an American-led defence of Taiwan), American strategists would have to contemplate deploying ground and naval forces in settings where they could come under sustained air attack. Indeed, although the loss of air supremacy does not necessarily mean that enemy forces would enjoy a decisive battlefield advantage, it does mean that the costs of conflict for US forces would quite likely increase, significantly and perhaps even dramatically. No one in the US armed forces has combat experience in such an exceedingly demanding environment. No living American political leader has had to make a use-of-force decision involving that cruel calculus. As it is, serious strategists consider the human toll of the Iraq War, which lasted eight years, to be devastating. Will American officials be willing to countenance combat operations when a butcher's bill of comparable magnitude could come due in mere days?

By complicating US decisions about how and where to use force, the straining of American primacy over the next 10–20 years will also have broader strategic ramifications. This trend will certainly make it harder for the United States to uphold its alliance commitments in Europe and Asia than at any time in the post-Cold War era. It may thereby unnerve US allies that have long depended on American protection, while tempting adversaries and rivals to pursue revisionist aims.[16] More broadly, because military power unavoidably casts a shadow over diplomacy and other international interactions, this trend could well mean that Washington and its allies will find it more difficult to get their way on important issues of regional or international order. The challenging of American military primacy, then, could introduce far greater uncertainties into the post-Cold War international system.

Assumption 2: US allies are the richest, most capable countries in the world

America's post-Cold War supremacy has not derived solely from its own strengths, but also from those of its core allies in Europe and Asia. In 1994, those allies commanded roughly 47% of global GDP and 36% of global defence spending, in addition to America's own 24% and 38%, respectively. And after the United States, America's closest allies – France, Germany, Japan and the United Kingdom – rounded out the top five in both of these categories.[17] Add in the fact that Russian power was in free fall during the early 1990s, and that other US competitors (or potential competitors) possessed mere fractions of global wealth and power, and this situation created great benefits for US policy.

It meant, for instance, that most key allies were less dependent on American protection than they had been during the Cold War, and that they were now security exporters that could contribute significantly to the out-of-area military interventions that figured prominently in US strategy. More broadly, it meant that the danger of serious counter-hegemonic balancing against the United States was assessed to be extremely low, and that Washington could generally (although not always) count on having the most powerful second-tier countries on its side on crucial issues of international order, from deterring aggression and preserving stability in key areas, to promoting democracy and human rights.[18] These advantages – and the core assumption of allied strength and vitality underlying them – have long played a key role in augmenting US superiority, and in enabling America's assertive approach to the post-Cold War world.

Since the early 1990s, however, a great deal has changed. Although a few US allies have increased their relative global wealth and power, the broader trend has been one of decline. The aggregate share of global GDP possessed by core US allies in Asia and Europe had fallen to 39% by 2014; the aggregate share of global defence spending had fallen to 26%. During this period, many US allies, particularly in Europe, slashed defence outlays as a percentage of GDP and shed large portions of their air, naval and ground forces.[19] This trend was somewhat masked by the vast increase in US defence spending after 9/11, which kept the aggregate 'United States plus allies' total very high, but which also left an increasingly imbalanced load on America's shoulders.

Meanwhile, the combination of rapid economic growth and double-digit annual percentage increases in defence spending has carried China rapidly up the global power rankings, giving it 11.4% of global GDP and 11.2% of global military spending in 2014, shares far larger than those of any single US ally. And while Russia remains an economic basket case, its own military modernisation, combined with European military decline, has allowed Moscow to reassert local primacy along NATO's eastern flank. With significant long-term demographic and economic problems on all sides, the long-term trajectory of America's allies and rivals alike remains uncertain. To date, moreover, US allies' loss of relative military power far outstrips any loss of relative economic power. Nevertheless, the assumption that America's allies are the most powerful, capable and dynamic countries in the world after the United States has become far more tenuous.

How might the relative decline of America's friends affect American strategy? Broadly speaking, it means that the advantages Washington has enjoyed by dint of having such powerful allies are waning, as the liabilities of its alliance relationships become more pronounced. As evidenced by the Libyan war of 2011 and the campaign against the Islamic State (also known as ISIS or ISIL) today, US allies have already become less capable of contributing meaningfully to out-of-area interventions than they were at the outset of the post-Cold War era, even as the Middle Eastern instability that has traditionally called forth such interventions is more pronounced than ever.[20] Moreover, as US allies' power declines relative to their chief competitors, those allies are becoming more dependent on the Pentagon to protect them at a time when American military power is also under strain. 'Europe's decision to abdicate on defense spending', one US official remarked in 2013, 'increasingly means it can't take care of itself.'[21] Not least, the relative decline of countries that share the US vision of a liberal international order can only weaken the foundation of that order at a time when illiberal powers such as Russia and China are starting to challenge it more assertively than at any time since the end of the Cold War.

Of course, complaints about the United States shouldering allied deadweight are as old as America's alliances themselves. And, to be clear, America's allies still add tremendously to US power, and provide pronounced geopolitical advantages over any challenger. But the relative power and dynamism of those allies, and thus the degree of American advantage, has been fading, and burden-sharing arrangements have become more skewed over time. This situation will only complicate the prospects of American statecraft at a time when America's own primacy is increasingly being contested.

Assumption 3: A richer and more globally integrated China will also be a freer and more peaceful China

A third assumption involves the possibility of a great-power challenge to the post-Cold War order. Since the mid-1990s, American officials have understood that an increasingly powerful China could eventually challenge US interests and dominance in East Asia, and perhaps globally as well. But a fundamental assumption has been that Washington can avert this danger by promoting constructive change in Chinese politics and policy. In particular, American officials have wagered that, as China becomes richer, it will also become more democratic, because an increasingly prosperous population will demand a greater say in how it is governed. US officials have equally wagered that, as China becomes more integrated into the global economy and other global interactions, it will also become more peaceful, because it will have less incentive to upset a system in which it plays such a significant and rewarding role. The dominant viewpoint, writes Aaron Friedberg, has been that, via intensive integration and engagement, 'the Beijing regime would come to see itself as having a substantial stake in supporting the prevailing order and a strong need to avoid actions that might lead to its disruption'.[22]

For roughly two decades, this assumption has pushed US policymakers to consistently emphasise the need to engage Beijing both economically and diplomatically, and to lay aside concerns that doing so might simply end up 'creating a monster'.[23] During this period, the US has done more than any other country to facilitate China's astounding rise, by opening US markets to Chinese goods, paving China's way into international institutions such as the World Trade Organization (WTO), involving China in myriad high-level diplomatic efforts and other measures.[24] As they have done so, US leaders have sought to balance this engagement with other efforts that would serve as a hedge if China's rise proved destabilising: deepening long-standing treaty relationships, developing new strategic partnerships with non-allied Asian powers and maintaining defence-modernisation programmes designed to meet future threats. Nevertheless, the balance between engagement and hedging has been tilted markedly in the direction of engaging China and cultivating it as a 'responsible stakeholder'.

But what if this great geopolitical wager does not pay off? China has indeed become far more prosperous: its GDP rose from $359 billion in 1990 to $10.35 trillion in 2014, and its per capita GDP skyrocketed from $316 to $7,587.[25] Yet politically, China has not become more liberal, and it may even be turning more repressive, particularly in recent years. Since the Tiananmen Square massacre in 1989, the Communist Party has rejected any opening toward a more competitive, pluralistic system; it has assiduously repressed civil society and human-rights activists; and it has so strictly censored information flows that in 2015 China was ranked last in the world in terms of internet freedom.[26] Meanwhile, the current government of Xi Jinping has ruthlessly centralised power to a degree not seen in decades. The widely used Polity IV dataset still lists China as one of the world's most repressive countries, with no positive change for nearly four decades.[27] Freedom House has labelled China 'a role model' for political repression.[28]

Nor does China seem to be becoming more peaceful, in the sense of becoming more reconciled to the existing order. China specialists dispute just how assertively China is now behaving, the extent of its geopolitical ambitions, and whether its behaviour is driven by offensive or defensive motives.[29] But the past several years have witnessed a pattern of increasingly disruptive Chinese behaviour, manifested in expansive maritime claims with little basis in international law; efforts to control and militarise disputed features in the South China Sea; the use of economic, military and paramilitary coercion against countries from Japan to Indonesia; and persistent efforts to undermine US alliances in East Asia. Moreover, for more than two decades, China has been undertaking a massive military build-up that seems to indicate dissatisfaction with the existing state of affairs in Asia, and a corresponding determination to develop the capabilities that might allow it to revise the status quo in its favour.[30]

Such behaviour may simply be what one should expect from a proud civilisation whose power has been growing rapidly. But since US policy has been premised on the idea that a richer China will be a tamer and more liberal China, this assumption would seem to be coming under real strain. If current trends continue, the resulting challenges could be profound. America's post-Cold War grand strategy has always identified the emergence of a hostile peer competitor as the principal long-term threat to be forestalled; China's recent trajectory raises the prospect that this eventuality may be materialising sooner than expected. At the very least, then, US strategists may soon have to confront sharper trade-offs between engagement with China and efforts to preserve American primacy and the US-led international order. Over time, the United States might find that, rather than facing a China that has become more democratic and more reconciled to the global status quo, it faces an authoritarian, revisionist China that American policy has done much to empower.

Assumption 4: Great-power war is obsolete

The shifting geopolitical balance, and the rise of an authoritarian and increasingly assertive China, bear on a fourth key assumption having to do with the prospect of great-power war. During the Cold War, the world lived in fear of a great-power conflict that could escalate to a nuclear cataclysm. Yet after the Cold War, it became increasingly common to think that great-power wars, and particularly the danger of a great-power nuclear war, were things of the past. George W. Bush gave expression to this belief in 2002: at no time since the 'rise of the nation state in the seventeenth century', he said, had there been such bright prospects 'to build a world where the great powers compete in peace instead of prepare for war'.[31]

This assumption that the world was turning the page on the great-power conflicts that had marked the twentieth century – and much of human history – was based on several sub-premises. In part, it was based on the idea that supranational institutions such as the European Union (EU) were reducing historical great-power rivalries, while leaps in economic interdependence were simultaneously making great-power war less profitable. In part, it was based on the fact that the United States and its powerful allies now formed a 'security community' in which war was almost unthinkable.[32] In part, it was based on the decline of rival ideologies, particularly communism, that had previously spurred international conflict. And in part, it was a reflection of America's sheer military dominance, which made it difficult to imagine any other major power seriously challenging the international order that Washington supported. 'America has, and intends to keep, military strengths beyond challenge', Bush declared in 2002, 'thereby making the destabilizing arms races of other eras pointless, and limiting rivalries to trade and other pursuits of peace.'[33]

This assumption is now being tested, however, as the spectre of great-power war revives. Russia and China – two key powers that were never fully reconciled to the post-Cold War order – are now pushing back against that order more assertively than ever before. Russian President Vladimir Putin has used force to halt the feared spread of Western influence and institutions into the former Soviet space. He has also used Russia's revived military power to intimidate US allies in the Baltics and Eastern Europe, and to harass US and NATO forces in international waters and airspace. China, as noted previously, is likewise using military and paramilitary forces to coerce US allies, to adjust maritime boundaries by force and to exert pressure on neighbours from Japan to Vietnam.

Both Moscow and Beijing, moreover, are developing warfighting capabilities and strategies designed to deny Washington access to their 'near-abroads', and to prevail in a limited military conflict with the United States and its allies. As one US Navy official has noted, Chinese forces have been training for a 'short sharp war' with Japan – and presumably, by extension, with America as well.[34] For its part, Moscow has regularly staged major military exercises along NATO's eastern flank, and has re-emphasised nuclear weapons in its rhetoric and planning.[35] In other words, neither Russia nor China is acting – or talking – like it believes that great-power war is obsolete. And neither, for that matter, is the United States, as the Pentagon invests in a Third Offset Strategy meant to re-establish American military dominance vis-à-vis great-power rivals.[36]

At present, few analysts believe that either Russia or China wants a war with Washington, and there are still powerful brakes on the possibility of great-power conflict. But it is clear that America once again has great-power rivals, that those rivals are increasingly willing to assert themselves even at risk of heightened geopolitical tensions, and that the risk of great-power conflict has therefore risen to a level higher than at any time since 1989. As the US National Military Strategy warned in 2015, 'Today, the probability of US involvement in interstate war with a major power is assessed to be low but growing.'[37] If great-power geopolitical competition continues to intensify in the coming 10–20 years – as most commentators expect it will – American assumptions about the obsolescence of major-power war, and the striking great-power peace that has characterised the post-Cold War era, will only be further challenged. We may find that the seeming respite from history that accompanied the end of the Cold War is finally coming to an end; the world, and the United States, may find itself heading 'back to the future' of international affairs, as John Mearsheimer predicted a quarter-century ago.[38]

Assumption 5: The advance of democracy is unstoppable and irreversible

Might the world be trending against the United States more generally? Although post-Cold War American strategists have found plenty of dangers to worry about in the short run, and plenty of more distant threats to hedge against in the long run, these concerns were always counter-balanced by the conviction that the world's deeper ideological, economic and technological trends favoured the United States. Indeed, there has been a certain whiggishness to post-Cold War grand strategy – a tendency to believe that the things that were good for America had also been proven to be good for the world, and that, despite the temporary disruptions of malevolent forces, we should expect those things to continue their advance. Yet that conviction is today being challenged on multiple fronts.

This can be seen, firstly, in the return to a more competitive ideological environment. When the Cold War ended, democracy was on a historic winning streak that saw the number of electoral democracies increase from 39 to 76 between 1974 and 1990, and eventually to 120 by the year 2000.[39] A guiding assumption of post-Cold War US grand strategy has been that this trend is unstoppable and irreversible – that with the support of the US and its liberal friends, the world will continue to move in a more democratic direction, and that this progression will also make the international environment more peaceful, prosperous, stable and congenial to US interests and ideals alike. This concept was expressed most forthrightly in the 2002 *National Security Strategy*, which proclaimed that the combination of 'freedom, democracy, and free enterprise' now represented the 'single sustainable model for national success'.[40] Throughout the post-Cold War era, this assumption has guided concrete policies, from the bipartisan, multi-administration commitment to promoting democracy and human rights overseas, to the broader US commitment to extending and deepening the liberal international order.[41]

Today, however, democracy's future has become cloudier. Over the past 10–15 years, authoritarian regimes have become more subtle and skilful at repressing dissent, and more tenacious in clinging to power.[42] In countries such as Venezuela and Turkey, illiberal leaders have taken power through democratic means and then set about dismantling the checks and balances that previously constrained them. Meanwhile, illiberal great powers such as Russia and China have been pushing back against the spread of democracy in their own geopolitical neighbourhoods, opposing anti-authoritarian regime change overseas (in Syria, for instance), and touting the benefits of their own centralised models. Even in the West, democracy's prospects now seem less certain. The rise of illiberal right-wing governments in Hungary and now Poland has created pockets of quasi-authoritarianism within NATO and the EU; Hungary's Viktor Orbán has proudly and openly proclaimed the weakness of liberal society and the rise of the 'illiberal state'.[43] Meanwhile, the 2008 financial crisis raised questions about whether democratic systems can deliver the economic goods as well as their authoritarian counterparts, and America itself has experienced levels of political gridlock and polarisation – as well as the rise of quasi-authoritarian sentiment in some quarters – that hardly speak well for the form of government it champions.

Nor is the stalling of democracy's advance merely an anecdotal phenomenon: the trend is evident in statistical measures of democracy's breadth and strength. The number of democracies in the world has roughly plateaued since around 2006, hovering between 114 and 119, while the rate of 'democratic breakdowns' has increased. And within a number of countries, the past decade has seen some degree of erosion in terms of political freedom, human rights and the rule of law. As one expert notes, Freedom House statistics show 'that in each of the eight consecutive years from 2006 through 2013 more countries declined in freedom than improved'.[44] At the very least, the world is experiencing democratic stagnation; a modest democratic recession may even be under way.

The rate of democratic breakdowns has increased

If assumptions about democracy's continued advance were to be further undermined in the coming 10–20 years, this phenomenon would complicate American strategy in meaningful ways. For example, it would confront US policymakers with the challenge of dealing with political illiberalism within America's core alliances, in a way that would force starker trade-offs between security and ideological issues than Washington has generally had to face in recent decades. A less liberal world might also be a world in which it is more difficult to rally opposition against authoritarian rivals – just look at how Vladimir Putin has reportedly sought to weaken NATO and the EU by supporting illiberal European politicians.[45] More broadly, this scenario would presumably heighten the difficulties and costs of promoting democracy and human rights overseas, and thus force American policymakers to reassess how much emphasis to place on these efforts. Finally, though no less significantly, the stalling or even moderately significant reversal of democracy's progress could undermine one of the fundamental enthusiasms underlying post-Cold War statecraft – the idea that history is moving inexorably in America's direction – and cast the country into an uncertain and adverse ideological climate.

Assumption 6: Globalisation is inexorable

Ominous developments in international politics are matched by troubling economic trends that seem to put at risk a sixth key assumption: that the advance of globalisation is inexorable, beneficial for humanity and beneficial for the United States, because it will ultimately lead to a more peaceful, prosperous and democratic world. This assumption firmly took root in the 1990s, when the end of the Cold War tore down geopolitical barriers to economic integration, just as technological advances were themselves enabling the integration of global finance and economics as never before. Since that time, US officials have acknowledged the dislocations that globalisation can bring, but they have nonetheless argued that its progression is inevitable and ultimately beneficial. 'Efforts to resist the powerful technological and economic forces behind globalization … are misguided and, in the long run, futile', Clinton administration officials first argued in the 1990s.[46] Subsequently, this belief has structured virtually all aspects of US foreign economic policy, from the creation of international economic institutions such as the WTO, to the promotion of free-trade and investment agreements meant to impel economic integration forward.

Most US officials would still aver that globalisation is a good thing, even as they would acknowledge all of the familiar ways that it also invites instability and insecurity. Less certain is whether that advance is really as inexorable as previously thought. From a historical perspective, the progression of globalisation has been neither linear nor uninterrupted – dramatic advances in one era have often been followed by stagnation or even abrupt reversals in subsequent periods.[47] It is therefore reasonable, at least, to consider the numerous indications that the current wave of globalisation may not actually be unstoppable.

Consider five specific issues. Firstly, although a truly epic economic disaster was ultimately averted in 2007–08, the global financial crisis did indicate that the international financial and economic system is perhaps more vulnerable than previously thought to the sort of systemic crisis that has disrupted globalisation before.[48] Secondly, the recent British vote to leave the EU, along with that institution's decade-long struggle to foster renewed economic growth, has shown that institutions commonly associated with globalisation may be more fragile than previously believed. Thirdly, in the US and throughout the West, political processes are revealing greater disillusion not just with economic integration per se, but also with the broader climate of national and societal openness that comes with globalisation.[49] The election of Donald Trump – following a campaign in which both major parties evinced strong scepticism of economic openness – is simply the most dramatic recent manifestation of this trend.

Fourthly, the return of serious great-power frictions – between NATO and Russia in Europe, and between the United States and its allies and China in East Asia – has revived the possibility that geopolitics might once again thwart globalisation, or simply cause leading powers to take a more zero-sum approach to foreign economic policy. If US–China tensions continue to rise, for instance, how long will the pursuit of unfettered economic integration between the two countries seem a wise policy? For that matter, what would a Sino-Japanese war over the Senkaku/Diaoyu Islands do to regional integration in Asia? Finally, some have argued that the internal engine of globalisation – the revolution in global supply-chain manufacturing and the distributed production of the information age – may itself be slowing, and could even reverse.[50] One can, perhaps, envision a retreat from 'off-shoring' back to 'on-shoring' as 3-D printing and robotics make manufacturing even in high-wage societies profitable.[51]

Admittedly, challenges to and changes in globalisation are still comparatively nascent, and the emphasis of government policy in the United States and other key nations remains on initiatives (such as the Trans-Pacific Partnership, or TPP) that are designed to drive globalisation forward. But it is nonetheless becoming easier to see how this progress might be challenged, or even potentially reversed, over the next 10–20 years, and to identify plausible scenarios – economic, political or geopolitical – that could fundamentally challenge this assumption. Were this to occur, it would significantly complicate a US foreign economic policy that has made promoting globalisation its overarching *raison d'être* in the post-Cold War era, while also significantly distorting the broader American conception of where the world is headed.[52]

Assumption 7: Technological innovation will lead to greater human flourishing and freedom, and will disproportionately favour the United States

A final source of long-term American confidence has been the belief that the benefits of technological innovation trump its dangers, both for humanity as a whole and for the US in particular. This idea has been a recurring theme in American strategy for generations, and has been particularly pronounced since the end of the Cold War. In the economic realm, this assumption was informed by the way that technological advances helped transform the global economy from the 1970s onward, simultaneously uplifting vast numbers of individuals around the globe and strengthening America's own economic power. In the realm of ideas, this assumption was fostered by the role of technological innovation in empowering people vis-à-vis states, and thereby contributing to the remarkable democratic wave from the mid-1970s to the early 2000s. In the security realm, this assumption was promoted by the way in which the United States harnessed information-age technologies to leap ahead of the Soviets during the 1980s, and to establish an astounding post-Cold War primacy. Throughout the post-Cold War era, the view that technological change has been basically good for the flourishing and freedom of people around the world – and that the United States is best placed to exploit and adapt to such change – has thus been central to the country's strategic outlook, and it has been fundamental to the belief that America and its guiding principles will ultimately win the future.[53]

It would be an enormous exaggeration to say that this optimism has been fully or even largely discredited in recent years. In many ways, a capacity for technological innovation remains a key comparative advantage for the US, both economically and militarily.[54] Technological innovation also continues to produce remarkable gains in human prosperity, and to create pathways for individuals to mobilise against dictatorial regimes, as demonstrated by the use of social media in recent anti-authoritarian uprisings. Yet there are nonetheless important respects in which this assumption is being tested – in which the balance sheet on technological advance may be shifting in unfavourable ways.

Technological advances are empowering individuals to challenge dictators, but they are also empowering dictators to monitor and repress citizens.

Internal-security services in Iran and other Middle Eastern countries have used activists' Facebook profiles to map and disrupt protest networks, and they have used advances in information technology more broadly to better surveil groups that threaten their rule.[55] For its part, China has emerged as a veritable case study in how autocrats can use technological change to fortify themselves in power. Communist Party officials have worked to seize the 'commanding heights' of the internet, by using the state's technological prowess to monitor emerging sources of discontent, to censor threatening information or commentary, to spread propaganda and misinformation, and to harass and intimidate dissidents. State employees flood the information battlespace, churning out social-media posts that praise party rule and attack regime opponents. 'Social media can allow autocrats to become stronger, more informed, and more adaptable', argues analyst Simon Denyer. It is 'a potential tool of subtle control and manipulation … that often works more effectively than brute-force suppression'.[56] Experts continue to debate whether the forces of liberalism or illiberalism are more effectively harnessing technology, but it can no longer simply be assumed that the former will triumph.

In the military sphere, too, it is increasingly unclear whether technological innovation will increase or decrease America's advantages. For all the discussion in the early post-Cold War era of a US-led 'revolution in military affairs', technological change now seems to act more as an equaliser for American adversaries. Since the 1990s, for instance, China has been a 'fast follower', using intensive resource investments (along with, reportedly, healthy doses of industrial theft and espionage) to catch up rapidly in several key areas. The People's Liberation Army has leapt forward by perhaps two generations in capabilities such as fighter aircraft, ballistic missiles and other key components of the precision-strike complex; these and other aspects of Chinese modernisation 'have come extraordinarily quickly by any reasonable historical standard', as RAND corporation analysts put it.[57] The Chinese build-up, in other words, is not simply a matter of numbers. Rather, Beijing is also cutting into America's lead, and contesting its customary advantages, by harnessing technological innovation to make some remarkable qualitative improvements.

Nor is this the only way in which the geopolitical results of innovation seem more adverse than advantageous. The spread of anti-satellite and cyber-warfare capabilities to a number of rivals and malign actors is complicating American superiority in, and unimpeded access to, the space and cyberspace domains. Hostile non-state groups such as Hizbullah have increasingly gained access to weapons systems, from man-portable air-defence systems (MANPADS) to guided surface-to-surface rockets, that allow them to mimic certain capabilities of technologically advanced powers. Meanwhile, the proliferation of 'lone-wolf' and 'wolf-pack' terrorism demonstrates how extremist groups have harnessed the power of the internet to achieve radicalisation and mount attacks over great distances, in a way that US and European security services have so far found devilishly difficult to forestall.[58] Across a variety of dimensions, then, technology is narrowing the power gap between the United States and its adversaries. Here as in the political realm, the darker side of technological advancement is increasingly coming into view, raising pointed questions about who will win the future after all.

The will to adapt

Since the end of the Cold War, American grand strategy has been rooted in generally bullish assumptions about where the world is headed and the feasibility of sustaining America's dominance. Now, however, the world is changing geopolitically, economically and ideologically, and central assumptions are being tested more strenuously than at any previous time in the post-Cold War era. There will be fewer favourable givens for the United States in the emerging international environment – America is entering an era in which global affairs will be more contested, more competitive and more uncertain.

This does not necessarily mean that America's post-Cold War strategy is doomed, or that radical retrenchment will soon be required. Key assumptions of US globalism have been tested before – in the period after the Vietnam War, for instance – and American leaders proved capable of gradually making the adjustments needed to reinvigorate US strategy in light of global changes.[59] Today, then, the fate of US strategy will depend in substantial measure on whether Washington can do so again – whether it will make the investments necessary to shore up US military primacy against growing challenges; whether it will offset the decline of traditional allies by forging more diverse partnerships with a range of other key international actors; and whether it will invest the political capital needed to revitalise the free-trade/globalisation agenda amid domestic resistance. In other words, the country has options: it need not simply be a bystander to a shifting international environment. The key policy question is thus whether the US can mobilise its still pre-eminent resources and energies to effectively adapt to a world in which its core strategic assumptions are being tested.

What if this time is different?

The answer to that question bears on a final core assumption – that decline is a choice that Americans can reject, because the US political system will ultimately support the decisions and sacrifices needed to sustain an effective, primacist grand strategy. This assumption significantly predates the post-Cold War period. Throughout the post-war era, the United States has confronted doubts about the resilience of its power, the validity and sustainability of its policies, and its ability to deal with new global challenges. This was the case following the first Soviet A-bomb test in the late 1940s, the launching of *Sputnik* in the 1950s, the traumas of Vietnam and the oil shocks in the 1970s, and in several other instances.[60] In each case, the US political system ultimately proved capable of taking the steps necessary to once again put America on an upward trajectory – for instance, by undertaking the military build-up associated with NSC-68 in the early 1950s, by rebuilding US military power after Vietnam, and by addressing budget deficits during the 1980s and early 1990s. And so for many political and policy elites, a bedrock intellectual assumption has been that, just as the US has overcome great challenges before, it can do so again. As former president Bill Clinton aptly put it in 2012: 'Every single person that's bet against America has lost money because we always come back.'[61]

But what if this time is different? What if this assumption does not hold, because the American political system has become less capable of enabling good grand strategy? One hardly needs to be an alarmist to wonder whether this may be the case.

Consider the issue of whether the US can adequately resource its grand strategy. By historical standards, the percentage of GDP devoted to the overall national-security budget – the combined costs of defence, foreign diplomacy, foreign aid and intelligence – is fairly small. American defence spending, for instance, has never been higher than 4.7% of GDP since the mid-1990s, compared to more than 12% at the height of the Cold War.[62] Yet in recent years, national-security spending has come under intense downward pressure. The culprit is not declining national wealth, but rather historically high levels of political gridlock and polarisation.[63] By most statistical measures, these forces are now at generational highs, and since 2011 in particular, they have made it essentially impossible for the country to address issues of deficits and spending in a reasonable way. Instead, they led to a sequestration mechanism that has inflicted significant defence cuts, caused crippling budgetary inflexibility and uncertainty, and played havoc with US force structure, modernisation and readiness – all at a time when threats to American primacy are becoming more severe. Looking ahead, if the United States does not find a way of overcoming surging polarisation and addressing spending issues more strategically, then exploding entitlement costs will consume ever-larger chunks of federal spending, crowding out defence and further corroding the military pillar of American strategy.

Nor is this the only issue about which there is cause for concern. As noted, the American political system seems to be becoming more resistant to free trade and globalisation. During the 2016 presidential campaign, both major parties' candidates opposed TPP, and anti-trade rhetoric loomed larger than at any time in at least a generation. The election ultimately brought to power a candidate who – in his campaign rhetoric, at least – had fundamentally critiqued key elements of American globalism, from US support for international institutions to the maintenance of US alliances. How Donald Trump actually governs remains to be seen, of course. Yet all of this is nonetheless enough to make one wonder whether America's post-Cold War strategy is running out of steam.

Of course, one should not overstate the degree to which this assumption has been invalidated. Public-opinion polling paints a somewhat brighter picture, with polls taken in 2015 and 2016 showing that public support for many key aspects of American internationalism remains (superficially, at least) fairly strong.[64] And it may be that the political system will, over the long run, continue to produce leaders and policies that will sustain US leadership.

But given recent trends, it is hard not to worry that this most fundamental assumption of US grand strategy – that the country can effectively cope with the problems before it – may be becoming shakier as well. And if this assumption is further undermined over the next 10–20 years, it would significantly compound the effects of all the other global changes discussed here – and augur a bleak future for both American grand strategy and the post-Cold War order it supports.

Notes

1 To be sure, US grand strategy was not premised *entirely* upon optimistic assumptions, as it also identified a range of threats and challenges that warranted an assertive response. But those problems stood out in sharp relief against a broader backdrop that was assumed to be basically favourable to US power, values and interests.

2 For a more comprehensive compilation of the assumptions underlying US grand strategy since the end of the Second World War, see Peter Feaver, William Inboden, Hal Brands and Paul Miller, 'Planning Assumptions in American Grand Strategy', paper prepared for the National Intelligence Council, August 2015. This longer list of assumptions was initially prepared for the National Intelligence Council in support of the *Global Trends 2035* report.

3 See Christopher Layne, 'The Unipolar Illusion: Why New Great Powers Will Rise', *International Security*, vol. 17, no. 4, Spring 1993, pp. 5–51.

4 'Grand strategy' is defined here as the 'purposeful and coherent set of ideas about what a nation seeks to accomplish in the world, and how it should go about doing so'. Hal Brands, *What Good Is Grand Strategy? Power and Purpose in American Statecraft from Harry S. Truman to George W. Bush* (Ithaca, NY: Cornell University Press, 2014), p. 3.

5 On post-Cold War grand strategy, see Peter Feaver, 'American Grand Strategy at the Crossroads: Leading from the Front, Leading from Behind, or Not Leading at All', in Richard Fontaine and Kristin Lord, *America's Path: Grand Strategy For the Next Administration* (Washington DC: Center for New American Security, May 2012), pp. 59–70; and Hal Brands, *Making the Unipolar Moment: US Foreign Policy and the Rise of the Post-Cold War Order* (Ithaca, NY: Cornell University Press, 2016), especially Chapter 6 and the conclusion. As this description indicates, we believe there was a coherent post-Cold War grand strategy, a position that is supported at greater length in the works cited here and other sources.

6 It has sometimes been argued that the terrorist attacks of 9/11 represented

such a change, but 9/11 did not fundamentally alter structural global power dynamics to anywhere near the same degree as did the end of the Cold War.

7 On the Bush administration's approach to counter-terrorism and grand strategy, see Brands, *What Good Is Grand Strategy?*, Chapter 4; and Peter Feaver and Stephen Biddle, 'Assessing Strategic Choices in the War on Terror', in James Burk (ed.), *How 9/11 Changed Our Ways of War* (Stanford, CA: Stanford University Press, 2014).

8 The argument we are making here is *not* that these seven assumptions are necessarily the seven most important assumptions in American grand strategy, although they are all fundamentally important. Rather, these are the seven most important assumptions that are now increasingly open to challenge.

9 See Barry Posen, 'Command of the Commons: The Military Foundation of US Hegemony', *International Security*, vol. 28, no. 1, Summer 2003, pp. 5–46.

10 See, for instance, Barton Gellman, 'Keeping the US First; Pentagon Would Preclude a Rival Superpower', *Washington Post*, 11 March 1992; and George W. Bush, 'Commencement Address at the United States Military Academy in West Point, New York', 1 June 2002, http://www.presidency.ucsb.edu/ws/index.php?pid=62730&st=&st1=.

11 Stephen G. Brooks and William Wohlforth, 'The Rise and Fall of the Great Powers in the Twenty-First Century', *International Security*, vol. 40, no. 3, Winter 2015–16, pp. 7–53.

12 Eric Heginbotham et al., *The US–China Military Scorecard: Forces, Geography, and the Evolving Balance of Power, 1996–2017* (Santa Monica, CA: RAND Corporation, 2015), especially p. xxxi.

13 David Shlapak and Michael Johnson, 'Reinforcing Deterrence on NATO's Eastern Flank: Wargaming the Defense of the Baltics', RAND Corporation, January 2016.

14 *Countering Air and Missile Threats, Joint Publication 3-01* (Ft. Belvoir, VA: Defense Technical Information Center, 23 March 2012). 'Air supremacy' is distinguished from 'air superiority', a lesser degree of advantage.

15 See Heginbotham et al., *US–China Military Scorecard*, chapters 3–6; David Barno and Nora Bensahel, 'The Catastrophic Success of the US Air Force', *War on the Rocks*, 3 May 2016; Elbridge Colby and Jonathan Solomon, 'Facing Russia: Conventional Defence and Deterrence in Europe', *Survival*, vol. 57, no. 6, December 2015–January 2016, pp. 21–50.

16 For a classic work on shifting balances and international statecraft, see Marc Trachtenberg, 'A "Wasting Asset": American Strategy and the Shifting Nuclear Balance, 1949–1954', *International Security*, vol. 13, no. 3, Winter 1988–89, pp. 5–49.

17 The defence-spending figures in this section are drawn from the Stockholm International Peace Research Institute's (SIPRI) annual data on global military spending. The GDP figures are drawn from Economic Research Service, US Department of Agriculture, 'GDP Shares by Country and Region Historical', http://www.ers.usda.gov/data-products/international-macroeconomic-data-set.aspx. The data used here were drawn

from these data sets in November 2015. Figures for US allies include the NATO countries, US treaty allies in the Asia-Pacific and Taiwan (thanks to its quasi-treaty-ally status).

18 US and allied interests did not always converge on particular issues: consider the growing divergence between French and US–British positions on Iraq as the 1990s progressed.

19 See F. Stephen Larrabee et al., *NATO and the Challenge of Austerity* (Santa Monica, CA: RAND Corporation, 2012); Adrian Croft, 'Defense Cuts "Hollowing Out" European Armies: US Envoy', Reuters, 17 June 2013.

20 See, for instance, Thom Shanker, 'Defense Secretary Warns NATO of "Dim" Future', *New York Times*, 10 June 2011.

21 Steven Erlanger, 'Shrinking Europe Military Spending Stirs Concern', *New York Times*, 23 April 2013. See also Michael Swaine et al., *Conflict and Cooperation in the Asia-Pacific Region: A Strategic Net Assessment* (Washington DC: Carnegie Endowment for International Peace, 2015), especially p. 2.

22 Aaron Friedberg, *A Contest for Supremacy: China, America, and the Struggle for Mastery in Asia* (New York: Norton, 2011), especially pp. 91–2.

23 See Thomas Christensen, 'Fostering Stability or Creating a Monster? The Rise of China and US Policy toward East Asia', *International Security*, vol. 31, no. 1, Summer 2006, pp. 81–126.

24 *Ibid*.

25 See World Bank, 'GDP at Market Prices (Current US$)', http://data.worldbank.org/indicator/NY.GDP.MKTP.CD?locations=CN; and World Bank, 'GDP Per Capita (Current US$)', http://data.worldbank.org/indicator/NY.GDP.PCAP.CD?locations=CN.

26 Edward Wong, 'China Ranks Last of 65 Nations in Internet Freedom', *New York Times*, 29 October 2015.

27 See 'Polity IV Individual Country Regime Trends, 1946–2013', http://www.systemicpeace.org/polity/polity4.htm.

28 Chantal Yuen, 'Freedom House Says China "Role Model" for Oppressive Countries, Flags SCMP Sale to Alibaba', *Hong Kong Free Press*, 28 January 2016.

29 For a sceptical take on the idea that there has recently been a significant change in China's policies, see Alastair Iain Johnston, 'How New and Assertive Is China's New Assertiveness?', *International Security*, vol. 37, no. 4, Spring 2013, pp. 7–48.

30 See Department of Defense, 'Annual Report to Congress: Military and Security Developments Involving the People's Republic of China 2016', http://www.defense.gov/Portals/1/Documents/pubs/2016%20China%20Military%20Power%20Report.pdf; and Andrew Erickson and Conor Kennedy, 'China's Maritime Militia: What It Is and How to Deal With It', *Foreign Affairs*, 23 June 2016, https://www.foreignaffairs.com/articles/china/2016-06-23/chinas-maritime-militia.

31 See Bush's introduction to *National Security Strategy of the United States of America* (Washington DC: White House, 2002).

32 Robert Jervis, 'Theories of War in an Era of Leading-Power Peace', *American Political Science Review*, vol. 96, no. 1, March 2002, pp. 1–14.

33 Bush, 'Commencement Address at the United States Military Academy in West Point, New York'.

34 'Navy Official: China Training for "Short Sharp War" with Japan', *USNI News*, 18 February 2014.

35 Max Fisher, 'How World War III Became Possible: A Nuclear Conflict with Russia is Likelier than You Think', *Vox*, 29 June 2015, http://www.vox.com/2015/6/29/8845913/russia-war.

36 See Robert Work, 'The Third Offset Strategy and its Implications for Partners and Allies', Washington DC, 28 January 2015, http://www.defense.gov/News/Speeches/Speech-View/Article/606641/the-third-us-offset-strategy-and-its-implications-for-partners-and-allies.

37 General Martin Dempsey, 'National Military Strategy of the United States of America', June 2015, p. 4.

38 John Mearsheimer, 'Back to the Future: Instability in Europe after the Cold War', *International Security*, vol. 15, no. 1, Summer 1990, pp. 5–55.

39 Statistics from Freedom House, 'Freedom in the World 2013: Democratic Breakthroughs in the Balance', 2013, p. 29, https://www.freedomhouse.org/sites/default/files/FIW%202013%20Booklet.pdf; Larry Diamond, *Developing Democracy: Toward Consolidation* (Baltimore, MD: Johns Hopkins University Press, 1999), p. 25.

40 See Bush's introduction to *National Security Strategy of the United States of America*.

41 Paul Miller, 'American Grand Strategy and the Democratic Peace', *Survival*, vol. 54, no. 2, April–May 2012, pp. 49–76.

42 On this point, see William J. Dobson, *The Dictator's Learning Curve: Inside the Global Battle for Democracy* (New York: Doubleday, 2012).

43 See Michael Boyle, 'The Coming Illiberal Order', *Survival*, vol. 58, no. 2, April–May 2016, especially pp. 35–6.

44 Larry Diamond, 'Facing Up to the Democratic Recession', *Journal of Democracy*, vol. 25, no. 1, January 2015, pp. 141–55, especially pp. 142, 147–8.

45 See Peter Foster and Matthew Holehouse, 'Russia Accused of Clandestine Funding of European Parties as US Conducts Major Review of Vladimir Putin's Strategy', *Telegraph*, 16 January 2016.

46 Joan Spero, 'The Challenges of Globalization', remarks at the World Economic Development Congress, Washington DC, 26 September 1996, http://www.state.gov/www/issues/economic/960926.html.

47 See Peter Stearns, *Globalization in World History* (New York: Routledge, 2010).

48 For an optimistic interpretation of the crisis, see Daniel Drezner, *The System Worked: How the World Stopped Another Great Depression* (New York: Oxford University Press, 2014). For more pessimistic interpretations, see Jonathan Kirschner, *American Power after the Financial Crisis* (Ithaca, NY: Cornell University Press, 2014); and Carmen Reinhart and Kenneth Rogoff, *This Time Is Different: Eight Centuries of Financial Folly* (Princeton, NJ: Princeton University Press, 2011).

49 See, for instance, Diego Zuluaga, 'Public Opinion Is Turning Against Free Trade and Globalisation', Institute of Economic Affairs, 27 June 2016, http://www.iea.org.uk/blog/public-opinion-is-turning-against-free-trade-and-globalisation.

50 T.X. Hammes, 'The End of Globalization? The International Security Implications', *War on the Rocks*, 2 August 2016.

51 See 'Made in America, Again: Fourth Annual Survey of US Based Manufacturing Executives', Boston Consulting Group, December 2015.

52 Conceivably, a reversal or major shift in globalisation could impact US grand strategy in an even more fundamental way. If the United States were to become less dependent on global supply-chain manufacturing, perhaps because of an accelerated return to 'on-shoring', then Washington might have less incentive to continue patrolling the global commons and taking other stabilising measures traditionally geared, at least in part, toward ensuring the smooth functioning of the global economy.

53 See, for example, Adam Segal, *Advantage: How American Innovation Can Overcome the Asian Challenge* (New York: W.W. Norton, 2011).

54 See Brooks and Wohlforth, 'The Rise and Fall of the Great Powers in the Twenty-First Century'; Michael Beckley, 'China's Century? Why America's Edge Will Endure', *International Security*, vol. 36, no. 3, Winter 2011–12, pp. 41–78.

55 See Dobson, *The Dictator's Learning Curve*.

56 Simon Denyer, 'The Internet Was Supposed to Foster Democracy. China Has Different Ideas', *Washington Post*, 10 July 2016. See also Seva Gunitsky, 'Social Media Helps Dictators, Not Just Protestors', The Monkey Cage, 30 March 2015, https://www.washingtonpost.com/blogs/monkey-cage/wp/2015/03/30/social-media-helps-dictators-not-just-protesters/.

57 Heginbotham et al., *US–China Military Scorecard*, especially p. xxx.

58 On this point, see Isaac Chotiner, 'A Lone-Wolf Terrorist Is Never Quite Alone', *Slate*, 13 June 2016.

59 See Peter Feaver (ed.), *Strategic Retrenchment and Renewal in the American Experience* (Carlisle, PA: Strategic Studies Institute of the Army War College, 2014); and Brands, *Making the Unipolar Moment*.

60 See Samuel Huntington, 'The US – Decline or Renewal?', *Foreign Affairs*, vol. 67, no. 2, Winter 1988–89, pp. 76–96.

61 'Transcript of Bill Clinton's Speech to the Democratic National Convention', *New York Times*, 5 September 2012.

62 See John Lewis Gaddis, *Strategies of Containment: A Critical Appraisal of American National Security Policy During the Cold War* (New York: Oxford University Press, 2005), p. 393; World Bank, 'Military Expenditure (% of GDP)', http://data.worldbank.org/indicator/MS.MIL.XPND.GD.ZS?page=3.

63 On these forces, see Pew Research Center, 'Political Polarization in the American Public', June 2014, especially pp. 6–15.

64 See Chicago Council on Global Affairs, *America Divided: Political Partisanship and US Foreign Policy*, October 2015. See also Craig Kafura and Dina Smeltz, 'On Eve of NATO Summit, Majority of Americans Say Alliance Is Essential', Chicago Council on Global Affairs, 6 July 2016, https://www.thechicagocouncil.org/publication/eve-nato-summit-majority-americans-say-alliance-essential.

Airpower in American Wars

R.D. Hooker, Jr

Since the Second World War, airpower has been seen as the crown jewel in America's strategic inventory.[1] No country has been able to match American dominance in the air since 1944, yielding clear air superiority to US forces in every conflict. This success has led to the belief that airpower is the dominant form of military power, and that US strategic and resource decisions should reflect that primacy. Yet a close reading of the history of modern warfare shows that airpower, while crucial, cannot by itself secure victory. Dominance and balance across the air, ground, maritime, space and cyber domains are the true basis of American military prowess. Increasingly, that balance is at risk.

Origins of airpower

The early experiences of the major combatants in the First World War established airpower as a military capability with far-reaching potential. Giulio Douhet's *The Command of the Air*, published in 1921, proffered a theory of the dominance of airpower over armies and navies that endures to this day. 'To conquer command of the air means victory', wrote Douhet. 'To be beaten in the air means defeat and acceptance of whatever terms the enemy may be pleased to impose.'[2] Building on Douhet's theories, the belief that wars can be won solely or primarily from the air became canonical for many airmen.

R.D. Hooker, Jr, is the Director of the Institute for National Strategic Studies at the National Defense University. A former career military officer, he served as a White House staff member in the administrations of George H.W. Bush, William J. Clinton and George W. Bush. This paper reflects the views of the author alone and not the official position of the National Defense University or the US Department of Defense.

US Air Force Colonel John Warden, for instance, has insisted that 'we must start our thinking by assuming we can do everything with air power, not by assuming that it can only do what it did in the past.'[3] Despite the inconclusive outcomes of the Korean, Vietnam, Iraq and Afghanistan wars – all conflicts in which the United States enjoyed an overwhelming edge in airpower – such views remain widespread.

A belief in the primacy of airpower carries a corollary: that airpower is by its very nature a strategic instrument, best applied against strategic targets such as industry or national command authorities far beyond the battlefield.[4] This implies that operational and tactical uses are less legitimate. From the very beginning, acceptance of this argument was seen as necessary if air forces were ever to become separate from, and equal to, the other services.[5] Though resisted by more traditional and conservative armies and navies, airpower offered dazzling advantages that were apparent as early as the 1920s. After the horror of the trenches, the prospect of rapid, decisive victory without huge casualties and expenditure proved almost irresistible.[6]

Airpower comprises much more than the nation's inventory of combat aircraft. It includes the industrial and technological foundation of that inventory; the pilots and other crew members that operate the aircraft, and the training bases that produce them; the intelligence, surveillance and reconnaissance (ISR), command and control, and tanker communities that enable combat missions; the strategic- and tactical-airlift communities that are so crucial to American power projection; the logistics, maintenance and targeting communities; basing facilities at home and abroad; and much else. The airpower provided by other services, partners and allies, though often overlooked, is also a critical part of the airpower equation.

Airpower in war

The Second World War provided the first opportunity to put ideas of the decisiveness of airpower to the test. Enormous resources were poured into British and American strategic bombing offensives in Europe, producing extraordinary losses among allied aircrews and civilians alike.[7] At great cost, the German air force was swept from the skies, despite the diversion of Germany's war industry for air defence. Looking back, it is clear that strategic bombing made a significant contribution to the outcome of the war, and that the allies' overwhelming strength in the air was a factor in their victory. Nevertheless, most scholars agree that airpower fell short of the more extreme claims made on its behalf. It had played a critical role in securing the victory, but had not won the war by itself. American and allied land and sea power were also important.[8]

In the Pacific, strategic bombing played a different role. Despite an early lead, the Japanese were quickly eclipsed in terms of the number and quality of US and allied planes and aircrew.[9] Only 160,800 tons of bombs were dropped on Japan's home islands (compared to 2,700,000 tons dropped on Europe), only 10% of which hit near their targets until the Army Air Forces shifted to low-level, night-time, area attacks against urban areas. Land-based bombers destroyed only a small fraction of vessels belonging to the Imperial Japanese Navy and the Japanese merchant fleet, with most sunk by tactical Navy and Marine aircraft and, above all, submarines.[10]

In both theatres, the prevailing theory of strategic bombing centred on bombing cities, in line with Douhet's proposition that destroying an enemy's will to resist through the deliberate targeting of civilian populations and the destruction of industry was the quickest and surest path to victory. General 'Hap' Arnold, commander of the US Army Air Forces, put it succinctly:

> America's air doctrine for years has been based solidly on the principle of long-range bombardment. Air forces are strictly offensive in character … Strategic air power is a war-winning weapon in its own right.[11]

In Korea and Vietnam, airpower played important roles, but true strategic bombing was not attempted for a variety of reasons – not least to avoid escalating the conflict. In both wars, the role of the Air Force as the principal airpower provider for a large-scale land campaign brought it into conflict with the Army over the proper use of airpower resources and their command and control. Naval and Marine commanders for the most part successfully retained operational control of their aviation. The inherent speed and power of fixed-wing aviation drove the most senior Army commanders to demand operational control of tactical Air Force assets for interdiction and close air support, as enjoyed by Marine commanders employing Marine air.[12] This tension would carry over into every future conflict.

Operation Desert Storm in 1991 presented an optimum test case for strategic airpower. The theatre of operations was largely devoid of built-up areas, with no forests or jungles to conceal the enemy. The Iraqi army was large but conventionally organised and relatively easy to target. Enemy air defence was not strong, and the Iraqi air force posed no real threat. Technology had advanced far beyond the Vietnam era, to include unmanned aerial vehicles (UAVs).[13] Air forces were enabled by global positioning satellites (GPS) and secure satellite communications, and possessed some advanced precision-guided munitions. If ever a war could be won solely from the air, the Gulf War was it.

The Gulf War presented a test case

Air operations commenced on 17 January 1991, with the 'air phase' of the campaign concluding on 23 February. The bulk of the air effort (some 70%) was focused on attacking Iraqi ground forces. More than 2,250 coalition aircraft ranged widely over Iraq, striking infrastructure and command-and-control targets. Iraqi air defences and the Iraqi air force were quickly overcome at low cost. Damage to Iraqi power and transportation systems, port facilities and oil refineries was extensive. However, a single attack against the Al Firdos command post in Baghdad on 13 February that resulted in many civilian deaths brought the strategic air campaign to an end.[14]

On Day 1 of the ground invasion, US Central Command assessed that air strikes had eliminated 39% of the Iraqi army's tanks and 47% of its artillery tubes.[15] Yet true 'decapitation' proved elusive: a resilient Iraqi command-and-control structure had demonstrated its ability to endure punishment and adapt. Likewise, an urgent effort to find and eliminate Iraqi mobile *Scud* launchers, intended to halt attacks aimed at drawing Israel into the war, was ineffective despite consuming up to one-third of the coalition air effort.[16] In the face of heavy punishment from the air, the Iraqi army did not decamp until coalition ground forces, numbering more than half a million, attacked. The application of airpower alone could not and did not force the Iraqi army to withdraw from Kuwait: powerful land forces were needed for that.[17] Yet the contributions of coalition airpower, if not decisive in and of themselves, should not be downplayed. Particularly significant was the use of airpower for air interdiction and close air support; more than strategic bombing, these missions dominated the allocation of air assets and contributed most significantly to the conflict's outcome. Strategic airlift, in-flight refuelling, tactical reconnaissance and bomb-damage assessment, cruise-missile strikes from naval platforms in the Persian Gulf, and intelligence, surveillance and reconnaissance functions performed by unmanned platforms and the Joint Surveillance Target Attack Radar System (JSTARS) were all key to the American campaign. Six US Navy carrier air wings and the 3rd Marine Aircraft Wing, along with significant air components from coalition partners, contributed heavily to the air effort.

The next opportunity to test Douhet's theory came with *Operation Allied Force*, the NATO campaign in 1999 to drive Serbian security forces from Kosovo. Perhaps even more than *Desert Storm*, the Kosovo air war was cited as proof that modern technology (in particular, precision-guided munitions) had vindicated Douhet. In ten weeks, from 24 March to 11 June, NATO aircraft flew more than 38,000 combat missions with 1,000 coalition aircraft. Initial air operations were focused on Serbian units in Kosovo, but poor weather, effective Serbian camouflage, dispersion and decoys limited battlefield effects. This led to an early shift in focus to strategic targets in Serbia proper, such as military bases, arms factories, road and rail networks, oil refineries, bridges and command posts. Two controversial strikes in particular drew worldwide criticism: an errant attack on the Chinese embassy in Belgrade, which killed three Chinese citizens, and a deliberate attack on the Serbian national television station, killing 14 Serbian civilians. Overall, however, civilian casualties were low.[18] Serbian air defences were hopelessly outmatched, and only two US jets were lost in combat.

The debate as to whether Serbian president Slobodan Milosevic withdrew from Kosovo due to the effects of NATO airpower alone continues to this day. Serbia gave in to NATO's demands after 78 days of bombing, without a ground invasion, but it is still unclear what lessons can be drawn from this. NATO, which enjoyed clear technological superiority, deployed massive airpower against a small, relatively backward state unsupported by any outside power. Whether airpower alone could produce similar outcomes against different opponents in different circumstances remains an open question.

Following 9/11, the invasions of Afghanistan in 2001 and Iraq in 2003 provided the next laboratories for airpower. Both campaigns saw an initial phase featuring the conventional deployment of airpower en masse, which then evolved into counter-insurgency and a much different role for the invader's air assets. Initial success in both campaigns was attributed largely to the effects of airpower, with ground forces (sent in far smaller numbers than during *Desert Storm*) playing only a secondary role.[19] Stealth technology and a new generation of unmanned ISR platforms now augmented the strongest, most advanced and most sophisticated air force on the planet. Soon, however, virulent insurgencies emerged. Hopes for 'rapid decisive victory' gave way to the Long War, a grinding, indecisive conflict that was decidedly different in character. As the campaigns evolved into counter-insurgency, structures and processes failed to optimise the delivery of airpower in distributed and low-intensity operations, in which close and continuous coordination with ground forces was imperative. Even where the air-defence threat was low, airpower had limited effects, and may at times have worked against campaign objectives by alienating the population through civilian casualties.[20] Early success led by airpower prompted some to declare a new era in warfare, but a decade later the prevailing view was more sober.[21]

Current trends

Douhet's premise that rapid, decisive victory in war can be achieved from the air, without the necessity for ground campaigns, continues to be widely accepted, despite the fact that it has so often fallen short. In war after war, the prospect of rapid enemy collapse through strategic bombing, at low cost, and without major ground fighting or casualties, has been seductive – and chimerical. While airpower has proven to be indispensable in state-on-state wars, by itself it is inadequate.

What accounts for this enduring belief in strategic bombing (now called 'strategic attack' in Air Force doctrine)[22] in the face of so much contradictory evidence? One explanation is that a coherent doctrine that offers the prospect of a single-service victory, controlled by airmen, without the need for protracted land or naval warfare, offers more than victory: it is a compelling argument for autonomy and freedom of action, which are highly prized by all large organisations. To an unusual degree, the Air Force has achieved these aims, both in terms of setting the conditions for employment of Air Force assets and in fielding new systems. While an important component of their parent services, Naval and Marine aviation complement the warfighting specialties of other services and do not consider themselves strategic communities in their own right.

The low priority assigned to close air support (CAS) also fits this hypothesis.[23] While strategic missions maximise the employment of Air Force assets under Air Force commanders, CAS requires close coordination and integration with ground commanders, violating a number of tenets deemed essential for the optimum employment of airpower.[24] Army doctrine is heavily dependent on airpower, which enables the flexible and powerful concentration of combat power more than any other capability on the battlefield. From the perspective of many airmen, however, CAS is seen as a wasteful dispersion of airpower for tactical, rather than strategic, ends.[25]

Air Force systems procurement, which clearly reflects a drive for independence, prioritises aircraft optimised for strategic attack to a marked degree. As a result, the costs of next-generation aircraft have exploded, driving inventories and flying hours down and crowding out other investment across the defence establishment. So-called fourth-generation fighters – the A-10, F-15 and F-16 – entered service in the 1970s at costs of $19 million, $75m and $36m respectively, and are still in service today.[26] F-117 stealth fighters, fielded in 1983 and retired in 2008, cost $179m each. In contrast, the fifth-generation F-22 and F-35 aircraft are priced at $441m and $138m per copy, with the F-35 programme described as the most expensive defence-procurement programme in history due to the planned high production run.[27] The cost to taxpayers for modern strategic bombers is even more extraordinary, with the B-1 priced at $413m per copy and the B-2 stealth bomber at an incredible $3 billion per plane.[28] By way of comparison, the F/A18 *Super Hornet* used by the US Navy and Marine Corps is priced at $113m per copy.[29]

It is clear that stealth or low-observable aircraft operating at medium and high altitudes represent the Air Force's preferred mode of breaching defended air space. This is problematic for several reasons. To achieve very small radar cross-sections, stealth-aircraft design compromises on manoeuvrability and flight performance. Stealth requires internally loaded weapons and fuel, dramatically reducing both weapons load and range. For example, the F-15E carries 70% more fuel and six times the weapons load of an F-22, and therefore costs six times as much with double the flying-hour costs. These are very heavy penalties.[30]

The Air Force's drive to field very costly aircraft in budget-constrained times is all the more questionable given the United States' overwhelming edge in airpower.[31] In quality and quantity, the US is by far the preponderant air power in the world, and will remain so for the foreseeable future. With no allies, Russia and China field far fewer and less capable combat aircraft, while their pilots receive fewer flying hours than US pilots.[32] Neither possesses true strategic capacity in their air forces; lacking tankers, airborne warning and control systems, and ISR, they are focused on conflict scenarios on their peripheries.[33] In terms of overall defence spending, the US defence budget of $581bn dwarfs China's ($130bn) and Russia's ($70bn).[34] Clearly, any argument that the US lead in airpower is at risk overstates the case by a wide margin.[35]

Of course, civilian leaders are attracted to the notion of surgical, precision warfare. Production is normally spread among many subcontractors located in many different states, a key consideration for congressional supporters. Three of the four services have very strong fixed-wing aviation communities with close ties to the defence industry. The movement of officers to industry and of industry officials into the Department of Defense is routine. These dynamics ensure that the linkages between the services, the Department of Defense, the US Congress, the defence industries and their lobbyists are strong enough to withstand most opposition to aviation procurement. Strategic or budgetary arguments – even from the defense secretary – are brushed aside relatively easily. Even in times of budgetary uncertainty and cutbacks, the power and momentum behind airpower-system acquisition is striking.

Another driver of costly airpower investment is the notion that the US should develop its ability to penetrate the world's strongest and densest air-defence networks with manned aircraft to attack high-value targets, such as nuclear-delivery systems or a regime's leadership, deep inside an adversary's homeland. While gaining and maintaining air supremacy is universally recognised as essential, these aims are more controversial. The historical record is ambiguous, the resources required are extraordinary, and opinion among the other services and the national-security establishment is divided. If such an effort were successful, the survival of an adversary's regime would be at risk, raising the possibility of a nuclear exchange that would yield no victor. If unsuccessful, as such efforts have often been historically, the massive investment would be wasted. Since 1945, the US has engaged in many armed conflicts, but never against the territory of a nuclear state. Washington and its allies should be prepared to engage in armed conflict with major powers such as China and Russia when vital interests are clearly at stake. But strategic bombing campaigns against an adversary's capital and nuclear infrastructure are far from the only choices available.[36]

* * *

The proper role for airpower in joint warfighting is, firstly, to secure air supremacy and eliminate the threat of enemy airpower; and, next, to apply airpower decisively as part of a joint effort to defeat enemy forces at the strategic, operational and tactical levels of war. The use of airpower against national strategic targets, far from the battlefield, requires enormous investments that have historically failed to deliver decisive results. Strategic attacks against water, power and transportation systems, or command-and-control targets in urban areas, both directly and indirectly lead to civilian casualties that call into question US moral leadership and standing. The probability of decapitation – that is, the elimination of an enemy's civilian and military strategic leadership – is low. Strategic attack against nuclear-armed, near-peer adversaries is unprecedented and highly dangerous, representing an escalatory approach fraught with risk.

It seems clear that the future of airpower will centre on long-range, precision-guided munitions and unmanned aircraft. These tools should be neither limited in number nor costly, and their use should be networked such that the entire joint force can exploit their capabilities. Nowhere is this more important than in overcoming integrated air defences and area-denial/anti-access systems. Continuing to field future generations of manned aircraft will undermine the development of this capability and deny the joint force the full benefits of America's edge in advanced technology.

At issue is not the importance of airpower to national security. That was settled long ago. Airpower is indispensable to success in war. For all its strengths, however, airpower can only complement, and not substitute for, land and sea power. Modern warfare has shown us that actors who lack airpower – the North Koreans and Chinese in the Korean War, the North Vietnamese in the Vietnam conflict, and the insurgents in Iraq and Afghanistan – can nevertheless contend successfully with the American military. Land and sea power are therefore equally important, and will remain so. Accordingly, a balanced approach to US grand strategy that acknowledges and supports the contributions of each of the services will best serve the common defence.

Notes

1 Though official US Air Force doctrine has used the term 'aerospace power' since 1992, analysts have confirmed that 'the most fundamental operational and strategic characteristics of air power are almost wholly absent in the space arena'. See Karl P. Mueller, 'Air Power', RAND Corporation, 2010, p. 16. This paper focuses on the employment of aircraft, manned and unmanned, at altitudes low enough to sustain aerial flight, hence the use of the more traditional term 'air power'. Aerial delivery of nuclear weapons also occupies a decidedly distinctive and separate space, and therefore lies outside this discussion.

2 Guilio Douhet, *The Command of the Air*, reprinted by the US Air Force History and Museums Program, Washington DC, 1998, p. 23.

3 Colonel John Warden, cited in John Olsen, *Strategic Air Power in Desert Storm* (London: Routledge, 2003), p. 150.

4 Channelling Douhet, US airpower theorists in the 1930s believed that aerial attack of transportation, power and water systems would 'quickly and efficiently destroy the people's will to resist'. See Howard D. Belote, 'Warden

and the Air Corps Tactical School', *Airpower Journal*, Fall 1999, p. 42.

5 According to Richard Kohn, 'The very creation of the Air Force as an independent service grew out of the U.S. effort in World War II to mount a decisive air campaign to destroy the enemy's capability to wage war and to decide the conflict independent of military operations on land and sea.' See Richard Kohn, 'U.S. Strategic Air Power 1948–1962', *International Security*, Spring 1988, p. 79.

6 Douhet wrote that 'those who daringly take to the new road first will enjoy the incalculable advantages of the new means of war over the old … Those who are ready first not only will win quickly, but will win with the fewest sacrifices and the minimum expenditure of means.' *The Command of the Air*, p. 30.

7 US and allied combat strength in the air peaked at 28,000 aircraft. A total of 40,000 aircraft were lost during the war in Europe. British and American personnel losses in the air were almost identical: 79,281 vs 79,265. See *The United States Strategic Bombing Survey (European War)* (Washington DC: US Government Printing Office, 1946), p. 1. US aircraft losses during the Second World War totalled 95,000, including 52,951 operational losses. See John Ellis, *World War II – A Statistical Survey*, Facts on File, October 1993. The Allies claimed 57,405 enemy planes downed in Europe with 40,379 allied planes lost. US Army Air Forces in Europe in August 1944 totalled 619,020 men. The Royal Air Force comprised 718,628 men. See 'Strategic Bombing Survey, Statistical Appendix to Overall Report (European War)', February 1947, table 1.

8 See, for example, Russell Weigley, *The American Way of War* (Bloomington, IN: Indiana University Press, 1973), p. 359.

9 US strength in the Pacific increased from some 200 planes in 1941 to 11,000 planes by August 1945. At war's end, the Japanese inventory still included 5,000 combat planes plus another 5,400 kamikaze suicide aircraft, though pilot training had badly deteriorated by then, and the quality of US aircraft was higher. US losses during the Pacific War totalled 27,000 planes, of which 8,700 were lost in combat. The Japanese lost approximately 50,000 planes, 40% of which were lost in combat. *United States Strategic Bombing Survey (Pacific War)* (Washington DC: US Government Printing Office, 1946), pp. 9–10.

10 Four-star admiral Raymond Spruance, the hero of Midway, was reported to have said, 'the submarine beat Japan'. Cited in Carl Builder, *The Masks of War: American Military Styles in Strategy and Analysis* (Baltimore, MD: Johns Hopkins University Press, 1989), p. 77.

11 General of the Air Force Henry H. Arnold, *Global Mission* (New York: Harper, 1949), p. 149.

12 The average response time for an Army request for CAS in Korea was 40–50 minutes, but only 10–15 for the Marines, who owned their own tactical air and who employed different procedures. Bryan K. Luke, 'Will Close Air Support Be Where Needed to Support Objective Force Operations in 2015?', US Army Command and

General Staff College, 2002, p. 20.

13 Further examples of new technologies include the F-15, F-16, F/A-18, F-117, B-1, B-2, the E-3 AWACS, the RC-135 *Rivet Joint*, and the E-8 JSTARS.

14 Williamson Murray with Wayne W. Thompson, *Air Power and the Persian Gulf* (Baltimore, MD: Nautical and Aviation Publishing Co., 1995), p. 190.

15 Thomas A. Keaney, 'Surveying Gulf War Airpower', *Joint Force Quarterly*, Autumn 1993, p. 33.

16 According to *Gulf War Survey*, 'There is no indisputable proof that Scud mobile launchers … were destroyed by fixed wing aircraft.' Thomas A. Keaney and Eliot A. Cohen, *Gulf War Air Power Survey*, Summary Report (Washington DC: USGPO, 1993), p. 237. This effort may have yielded political benefits, however, in helping to prevent Israel's entry into the war.

17 As Leon Elsarelli has written, 'despite the success of air power, the introduction of ground troops was ultimately required to bring the war to a successful conclusion'. Leon E. Elsarelli, 'From Desert Storm to 2025: Close Air Support in the 25th Century', US Air Command and Staff College, Maxwell Air Force Base, Montgomery, AL, April 1998, p. 18.

18 Human Rights Watch estimated that 500 civilians were killed during the campaign. See Human Rights Watch, *Civilian Deaths in the NATO Air Campaign,* vol. 12, no. 1, February 2000.

19 See Joseph J. Collins, *Understanding War in Afghanistan* (Washington DC: National Defense University Press, 2011), p. 48; and Benjamin S. Lambeth, *The Unseen War* (Annapolis, MD: Naval Institute Press, 2013), p. 305.

20 According to Anthony Carr, 'operational trends in Afghanistan showcase an increasing reliance on CAS to proxy for ground troops … This is driven by economy of force, but has generated a number of high-profile collateral damage incidents that threaten the entire enterprise.' Anthony B. Carr, 'America's Conditional Advantage: Airpower, Counterinsurgency and the Theory of John Warden', School of Advanced Air and Space Studies, Air University, Maxwell Air Force Base, Montgomery, AL, June 2009, p. 127.

21 See, for example, Stephen Biddle, 'Allies, Airpower and Modern Warfare: The Afghan Model in Afghanistan and Iraq', *International Security*, vol. 30, no. 3, Winter 2005–06, pp. 161–76.

22 US Air Force, 'Strategic Attack', Air Force Doctrine Document 3-70, with changes, 1 November 2011.

23 James G. Burton, *The Pentagon Wars* (Annapolis, MD: Naval Institute Press, 1998), p. 22.

24 These include the beliefs that 'airpower is an inherently strategic force', that it is 'primarily an offensive weapon' and that 'airpower's unique characteristics necessitate that it be centrally controlled by airmen'. See Phillip Meilinger, *Ten Propositions Regarding Airpower*, US Air Force History and Museums Program, Washington DC, 1995.

25 Builder, *The Masks of War*, p. 137.

26 The numbers cited here reflect the Program Acquisition Unit Cost (PAUC), computed by dividing the total cost of each programme by the number of units to be produced. As

the website Defense-Aerospace.com explains, 'PAUC includes research and development costs, and some support costs. It is thus not an indication of actual acquisition prices. It is, however, the simplest, clearest and most accessible measure of real weapon costs that is publicly available.' See 'Costs of Selected US Military Aircraft', Defense Aerospace.com, 3 April 2010. The F-35's $138m PAUC is based on a large production run of more than 2,000 aircraft; if subsequently reduced, as with the B-1, B-2 and F-22 programmes, the PAUC will rise dramatically. All figures via the General Accounting Office (GAO). All costs are cited in 2015 dollars. See GAO, 'Defense Acquisitions' reports, 1999, 2003, 2009, 2011 and 2015; and GAO, 'Operation Desert Storm: Evaluation of the Air Campaign', 1997.

27 See Andrea Shalal-Esa, 'US Sees Lifetime Cost of F-35 Fighter at $1.45 Trillion', Reuters, 29 March 2012.

28 US General Accounting Office, 'Defense Acquisitions: Achieving B-2A Bomber Operational Requirements', GAO/NSIAD-99-97, p. 7; and US Air Force AFCAP Data 2008–12, https://timemilitary.files.wordpress.com/2013/04/afcap-data-for-2008-2012.xlsx.

29 GAO figures.

30 See Colonel Mike Pietrucha, 'The U.S. Air Force and Stealth: Stuck on Denial', *War on the Rocks*, 24 March 2016.

31 See David Axe, 'Pentagon's Big Budget F-35 Fighter "Can't Turn, Can't Climb, Can't Run"', Reuters, 14 July 2014. For these reasons, a full production run is no more likely than for other recent programmes. As the size of the programme buy comes down, the unit cost will climb, probably dramatically.

32 China has one fifth-generation fighter nearing fielding, the J-20, scheduled to enter production in 2018. See Roger Cliff, *China's Military Power: Assessing Current and Future Capabilities* (Oxford: Oxford University Press, 2015), p. 98. Russia's first fifth-generation fighter, the Sukhoi T-50 PAK FA, will enter service in 2016.

33 Thomas Gibbons-Neff, 'This Is the Airpower Russia Has in Syria', *Washington Post*, 21 September 2015. Russia announced that most of these would be withdrawn in March 2016.

34 *Ibid.*

35 Typical of this genre is a recent report by the Heritage Foundation that describes the Air Force as 'geriatric', 'obsolescent' and 'in a death spiral'. Robert P. Haffa, Jr, 'Full Spectrum Air Power: Building the Air Force America Needs', Special Report #122, The Heritage Foundation, 12 October 2012. This paper 'argues for building an Air Force to support a force capable of meeting current and future threats to American security without regard for arbitrary fiscal guidelines and ceilings' (p. v).

36 For alternatives, see R.D. Hooker, Jr and T.X. Hammes, 'America's Ultimate Strategy in a Clash with China', *National Interest*, 10 June 2014; and R.D. Hooker, Jr, 'Baltic Fortress: NATO Confronts Russia 2016', *Royal United Services Institute Journal*, Summer 2015.

Little Grey Men: China and the Ukraine Crisis

Lora Saalman

Russia's annexation of Crimea and the crisis in Ukraine have affected Chinese views of territorial sovereignty and peripheral stability. Chinese analysts are applying lessons learned from Ukraine to their own regional and international environment. An examination of 434 Chinese-language documents on the Ukraine crisis provides insights into how Chinese academics, economists, engineers, officials and military personnel view Russian tactics and strategy, as well as Western intentions, and suggests that China is moving towards a more holistic and 'Russian' view of hybrid and proxy warfare – particularly in cyberspace.

Identification with Russia

Chinese coverage of the Ukraine crisis, although it is geographically distant, extends beyond simply recounting its impact on Russia, Ukraine and the United States, and frequently addresses the implications of the crisis for China.[1] Using the oft-touted accusation of 'Cold War thinking' (*lengzhan siwei*) on the part of Western powers, Chinese analysts frame the Ukraine crisis as a 'great-power game' (*daguo boyi*) between Washington and Moscow.[2] In a number of cases, Chinese writers are conflicted on how to evaluate the costs and benefits of the Ukraine crisis for Beijing.

In terms of advantageous fallout, a range of Chinese studies note that the Ukraine crisis distracted Washington from its rebalance to the Asia-

Lora Saalman is the Director of, and Senior Researcher at, the China and Global Security Programme at the Stockholm International Peace Research Institute (SIPRI).

Survival | vol. 58 no. 6 | December 2016–January 2017 | pp. 135–156 DOI 10.1080/00396338.2016.1257201

Pacific, created questions over US commitments to its regional partners and carved out space for Beijing to shape its own regional interests.[3] However, a number of negative trends are also identified in these writings. Academics from the China Foreign Affairs University and the University of International Business and Economics in Beijing note that the Ukraine crisis has threatened Asia-Pacific stability by accelerating Washington's efforts to bolster China's neighbours to forestall a Crimea scenario emerging via Beijing's territorial and maritime disputes in the Asia-Pacific region. A counsellor in China's Ministry of Foreign Affairs has suggested that Beijing remains concerned about Ukraine setting a negative precedent for its own regional claims, threatening long-held precepts of territorial sovereignty and non-intervention,[4] and potentially inspiring Taiwan, Xinjiang, Tibet and Hong Kong to engage in independence votes like that held in Crimea.[5]

Chinese analysts applaud Russian defiance

Pulled between Washington and Moscow, the Chinese government has opted for neutrality at the official level, in part by abstaining from the March 2014 vote on Crimean annexation at the United Nations Security Council.[6] Yet, digging deeper, this official stance is muddied by a broader discourse in China that indicates support for Russia's decision-making process and actions in Ukraine.[7] In stark contrast to coverage on the Ukraine crisis in the West, Chinese experts across a wide spectrum of official and non-official backgrounds express appreciation for Moscow's culture of heroism and patriotism; social cohesion and political support; unity and decisiveness of the central government and leadership; strong military and nuclear deterrence; cyber and information security; clarity of national and international stance; maintenance of sovereignty and stability; protection of national interests and territorial claims; resistance to external interference; and grand national strategy and global strategic vision.

Rather than seeing a nation hobbled by sanctions, Chinese analysts applaud Russia for its defiance. In fact, Chinese experts repeatedly emphasise that Russia and China maintain common interests and pursuits when it comes to 'national security, anti-hegemony, and promotion of democratization and multilateralization of international relations'.[8] Analysts from the China Institutes of Contemporary International Relations (CICIR) note Moscow's efforts in the past few years to restore some of the strategic balance between Russia and the United States, particularly when it comes to missile defence, cyber and space warfare.[9] In their view, the Ukraine crisis is part of this recalibration.

As a result, countless Chinese experts view Russia's actions in Ukraine as a decisive and largely justifiable reaction to instability and unrest at its borders, foreign stationing of military systems closer to its territory and loss of access to resources in the face of unrest, as well as the wrongs of history and territorial losses.[10] In making this assessment, these experts highlight China's own concerns over US military deployments to the Asia-Pacific region, citing Washington's threat to Beijing's own territorial claims and freedom of action in the South China Sea and East China Sea.[11]

Chinese historical accounts of the Ukraine crisis further promote identification with Russia's dilemma. Terms like 'invasion' (*ruqin*) and 'encirclement' (*baowei*) are used to express concerns faced by both Beijing and Moscow. Similar to their own territorial claims, Chinese experts detail centuries of Russian history to provide explanations for Moscow's linkages to Crimea.[12] Nearly a quarter of the writings surveyed use the term 'return' (*huigui*) to describe Russia's annexation of Crimea.[13] This term indicates the reappropriation of territories that have been unlawfully or forcibly seized and broken away. It is generally reserved for Hong Kong or Macao finding their rightful place back within China's fold. Its use reflects an overall acceptance of the fact that Moscow had historical, political and strategic impetus and cause to reclaim Crimea.[14]

Furthermore, Chinese writers detail the manner in which Ukraine's 'extreme nationalism' (*jiduan minzuzhuyi*) and inclination towards the West threaten Russia's emergence.[15] They draw ties to the ethno-nationalism in the strategic buffer zones of Xinjiang, Tibet and Taiwan that they believe makes China susceptible to external interference and propaganda.[16] Research conducted in conjunction with an event held by the China Institute of International Studies' Department for European Studies also indicates that Western co-opting of Kiev makes details on Moscow's nuclear programme vulnerable, by offering both proximity and access to formerly active nuclear facilities and researchers, while at the same time erasing Russia's strategic buffer zone.[17] Given China's own testing of nuclear and advanced conventional weaponry in its own integral buffer zone and border region of Xinjiang, Beijing is seen as facing similar intelligence threats at its restive and porous borders.

Overall, when detailing these threats to territorial integrity, sovereignty and overall security, the majority of Chinese authors posit that the primary concern remains Washington, not Moscow. A number of analyses allege hypocrisy in US policies on Ukraine versus Kosovo: Washington argued for elections in Kosovo under the guise of human rights, while denouncing elections in Crimea under the argument of sovereignty. These analyses laud how Russia has managed to turn the tables on Washington's 'double standards' (*shuangzhong biaozhun*) in using humanitarian intervention as an excuse to incite regional instability and government overthrow.[18] Chinese assessments use such linguistic parallels to connect the challenges faced by both Moscow and Beijing. And in both cases, the primary threat comes from Washington.

Criticism of US proxies

In contrast to their conflicted, but ultimately sympathetic, coverage on Moscow's role in Ukraine,[19] Chinese analysts are much less oblique about how Washington has violated principles of sovereignty and non-intervention. They compare the way in which the United States has exploited tensions between Russia and Europe with how it has divided ethnic and religious groups such as Sunnis and Shi'ites, and countries such as China and Japan.[20] Chinese authors describe the United States' attempts to use the Ukraine crisis to expand its transatlantic influence and to mitigate its 'hegemonic system crisis' (*baquan de jiegouxing weiji*) of decreasing control and relevance.[21]

NATO members are seen as proxies through which Washington is able to provide military and cyber assistance to Kiev,[22] while pursuing political and economic objectives via sanctions on Moscow.[23] NATO Secretary-General Jens Stoltenberg's statement on 16 June 2016 that 'a severe cyber attack may be classified as a case for the alliance' to respond suggests that Chinese criticisms of American use of allies in Europe and Asia as tools for interference and escalation will only grow.[24] By contrast, Chinese references to Moscow's use of 'proxies' (*dailiren*) often place the term in quotation marks to question its veracity.[25] They make relatively few references to the downing of Malaysian Airlines Flight MH17 by pro-Russian rebels. In fact, some of these writings refer to key details of the crash as conjecture,[26] choosing instead to focus on how propaganda has reframed global opinion.[27] In their view, the true 'little green men' are not deployed by Russia, but rather by the United States.

Chinese discussions stress that the Ukraine crisis is rooted in Washington's aim to provoke Moscow into a war with its European neighbours by eliminating its buffer zone and fomenting instability and opposition in its periphery. These articles create a link between Washington and myriad colour revolutions in the guise of proxy warfare, whether through US partner nations and allies, non-governmental organisations, online propaganda or other means.[28] In highlighting these claims, Chinese writings note that Russia made an initial pledge not to intervene in Ukraine, until forced to react to provocation from Western powers.[29]

When it comes to the Asia-Pacific, this assertion echoes how Chinese authors emphasise Beijing's 'reactive' (*beidong*) or 'forced' (*beipo*) approach when confronting Washington and its proxies in the Asia-Pacific region. Analyses contend that the Ukraine crisis allows Washington to expand its access to alliances and resources.[30] Similarly, they suggest that tensions in the South China Sea are used by the United States to enlist such countries as the Philippines and Vietnam in threatening Beijing's 'Maritime Silk Road' initiative.[31] As in the case of European nations, Washington is seen as aiding smaller Asia-Pacific countries to enhance their military interoperability, weakening Beijing's territorial stance via the Permanent Court of Arbitration at The Hague and isolating China economically with the Trans-Pacific Partnership.[32]

Overall, these Chinese analyses highlight political, legal, military and economic challenges that are similar to those faced by Russia. They posit US strategy in both Europe and Asia as spreading instability to maintain relevance and to avoid marginalisation; driving a wedge between regional players to strengthen America's grasp on the global system; and containing, weakening and destabilising the rise and re-emergence of countries such as China and Russia.[33] A number of Chinese experts argue that the United States' greatest failure has been to push Beijing away from Washington and towards Moscow.[34] US policy documents, such as the 2010 Nuclear Posture Review and 2013 Air–Sea Battle Concept, exacerbate these trends by making explicit connections between China, the former Soviet Union and Russia.[35]

Widening this gulf even further, Chinese academics and officials increasingly argue for distancing their own capital from Washington and the democratic precepts of 'so-called' (*suowei*) freedom, democracy and human rights,[36] as well as external 'interventionism' (*ganshe zhuyi*), which are seen as divisive and bringing instability to Ukraine.[37] They argue that democratic principles and trends are out of sync not only with Ukraine's development needs, but also with China's own culture and emergence.

In looking toward a different model, Chinese writings note that Russia has been able to domestically capitalise on its hard power of military modernisation to enhance its sense of national pride. In terms of soft power, they point to Russia's heroic traditions as integral to strengthening domestic cohesion and popular opinion to combat Western influences.[38] Moscow has worked to reinvigorate its own national power and to shape the international system by standing up to the West. Chinese analysts entreat Beijing to position itself as a pole in the global structure to counterbalance US influence in the Asia-Pacific region, and to make China a great power. In this effort, hybrid warfare plays a central role.

Future of hybrid warfare

Hybrid and proxy warfare are hardly new concepts in China. Decades ago, Beijing followed Moscow in supporting revolution that spanned the breadth of society. More recently, in 2003, China's Central Military Commission and Communist Party codified the 'three warfares' as psychological, media and legal operations. Beyond the similarity with Russian views on holistic campaigns that penetrate multiple levels of society, the deputy secretary general of the China National Security Forum notes that, similar to Ukraine, in the

Asia-Pacific, 'small to medium scale military conflict or tensions are difficult to completely rule out, particularly given the U.S. soft war of economic penetration and political subversion of China, combined with instigation of proxy warfare against China by neighboring countries with which it has historical disputes'.[39]

While hybrid warfare may be a well-worn concept, a new key element in this 'soft war' and the future of hybrid warfare is cyberspace. An expert in the Unit of Engineers in China's National Security Policy Committee points to 'network warfare' (*wangluo zhan*) conducted by the West in Ukraine through its use of cyberspace to control and manipulate public opinion and to attack the government; conduct network monitoring and information attacks on government and military systems; and provide substantial funding and information to support opposition groups.[40] His use of the term 'warfare' when describing these activities suggests Chinese application of a broader Russian definition to characterise conflict in cyberspace.

Using this broadened definition of warfare, a number of Chinese experts denounce the negative impact of Western influence via ethnic and religious nationalism and democratic principles that are spread via exchange students, non-governmental organisations and economic interactions within a globalised market economy.[41] All of these trends are facilitated by information flows that occur through cyberspace. Many Chinese analyses discuss the role of external propaganda and elections in Ukraine. Some pinpoint how Washington has used its own proxies in the form of non-government agencies and online propaganda to infiltrate and influence local opinion.[42] Others provide detailed accounts of how platforms such as Facebook, Twitter, Vkontakte, YouTube and others have been put to the use of the Euromaidan movement.[43] On this basis, Beijing and Moscow have increasingly aligned on such issues as internet sovereignty, under which cyberspace is regarded as a territorial domain that can be controlled and regulated in terms of its information flows.[44]

In fact, experts from China's Second Artillery Corps and the National Security Policy Committee, among others, have directly linked instability in Ukraine to US and European cyber operations to control and manipulate online content, opposition parties and domestic public opinion.[45] In the face of the revelations of former US government contractor Edward Snowden on US cyber-espionage programmes, the prevailing sense in China is that it remains especially vulnerable and needs to make advances in not just detection, but also defence, retaliation and offence.[46] These analysts argue that Washington sees Beijing as a 'new rival' (*xin duishou*) on a par with, or even exceeding, Moscow, citing Western references to a 'new Cyberspace Cold War' (*wangluo kongjian xin lengzhan*).[47] In doing so, they mimic Russian sources by referring to threats from 'external cyber terrorism' (*waibu wangluo kongbuzhuyi*) and 'Western hacker attacks' (*xifang wangluo heike de gongji*).[48]

At the national level, Chinese experts decry how the West has used cyberspace to control civilian networks and infrastructure, to demonise national leaders and their policies, and to spread rumours that result in ethnic conflicts and social disorder.[49] Zhu Zhihua, deputy director of the Association of Contemporary International Studies, points to how external powers have used incidents such as the 5 July 2009 unrest in Xinjiang, the 3 July 2011 train collision in Wenzhou and the 8 March 2014 Malaysia Airlines flight disappearance to wage online campaigns to undermine Beijing.[50] In doing so, Zhu notes that the stronger cyber capabilities of the Five Eyes countries – Australia, Canada, New Zealand, the United Kingdom and the United States – allow them to work in concert with the US rebalance to the Asia-Pacific to attack the Chinese Communist Party and the Central People's Government from within, by fabricating rumours, inciting extreme emotions, intensifying ethnic conflicts and encouraging social chaos.[51]

At the regional level, Chinese analysts see cyberspace as a key mechanism used by Washington to reinforce its hegemonic role, exacerbating a spectrum of concerns in Taiwan, Xinjiang and Tibet, as well as the East and South China seas. As a result, they argue that Beijing must learn from how the US and European powers infiltrated and controlled the Ukrainian government and military networks. In confronting these threats, Chinese experts emphasise development of civil–military integration and interoperability in cyber-command countermeasures and mitigation techniques, as well as in cyber-reconnaissance and -attack capabilities.[52] They advocate China strengthening its public and private networks, exerting greater control over content and hardening broadband networks to close technical loopholes used by other countries to undermine China's 'sovereignty security' (*zhuquan anquan*), 'political security' (*zhengzhi anquan*) and 'social stability' (*shehui wending*).[53]

Overall, Chinese analysts note that, in the face of Western encirclement on land and sea, and now in cyberspace, Beijing must follow Russia's example by placing a greater emphasis on both the reputation and modernisation of its own military to ensure its security and national interests. In the words of Ministry of Foreign Affairs Counsellor Chu Maoming, China must learn from Russia's actions in Ukraine to be confident in its theory, path and system to unswervingly forge ahead in its 'emergence' (*fuxing*).[54] To this end, Moscow's own prioritisation and modernisation of its military could be equated with what Beijing's official and non-official discourse labels its 'Strong Military Dream' (*qiang jun meng*), an extension of the 'China Dream' (*zhongguo meng*).[55]

Little grey men

As the 'China Dream' and 'Strong Military Dream' play out in cyberspace, China's and Russia's tactics and strategies are showing signs of convergence. Beyond China's alleged use of their own variant of 'little green men' (nomads and paramilitaries at land borders) and 'little blue men' (fishermen and coastguard vessels at maritime borders),[56] Chinese and Russian views are increasingly aligned in cyberspace, which cuts across both of these spheres. The holistic nature of cyberspace lends itself to more pervasive, and ultimately punishing, political, economic and military campaigns against broader populations and non-combatants.

Indeed, in cyberspace the line between combatants and non-combatants is blurred, making it the perfect environment for carrying out hybrid warfare. Nonetheless, despite the centrality of this sphere for future proxy activities,[57] it remains the least understood. This is, in part, due to the difficulty of attribution and the number of patriotic hackers and proxy entrants into this field. Determining the actions of a proxy individual or group versus a military or government remains difficult. This is a point frequently made by Chinese analysts, such as Dong Qingling at Beijing's University of International Business and Economics, when discounting allegations against Russia and China, whether pertaining to alleged cyber intrusions and attacks in Ukraine or in other networks.[58]

With advancements in forensics, such dilemmas may diminish in the future. In the meantime, however, civilian and military analysts in China have pushed for and made improvements to cyber security, military and civilian integration and legal structure, as well as better regulation of and jointness within cyber-attack and defence mechanisms.[59] They have also advocated for comprehensive cyber-warfare practices that place an emphasis on counter-attack capabilities and interference, as well as protection and monitoring of networks improved via defensive and offensive exercises.[60]

Cyber-intrusion campaigns are likely to become more common

China's integration of proxies into information operations is apparently already under way, with the alleged involvement of domestic universities, foundations and industries – thought to often have support from the People's Liberation Army or Ministry of State Security – in broader campaigns that intrude on the networks of multiple countries in Southeast Asia and South Asia, as with Advanced Persistent Threat 30 (APT30).[61] The latter series of incidents, alleged to have come from within China given its scope, duration and focus on the South China Sea, lasted more than ten years and compromised government, media and industry in 17 countries.[62]

Much like Russian hybrid warfare, which prioritises controlling and shaping the flow of information, such campaigns are likely to become more common in the future. They allow for military operations short of war and for information to be leveraged prior to and during conflict. In essence, they take the contemporary US model in command, control, communications, computers, intelligence, surveillance and reconnaissance (C4ISR) and look to shape it to Chinese requirements both on and off the battlefield. Since, once again, cyberspace does not discriminate in the same way between combatants and non-combatants, this new realm of engagement allows for a permanent campaign.

The connections between persistent Chinese and Russian multilayered tactics, cyber-command countermeasures and cyber-attack capabilities also appear to be growing. Similar malware campaigns are alleged to have emerged from within both China and Russia with an emphasis on using spear-phishing, man-on-the-side, man-in-the-middle and watering-hole attacks to exploit browser, VPN and social-engineering vulnerabilities.[63]

Among these, a 2015 distributed denial-of-service (DDoS) attack, allegedly using an Adobe Flash exploit, was conducted against the website of the Permanent Court of Arbitration at The Hague, while it was adjudicating the Philippines' case against China on the South China Sea.[64] While often considered a nuisance attack to take down systems, this kind of DDoS attack could also have been used to weaken the perimeter of the system to access and to potentially exfiltrate information on the proceedings. While employing different tactics, this incident is similar in nature to a 2015 intrusion and exfiltration of data, allegedly using a fake VPN server, against the Dutch Safety Board investigating the MH17 crash, which was thought to have come from the hacker group Pawn Storm in Russia.[65]

By 2016, the mass theft of data from the Democratic National Committee, reminiscent of the exfiltration of the clearance data of an estimated 25 million US employees from the US Office of Personnel Management discovered in 2015, pointed again to a basic form of cyber intrusion – spear-phishing and remote-access Trojans – as a means of creating domestic crises of confidence, damaged political systems and potential future blackmail.[66] From The Hague to Washington, these cases show organisations and individuals with political and legal significance to Beijing and Moscow finding themselves subject to cyber intrusion and attack.

Similar malware campaigns thought to be emanating from within China and Russia include *Clandestine Fox* and *Russian Doll*, which are both thought to use spear-phishing and Adobe Flash exploits to target aerospace and defence, construction and engineering, high-tech industry, telecommunications and transportation infrastructure.[67] Not only are the tactics and intent behind these campaigns convergent, but they are also likely to become increasingly commonplace. The challenges associated with identification of the perpetrators – whether at the technical-attribution level or the political–diplomatic level – suggest that cyberspace will be the crux of future hybrid warfare.

That this type of warfare is expanding from simple data exfiltration to kinetic attacks on critical infrastructure was demonstrated in a 2015 cyber attack on electric utilities in Ukraine. Forensic reports on the malware, staging and coordination of the attack suggest that the hackers were either based in or supported by Russia.[68] BlackEnergy malware, used in combination with denial-of-service attacks and the wiping tool KillDisk, not only severed the electricity supply of an estimated 225,000 people, it also created confusion and panic among the provider and users alike. Studies suggest that part of the motivation behind the attack was not simply to test out the ability to comprehensively take down critical infrastructure, but also to cause embarrassment.[69]

So while this particular campaign lasted only four hours and was mitigated in part by the utility's ability to use analogue equipment to restore functionality, it shows that cyber attacks can be used in broader campaigns to cut a population's vital services and to raise questions about the competence of first responders and government. Given the level of penetration of campaigns such as APT30 into Southeast Asia and South Asia, the likelihood of similar tactics reappearing in the Asia-Pacific region is significant.

Even with the improvement of bilateral China–Philippines relations under the leadership of Filipino President Rodrigo Duterte, the level of Chinese involvement in the Philippines' critical infrastructure, including power plants and other facilities,[70] means that there remains the potential for their exploitation in the event of future tensions on the South China Sea. Whether from government entities or patriotic-hacker proxies, campaigns that target society as a whole can supplement the conduct of more conventional military campaigns by supporting not only a shutdown in basic services, but also critical infrastructure from electricity plants to nuclear facilities.[71]

* * *

China's current behaviour and rhetoric does not match the violence of Russia's little green men in Ukraine. Still, government-linked Chinese analysts draw enough parallels between the two countries to suggest that China may take that model and craft it into a more penetrating and persistent campaign. Much as in the case of Moscow's dealings with Ukraine, Beijing has repeatedly pointed to Washington's enabling of China's neighbours. Chinese analysts categorise Beijing's actions in the East China Sea, South China Sea and elsewhere as 'reactive' or 'forced' behaviour driven by American actions.

Both Beijing and Moscow find what the Chinese call a 'dark hand' (*hei shou*) in Washington to be manipulating public sentiment and conditions on the ground in their near abroad. Given the two capitals' solidarity and concerns over American 'interference' (*ganshe*), it should not come as a surprise that China's own tactics increasingly resemble Russia's,[72] and that Chinese analysts have learned from Russian experience.[73] As hybrid warfare in cyberspace develops, little green men on land and little blue men at sea may increasingly be joined by China's little grey men online.

Notes

1 See, for example, Zhang Wenmu, 'Wukelan shijian de guoji yiyi' [International Importance of the Events in Ukraine], in 'Wukelan weiji de zhongguo sikao' [Chinese Reflections on the Ukraine Crisis], *Jingji daokan* [*Economic Herald*], April 2014, pp. 57–67. Zhang Wenmu is a professor in the Center for Strategic Studies at Beihang University, formerly known as the Beijing Institute of Aeronautics.

2 Zhang Yi, 'Wukelan weiji: E ou ying shili yu ruan shili de duijue' [The Ukraine Crisis: Contrasting Russia's and Europe's Hard Power and Soft Power], *Shijie taishi* [*World Perspectives*], pp. 52–4. Zhang Yi is an associate researcher in the Institute of Russian, Eastern European and Central Asian Studies at the Chinese Academy of Social Sciences.

3 Li Ling, 'Zhongguo de fuxing xuyao yici xin qimeng yundong' [China's Emergence Needs a New Enlightenment], in 'Chinese Reflections on the Ukraine Crisis', pp. 66–7. Li Ling is professor in the Institute of Economic Research at Peking University. Xu Zhaofeng, 'Jiedu meiguo 2014 nian 'si nian fangwu pinggu baogao' [Interpreting the United States' 2014 "Quadrennial Defense Review"], *Xiandai guoji guanxi* [*Contemporary International Relations*], May 2014, p. 32.

4 Chinese analysts tend to argue that Beijing's abstention from the UN Security Council vote was a reflection of its responsible attitude and pursuit of peace and stability. Gao Fei and Zhang Jian, 'Wukelan weiji beijing xia de daguo boyi ji qi dui guoji anquan geju de yingxiang' [Great-Power Game Behind the Ukraine Crisis and its Impact on the International

Security Structure], *Heping yu fazhan* [*Peace and Development*], June 2014, p. 97; Dai Changzheng and Zhang Zhongning, 'Guonei youyu xia wukelan weiji de genyuan ji qi yingxiang' [Roots of the Ukraine Crisis in the Domestic Domain and their Impact], *Dongbeiya luntan* [*Northeast Asia Forum*], May 2014, p. 96. Gao Fei is director and Zhang Jian is an assistant researcher at the Russia Research Center at the China Foreign Affairs University, which trains many of China's future diplomats. Dai Changzheng is the head and Zhang Zhongning is a graduate student within the China Institute for WTO Studies of the Institute of International Studies at Beijing's University of International Business and Economics.

5 Chu Maoming, 'Wukelan weiji yu zhongguo de xuanze' [The Ukraine Crisis and China's Options], *Zhanlue juece yanjiu* [*Strategic Decision-Making Studies*], no. 3, March 2014, p. 12. Chu Maoming is a counsellor in China's Ministry of Foreign Affairs and a visiting researcher at the Guangdong Research Institute for International Strategies. See also Liao Qiang, 'Wukelan weiji yinian: Huigu, fansi, yu zhanwang' [One Year of the Ukraine Crisis: A Look Back, Reconsideration, and Prospects], *Eluosi yanjiu* [*Russia Studies*], no. 1, February 2015, pp. 28–58; and Dai and Zhang, 'Roots of the Ukraine Crisis in the Domestic Domain and their Impact', p. 97.

6 See Dai and Zhang, 'Roots of the Ukraine Crisis in the Domestic Domain and their Impact', p. 94; and Jiang Shixue, 'The Ukrainian Quandary', *Beijing Review*, 6 November 2014, pp. 22–3. Jiang Shixue is deputy director of the Institute of European Studies at the Chinese Academy of Social Sciences.

7 Chen Xiaolu, 'Kelimaya shijian dui zhongguo de qishi' [Implications of Crimea Events for China], *Junshi lishi yanjiu* [*Military History Studies*], no. 4, April 2014, pp. 1–12. Chen Xiaolu is head of the South China Sea Research Collaborative Innovation Center and a professor in the Department of History at Nanjing University.

8 Dai and Zhang, 'Roots of the Ukraine Crisis in the Domestic Domain and their Impact', p. 94.

9 CICIR Task Force, '2013 nian eluosi zhanlue xingshi pinggu' [2013 Russia Strategic Situation Assessment], *Eluosi dongou zhongya yanjiu* [*Russia, Eastern Europe, Central Asia Studies*], no. 2, February 2014, pp. 1–9. China Institutes of Contemporary International Relations (CICIR) Task Force members include Feng Yujun, Li Dongfu, Jiang Li, Wang Lijiu, Miao Lijiu, Miao Songfu and Chen Yu. CICIR is among China's largest and most influential civilian research institutes for international studies. It is affiliated with China's Ministry of State Security, which is an intelligence and security agency responsible for counter-intelligence, foreign intelligence and political security.

10 See Wang Xiangsui, 'Cong sange weidu dui weiji zuochu zhengti bawo' [From Three Dimensions of the Crisis Making an Overall Grasp], in 'Chinese Reflections on the Ukraine Crisis', pp. 57–9; and Cao Yongsheng, 'Eluosi dui wukelan qiangying zhanlue muhou

de jige yinsu' [Several Factors Behind Russia's Strong Strategy toward Ukraine], *Zhongguo jun zhuanmin* [*Defense Industry Conversion in China*], 2014, p. 83. Wang Xiangsui is the director of the Center for Strategic Studies at Beihang University. Colonel Cao Yongsheng is a professor in China's National Defense University's Strategic Research Bureau and an expert on Russia.

11 Chen Xulong and Su Shaojun, 'Zhongguo mianlin geng wei fuza de zhoubian he guoji huanjing' [China Faces More Complex Surroundings and International Environment], *Heping yu fazhan* [*Peace and Development*], no. 4, April 2014, pp. 1–10. Chen Xulong is head of the International Strategic Studies Institute at the China Institute of International Studies.

12 'Wukelan de qianshi jinsheng – Zhuanfang zhongguo shehui kexueyuan shijie lishi suo yanjiuyuan wenyi' [Ukraine's Past and Present – Interview with Chinese Academy of Social Sciences World History Researcher Wen Yi], *Lingdao wencui* [*Leadership Digest*], August 2014, pp. 7–22.

13 See, for example, Zhang Wenru, 'Kelimiya: Eluosi de zhengce xuanze' [Crimea's Return: Russia's Political Choice], *Heping yu fazhan* [*Peace and Development*], February 2014, pp. 19–29. Zhang Wenru was a visiting scholar at the Russian Foreign Affairs University at the time of writing this article.

14 *Ibid.*, p. 22.

15 Huang Dengxue, 'Xin "lengzhan": Yixiangyi huoshi xianshi – Wukelan weiji beijing xia de emei boyi toushi' [The New 'Cold War': Imagined or Real? – Perspectives on US–Russian Games Under the Ukraine Crisis], *Dongbeiya luntan* [*Northeast Asia Forum*], no. 3, March 2015, pp. 20–30. Huang Dengxue is a professor of Political Science and Public Administration at Shandong University, and a researcher within its Russia and Central Asian Studies Center.

16 Chu, 'The Ukraine Crisis and China's Options', pp. 3–12.

17 The use of the term 'lean' (*yibian dao*) within this writing reflects terminology used to describe countries leaning either towards the United States or the Soviet Union during the Cold War. Bu Shaohua, 'Wukelan weiji, ouzhou xingshi yu zhongou guanxi' yantaohui zongshu' [Summary of a Seminar on 'The Ukraine Crisis, European Trends, and China–Europe Relations'], *Guoji wenti yanjiu* [*International Relations*], January 2015, pp. 132–4; Wang, 'From Three Dimensions of the Crisis Making an Overall Grasp', pp. 57–9; Gao and Zhang, 'Great-Power Game Behind the Ukraine Crisis and its Impact on the International Security Structure', p. 83; Dai and Zhang, 'Roots of the Ukraine Crisis in the Domestic Domain and Their Impact', p. 85. Wang Xiangsui is the director of the Center for Strategic Studies at Beihang University.

18 See Hao Shiyuan, 'Daguo chengchang yu minzu wenti: Zhongguo ji qi guoji bijiao' [Great-Power Growth and Ethnic Issues: China and International Comparison], *Guoji jingji pinglun* [*International Economic Review*], May

2014, p. 14; and Zhang, 'Crimea's Return: Russia's Political Choice', p. 21. Hao Shiyuan is assistant dean of the Chinese Academy of Social Sciences and secretary general of the faculty bureau.

19 See Pan Guoshao, 'Jingguan qibian zhengqu you suo zuowei – Fudan daxue shijie jingji yanjiusuo shen guobing jiaoshou tan wukelan weiji' [Examining Changes and Their Impact on the Ground – Fudan University Institute of World Economics Professor Shen Guobing Discusses the Ukraine Crisis], *Zuguo* [*Motherland*], no. 3, March 2014, pp. 17–8; and Gu Xinyang, 'Diyuan zhengzhi yujingxia de wukelan weiji yu zhongguo jueqi' [Analysis of Ukraine Crisis and China's Rise in Geopolitical Context], *Hefei gonye daxue xuebao (Shehui kexue ban)* [*Journal of Hefei University of Technology (Social Sciences*], no. 4, August 2014, pp. 45–50. Shen Guobing is a professor in Fudan University's Institute of World Economy. Gu Xinyang is affiliated with the College of Humanities and Social Science, Beijing Language and Culture University.

20 Chen Xulong and Su Shaojun, 'Zhongguo mianlin geng wei fuza de zhoubian he guoji huanjing' [China Faces More Complex Surroundings and International Environment], *Heping yu fazhan* [*Peace and Development*], no. 4, April 2014, p. 6.

21 See Yu Zhengliao, 'Jiangou zhongmei xin xing daguo guanxi de jiegoux-ing zhangai' [Structural Obstacles to Building a China–US New Type of Great-Power Relations], *Mao zedong deng xiaoping lilun yanjiu* [*Mao Zedong and Deng Xiaoping Theoretical Studies*], June 2014, p. 82; and Gao and Zhang, 'Great-Power Game Behind the Ukraine Crisis and its Impact on the International Security Structure', p. 97. Yu Zhengliao is a professor in the International and Public Policy Institute of the Shanghai Communications University.

22 Zhang Wenzong, Xue Wei and Li Xuegang, 'Shixi wukelan weiji de zhanlue yingxiang' ['Analysis of the Strategic Impact of the Ukraine Crisis], *Xiandai guoji guanxi* [*Contemporary International Relations*], no. 8, August 2014, pp. 20, 26. Zhang Wenzong is a research associate at CICIR. Xue Wei is an associate researcher and Li Xuegang is an assistant researcher at the Harbin Institute of World Economic and Trade Research.

23 Cao, 'Several Factors Behind Russia's Strong Strategy toward Ukraine', p. 83; Gao and Zhang, 'Great-Power Game Behind the Ukraine Crisis and its Impact on the International Security Structure', p. 90.

24 In determining the potential for escalation, this statement may also be combined with indications that the United States will separate Cyber Command and Strategic Command, allowing the former greater speed and flexibility of response. See Francois Lenoir, 'Massive Cyber Attack Could Trigger NATO Response: Stoltenberg', Reuters, 16 June 2016, http://www.reuters.com/article/us-cyber-nato-idUSKCN0Z12NE?m...d1FFaHZNRld Gb3BEd01LQk1QeFprWWxDWVAyc TRNdlNLaVU4WToifQ%3D%3D.

25 'Hei tiane xiaoying' yu wukelan weiji yanhua de keneng qingjing' ['Black

Swan Effect' and Possible Scenarios for the Evolution of Ukraine Crisis], *Shijie zhishi* [*World Affairs*], May 2015, p. 53; Gao and Zhang, 'Great-Power Game Behind the Ukraine Crisis and its Impact on the International Security Structure', p. 80.

26 Jiang, 'The Ukrainian Quandry', pp. 22–3; Cao, 'Several Factors Behind Russia's Strong Strategy toward Ukraine', p. 84.

27 Xu Hua, 'Cong wukelan weiji kan eluosi de guoji chuanbo li – Jianyi guoji zhengzhi boyi zhong de chuanbo zhizheng' [The Ukraine Crisis: Russia's Propaganda War – With a Concurrent Comment on the Communication Rivalry in International Political Games], *Eluosi xuekan* [*Russia Journal*], no. 3, March 2015, pp. 61–8.

28 Han Yuhai, 'Nuli kaituo lushang sichou zhilu' [Work Hard to Open the Terrestrial Silk Road], in 'Chinese Reflections on the Ukraine Crisis', pp. 65–7. Han Yuhai is a professor at Peking University.

29 Gao and Zhang, 'Great-Power Game Behind the Ukraine Crisis and its Impact on the International Security Structure', p. 86.

30 She Shaohua, '"Wukelan weiji, ouzhou xingshi yu zhongou guanxi" yanjiuhui zongshu' ['Ukraine Crisis, European Trends and China-Europe' Research Meeting Summary], *Guoji wenti yanjiu* [*China International Relations*], January 2015, pp. 132–4; Dai, 'Roots of the Ukraine Crisis in the Domestic Domain and their Impact', p. 97.

31 Dai, 'Roots of the Ukraine Crisis in the Domestic Domain and their Impact', p. 97.

32 Yu, 'Structural Obstacles to Building a China–US New Type of Great-Power Relations', p. 84.

33 See 'Chinese Reflections on the Ukraine Crisis'; Zhang, 'Crimea's Return: Russia's Political Choice', p. 23; Yu, 'Structural Obstacles to Building a China–US New Type of Great-Power Relations', p. 82; Gao and Zhang, 'Great-Power Game Behind the Ukraine Crisis and its Impact on the International Security Structure', p. 97; Bu, 'Summary of a Seminar on "The Ukraine Crisis, European Trends, and China–Europe Relations"', p. 133; Wang Zhiyuan, 'Baquan yu zhicai: "Eluosi dongyao" nengfou gandong shijie xin pingheng' [Hegemony and Sanction: Can "Russian Turmoil" Shake the New Balance in the World], *Eluosi xuekan* [*Russia Journal*], no. 4, April 2015, pp. 58–68; Liang Qiang, 'Meiguo zai wukelan weiji zhong de zhanlue mubiao-Jiyu meiwu guanxi de fenxi (1992–2014)' [US Strategic Aims in the Ukraine Crisis – Based on US–Ukraine Relations (1992–2014)], *Eluosi dongou zhongya yanjiu* [*Russia, Eastern Europe, Central Asia Relations*], no. 2, February 2015, pp. 10–19; and Chu, 'The Ukraine Crisis and China's Options', p. 7.

34 Zhang, 'International Importance of the Events in Ukraine', pp. 59–62; Yu, 'Structural Obstacles to Building a China–US New Type of Great-Power Relations', p. 83.

35 See US Department of Defense, 'Nuclear Posture Review Report', April 2010; and Air–Sea Battle Office, 'Air-Sea Battle Concept: Service Collaboration to Address Anti-Access

& Area Denial Challenges', May 2013. Air–sea battle has been renamed 'Joint Concept for Access and Maneuver in the Global Commons' (JAM-GC).

36 Chu, 'The Ukraine Crisis and China's Options', p. 7.

37 Han, 'International Importance of the Events in Ukraine', pp. 65–7; Zhao Minghao, '"Qiao touzi" yu "xin gongshi": Aobama de yazhou zhixing' ['Clever Investment' and 'New Offensive': Obama's Trip to Asia], *Dangdai shijie* [*Contemporary World*], June 2014, p. 29; Cao, 'Several Factors Behind Russia's Strong Strategy toward Ukraine', p. 83.

38 Xu, 'The Ukraine Crisis: Russia's Propaganda War – With a Concurrent Comment on the Communication Rivalry in International Political Games', pp. 61–8.

39 Peng Guangqian, 'Lengzhan hou ouya dalu shouci chuxian diyuan zhanlue nixi' [The First Appearance of Geostrategic Counter Attack in Eurasia Following the End of the Cold War], *Jingji daokan* [*Economic Herald*], July 2014, pp. 85–6.

40 Yu Zhonghai, 'Wukelan shouxian zai wangluo bei wajie' [Ukraine First Disintegrated Online], *Lilun daobao* [*Theory Herald*], p. 63.

41 Ge Hanwen and Ding Yanfeng, 'Wukelan minzu zhuyi: Lishi yanjin, zhengzhi suqiu yu jiduan fazhan' [Ukrainian Nationalism: Historical Evolution, Political Demands, and Extreme Development], *Eluosi yanjiu* [*Russian Studies*], no. 3, June 2014, pp. 62–76; Zhang Yanbing and Zeng Zhimin, 'Wukelan weiji ji qi dui zhongguo fazhan de qishi' [The Ukraine Crisis and its Impact on China's Development], *Heping yu fazhan* [*Peace and Development*], no. 1, January 2015, pp. 72–83. Zhang Yanbing is deputy director of the Institute of International Strategies and Development of the School of Public Policy and Management, Tsinghua University; Zeng Zhimin is a graduate student at Tsinghua University.

42 Zhu Zhihua, 'Wukelan weiji beihou zheshe de daguo boyi ji jiaoxun qidi' [Reflections on the Great-Power Game and Lessons Behind the Ukraine Crisis], *Zhanlue juece yanjiu* [*Strategic Decision-making Studies*], no. 6, June 2014, pp. 20–9. Zhu Zhihua is Deputy Director of the Association of Contemporary International Studies.

43 See Fang Xingdong, Pan Feifei, Liu Kaiguo and Zhang Qing, 'Hulianwang zai wukelan chongtu zhong de zuoyong' [The Use of the Internet in the Ukraine Conflict], *Wangshi zongheng* [*Network Latitude*], July 2014, pp. 67–71; and Hu Yong and Li Na, 'Shejiao wangluo yu wukelan kangyi yundong' [Social Networking and the Ukraine Protests], *Shejiao meiti yu gonggong shijian* [*Social Media and Public Events*], no. 6, June 2014, pp. 17–24. Hu Yong and Li Na are affiliated with Peking University's School of Journalism and Communication.

44 See People's Republic of China, 'Zunzhong guojia wangluo zhuquan' [Respect National Network Sovereignty], 17 February 2016, http://www.gov.cn/zhengce/2016-02/17/content_5042042.htm; S.I. Bazylev et al., *The State and Prospects of Russian Military Cooperation on International Information Security* (Moscow: Ministry

of Defense of the Russian Federation, 2014); and Yu Xiaoqiu, '"Xin lengzhan" tiaozhan xia wangluo kongjian de yingdui zhice' [Cyberspace Countermeasures Under 'New Cold War' Conditions], *Guandian* [*Viewpoint*], July 2014, p. 117.

45 Yang Chengjun, 'Cong wukelan jubian kan wangluozhan dui guojia anquan de yingxiang' [From Ukraine's Upheaval Viewing the Impact of Cyber Warfare on National Security], *Zuguo* [*Motherland*], March 2014, pp. 14–15. Yang Chengjun is a professor and researcher within the Army Research Department of the Second Artillery Corps. He has also held affiliations with the Ministry of Foreign Affairs National Security Policy Committee. See also Yu, 'Ukraine First Disintegrated Online', p. 63. The author of this article is a senior fellow within the Unit of Engineers in China's National Security Policy Committee.

46 Jiang Lingfei, 'Miandui shijie luanju, zhongguo yao chenzhuo yingdui' [Facing Chaos in the World, China Should Calmly Confront It], *Dangdai shijie* [*Contemporary World*], May 2014, pp. 19–21.

47 Yu, 'Cyberspace Countermeasures Under "New Cold War" Conditions', p. 117.

48 Fang et al., 'The Use of the Internet in the Ukraine Conflict', p. 69.

49 Yu, 'Ukraine First Disintegrated Online', p. 63.

50 Zhu, 'Reflections on the Great-Power Game and Lessons Behind the Ukraine Crisis', p. 28.

51 *Ibid.*, p. 28.

52 Yu, 'Ukraine First Disintegrated Online', p. 63.

53 Fang et al., 'The Use of the Internet in the Ukraine Conflict', p. 71.

54 The increase in the use of the term 'emergence' (*fuxing*) in connection with both China and Russia is noteworthy, since it indicates not only greater connectivity between the two, but also how 'rise' (*jueqi*) has increasingly fallen out of favour in describing China. Chu, 'The Ukraine Crisis and China's Options', p. 11.

55 See Chu, 'The Ukraine Crisis and China's Options', p. 11; Zhang Jinying and Nan Weihua, 'Qiangjun xingjun shi zhongguo jundui de weiyi xuanxiang – Wukelan dongyao de fansi' [Building a Powerful Army Is the Only Option for the Chinese Military – Reflections on Ukraine's Turmoil], *Junshi zhengzhi xue yanjiu* [*Military Political Study*], no. 1, January 2014, pp. 146–9; and '2015 Zhongguo guofang baipishu (Zhongguo de junshi zhanlue) (Quanwen)' [2015 China's National Defence White Paper (China's Military Strategy) (Complete Text)], *Zhongguo ribao* [*China Daily*], 26 May 2015, http://world.chinadaily.com.cn/2015-05/26/content_20821000.htm. Zhang Jinying is affiliated with PLA Unit 69223 as a deputy political teacher and as a PhD candidate at Xi'an's Political School. Nan Weihua is a military training instructor at the Border Defense College.

56 See 'Chinese Pressure Sees Pakistan Mull Constitutional Status of Gilgit-Baltistan', *Express Tribune*, 7 January 2016, http://tribune.com.pk/story/1023523/chinese-pressure-sees-pakistan-mull-constitutional-status-of-gilgit-baltistan; Luisa

Lam, 'The Thugs of Mainland China', *New Yorker*, 8 October 2014, http://www.newyorker.com/news/news-desk/thugs-mainland-china-hong-kong-protests; Tom Porter, 'Hong Kong: "Hired Triad Thugs Attacked Demonstrators", Claims Legislator', *International Business Times*, 4 October 2014, http://www.ibtimes.co.uk/hong-kong-hired-triad-thugs-attacked-demonstrators-claims-legislator-1468529; Peter Popham and James Legge, 'Beijing Allegedly Call Hired Thugs to Incite Hong Kong Riots', *Morning Bulletin*, 4 October 2014, http://www.themorningbulletin.com.au/news/beijing-allegedly-call-hired-thugs-incite-hong-kon/2408957/#/0; Megha Rajagopalan, 'China Trains "Fishing Militia" to Sail into Disputed Waters', Reuters, 30 April 2016, http://www.reuters.com/article/us-southchinasea-china-fishingboats-idUSKCN0XS0RS; James C. Bussert, 'Chinese Maritime Assets Enforce Ocean Territorial Claims', *Signal*, 1 July 2014, http://www.afcea.org/content/?q=chinese-maritime-assets-enforce-ocean-territorial-claims; and Paul J. Leaf, 'Learning From China's Oil Rig Standoff With Vietnam', *Diplomat*, 30 August 2014, http://thediplomat.com/2014/08/learning-from-chinas-oil-rig-standoff-with-vietnam.

57 Wang Zhijun and Zhang Yaowen, 'Xifang diyuan zhanlue lilun pipan yu zhongguo diyuan zhanlue lilun gou-jian' [Critique of Western Geostrategic Theory and Construction of China's Construction Geostrategic Theory], *Xueshu tansuo* [*Academic Exploration*], Issue 2, February 2015, p. 32. Wang Zhijun is a professor, and Zhang Yaowen is a lecturer, at the Nanjing Army Command College.

58 Based on a panel moderated by Dr Lora Saalman on 'Cyber Security and Arms Control' at Tsinghua University's 2016 Annual Conference of the Chinese Community of Political Science and International Studies. See also 'San yue guoji wangluo he xinxi anquan fazhan dongtai' [March International Networks and Information Security Developments], *Xinxi anquan yu tongxin baomi* [*Information Security and Communications Privacy*], no. 4, April 2014, pp. 14–17.

59 Chen Hongchao, Duan Benqin and Li Tao, '21 shiji zhanzheng xin gai-nian – Wangluo zhan' [New Concept of Wars in the Twenty-First Century – Network War], *Junshi tongxin jishu* [*Journal of Military Communications Technology*], no. 4, April 2001. Chen Hongchao, Duan Benqin and Li Tao are affiliated with the 1st Military Representatives Office of the Communication Division of PLA General Staff Headquarters in Tianjin.

60 Yu Zhonghai, 'Ukraine First Disintegrated in Cyberspace', p. 63; Ma Liangli, Wu Qingzhi, Su Kai and Ren Wei, *Wulianwang ji qi junshi yingyong* [*The Internet of Things and Its Military Applications*] (Beijing: National Defense Industry Press, 2014), p. 187; Zheng Ruobing, *Junshi xinxi anquan lun* [*Military Information Security Theory*] (Beijing: National Defense Industry Press, January 2013), p. 101; Tang Yueping, Zhao Weifeng, Yu Maizheng, Sun Jian, Han Ping and

Tang Shaoqing, *Keji xinxi yun fuwu ji junshi yingyong* [*Science and Technology Information of Cloud Services and Military Application*] (Beijing: National Defense Industry Press, January 2015), p. 258; Song Zhongping, *Daguo wuqi* [*Major Power Weapons*] (Beijing: New World Press, September 2013), p. 140.

61 See 'APT30 and the Mechanics of a Long-Running Cyber Espionage Operation: How a Cyber Threat Group Exploited Governments and Commercial Entities across Southeast Asia and India for over a Decade', FireEye, April 2015, https://www2.fireeye.com/rs/fireye/images/rpt-apt30.pdf; and Bryan Krekel, Patton Adams and George Bakos, 'Occupying the Information High Ground: Chinese Capabilities for Computer Network Operations and Cyber Espionage', Northrop Grumman Corporation, 7 March 2012, http://nsarchive.gwu.edu/NSAEBB/NSAEBB424/docs/Cyber-066.pdf.

62 Countries thought to have been compromised by the APT30 campaign include Bhutan, Brunei, Cambodia, India, Indonesia, Japan, Laos, Malaysia, Myanmar, Nepal, Philippines, Saudi Arabia, Singapore, South Korea, Thailand, the United States and Vietnam.

63 Spear-phishing is email fraud that targets an individual or organisation to gain unauthorised access to confidential data. A man-on-the-side attack and a man-in-the-middle attack are similar. However, in the former case, rather than controlling a network node as in the latter case, the attacker has regular access to the communication channel, allowing him or her to read the traffic and to insert new messages, rather than modifying or deleting messages sent by other participants. A watering-hole exploit compromises a specific group of end users by infecting websites that members of the group are known to visit, so that the attacker can gain access to the network at the target's place of employment.

64 'Nation-State Sponsored Cyberwarfare Campaign', TruShield, 2 November 2015, https://trushieldinc.com/wp-content/uploads/2015/11/TS_Advisory_11022015_AD.pdf.

65 Feike Hacquebord, 'Pawn Storm Targets MH17 Investigation Team', TrendMicro, 22 October 2015, http://blog.trendmicro.com/trendlabs-security-intelligence/pawn-storm-targets-mh17-investigation-team/.

66 See Max Fisher, 'Why Security Experts Think Russia Was Behind the D.N.C. Breach', *New York Times*, 26 July 2016, http://www.nytimes.com/2016/07/27/world/europe/russia-dnc-hack-emails.html; 'Here's What We Know about Russia and the DNC Hack', *Wired*, 27 July 2016, https://www.wired.com/2016/07/heres-know-russia-dnc-hack; and 'OPM Breach Analysis', *Threat Connect*, 2015, https://www.threatconnect.com/blog/opm-breach-analysis-update.

67 'Pinpointing Targets: Exploiting Web Analytics to Ensnare Victims', FireEye, November 2015, https://www2.fireeye.com/rs/848-DID-242/images/rpt-witch-coven.pdf.

68 'Analysis of the Cyber Attack on the Ukrainian Power Grid – Defense Use Case', SANS Institute Industrial

Control Systems, Electricity Information Sharing and Analysis Center, 18 March 2016, pp. 1–23, https://ics.sans.org/media/E-ISAC_SANS_Ukraine_DUC_5.pdf.

69 *Ibid.*

70 Based on not-for-attribution conversations with a Philippines expert at the Daniel K. Inouye Asia-Pacific Center for Security Studies in 2016.

71 The discovery in 2010 of the use of the Stuxnet worm against Iran's nuclear facility at Natanz to cause damage to its centrifuges was among the first harbingers of the kinetic role of a cyber attack against critical infrastructure.

72 For more information, see Lora Saalman, 'Pouring "New" Wine into New Bottles: China–U.S. Deterrence in Cyberspace', *Seton Hall Journal of Diplomacy and International Relations*, Fall/Winter 2015.

73 Hu Hao, 'Eluosi lianbang anquan huiyi de lishi yanjin ji dui zhongguo de qishi' [Evolution of the Russian Federation Security Council and Its Implications for China], *Guoji anquan yanjiu* [*International Security Studies*], no. 5, May 2014, pp. 3–15.

The War in Yemen

Emile Hokayem and David B. Roberts

Since the turn of the millennium, the states of the Gulf Cooperation Council (GCC) – Bahrain, Kuwait, Oman, Qatar, Saudi Arabia and the United Arab Emirates (UAE) – have spent over $1 trillion on mostly high-end, Western military equipment. On paper, this has left the countries' military kit without peer in the Arab world. Intensive military modernisation has been accompanied by joint operations and some small interventions, notably by the UAE. Nevertheless, *Operation Decisive Storm*, the Saudi- and UAE-led intervention in Yemen that began in March 2015, took many by surprise. Neither Saudi Arabia nor the UAE were believed to possess the capability, the skill or the will to engage in as large, dangerous and offensive a mission as the operation in Yemen. Never before had any of the Gulf states, under GCC command, so proactively, provocatively and assertively deployed their military forces on such a scale. It seems that the Yemen intervention has ushered in a new era in the Gulf's security discourse and, perhaps, praxis.

A unique combination of factors, most notably the perception of the convergence of an unprecedented regional menace (Iran) and the rise of a hostile non-state actor on the Arabian Peninsula (the Houthis), as well as a sense of greater ownership among the participants of their own security at a time of US retrenchment, provided the impetus to intervene in Yemen. Yet it is important not to oversimplify the regional dynamics that underpinned the operation. Commentary in the Arab media and government statements

Emile Hokayem is the Senior Fellow for Middle East Security at the International Institute for Strategic Studies. **David B. Roberts** is a Lecturer in the Defence Studies Department at King's College London.

Survival | vol. 58 no. 6 | December 2016–January 2017 | pp. 157–186 DOI 10.1080/00396338.2016.1257202

have overemphasised the pernicious influence of Iran expanding through the rebel Houthi movement.[1] Meanwhile, the narrative in Western media and policy circles focuses on personalities at the expense of more structural factors.[2] In particular, the ascendancy of King Salman bin Abdulaziz al-Saud in January 2015, and the simultaneous promotion of his ambitious son, Prince Mohammed bin Salman al-Saud, to minister of defence, are treated as factors of immediate causation, not correlation.

The 2015 intervention, which has relied heavily on airstrikes, as well as on local proxy and allied forces, has allowed the participating states to achieve significant, though incomplete and possibly unsustainable, military gains, and, at times, to register better-than-expected operational accomplishments. However, the overall performance of the Saudi and Emirati forces remains mixed, because of the absence to date of political returns, and controversial, because of the heavy civilian toll. The still-unclear outcome of this intervention will likely weigh heavily on whether similar interventions will be conducted in the future in an increasingly volatile Middle East.

All that glitters

The literature examining the militaries of the GCC is far from voluminous, but such studies as do exist raise serious questions about their performance. The critiques can be separated into two types. The first focuses on the lack of appropriate training, professionalism and overall skills of the forces. The second questions the underlying *raison d'être* and organisation of these militaries, as well as the rationales for acquiring expensive Western military equipment.

The most exhaustive study of Arab militaries, *Arabs at War*, was conducted by Kenneth Pollack, who sought to examine why 'since 1945 Arab states have experienced problems that have denied their armed forces the success on the battlefield that objective factors suggest should be within their grasp'.[3] He concluded that Arab forces faced 'consistent and crippling problems' in four areas of military effectiveness: tactical leadership, information management, weapons handling and maintenance.[4] Tellingly, and in part owing to the newness of the Gulf states, the only Gulf military covered in this study was Saudi Arabia's, which was allocated a mere 22 pages.

Authors with vast experience in training missions throughout the Middle East have drawn similar conclusions. Norvell De Atkine, a retired US Army colonel, has argued that there are vast and fundamental cultural differences between Western and Arab militaries. As such, the decades of Western-led military training on Western military kit has been – and will continue to be – an exercise in 'pounding square pegs into round holes'.[5] Other critiques focus on inappropriate and unrigorous training methodologies, the over-promotion of royal individuals and the lack of a military ethos.[6] Indeed, some critics charge that the purpose of armed forces in the Gulf is more about cultivating loyalty through patronage than serving as an actual military instrument.[7] In this view, many Arab leaders deliberately designed, staffed and resourced their security and military apparatuses to balance praetorian guards and a national force, thus coup-proofing their regimes; external defence and power projection were just two of several less important rationales underpinning security policy.[8] In this context, massive arms procurement is cynically seen as a strategy to bankroll continuing Western security commitment, as well as a way for regimes to acquire and display prestige – the so-called 'glitter factor'.[9]

Such assumptions have been challenged by the 2015 Emirati- and Saudi-led war in Yemen. The scale and complexity of this intervention belie critiques that implicitly – or even explicitly – assert that such warfare is beyond the capabilities of GCC states. The dangerous nature of the war, with GCC nationals being inserted into a deadly theatre and incurring significant casualties, further challenges existing conceptions of the built-in constraints on the role of the GCC militaries.

Though the Yemen intervention may have come as a surprise to some, it followed a gradual defence build-up and escalation in the use of force by GCC states such as Saudi Arabia and, in particular, the UAE.[10] Under the leadership of Mohammed bin Zayed al-Nahyan, the crown prince of Abu Dhabi and the Emirati president-in-waiting, the UAE has kept its military busy with numerous small training missions abroad, as well as some joint operations. These started with low-key contributions to peacekeeping missions in the 1990s in East Africa and Kosovo, and continued from 2008 with the NATO-led International Security Assistance Force (ISAF) operation in

Afghanistan.[11] Joining the effort in Afghanistan was a significant step for the UAE. Though the deployment was small and the Emiratis did not take an aggressive front-line role, they provided niche capabilities in a hostile, internationalised and politically important environment.[12] Emirati leaders sought to demonstrate the country's strategic and operational utility as a small state, garner approval from crucial international allies, and harden and test in hostile conditions brigades that would later form the elite UAE Presidential Guard. Throughout the 1990s, and particularly from the 2000s onwards, the UAE also modernised its air force, procuring F-16s from the United States that were more advanced than those operated by the US Air Force.[13] With the UAE Air Force leading the way, the Emirati military developed an unrivalled reputation throughout the Gulf region.[14] This military prowess was put on display during the 2011 NATO-led operation in Libya (*Unified Protector*) and the coalition airstrikes against Islamic State targets in Iraq and Syria starting in 2014.[15] The UAE also launched its own near-unilateral missions, attacking targets in Libya in 2015 and 2016 with limited Egyptian assistance.[16] These demonstrated the country's increasing military confidence and capacity.

In comparison, the Saudi military forces had considerably less experience. Though Saudi Arabia made important contributions to operations *Desert Storm* and *Desert Shield*, these were mostly financial and political in nature.[17] The overall state of readiness of Saudi forces entering these operations was deeply lacking: according to the authors of *The Lessons of Modern War*, Volume IV: *The Gulf War*, 'only a small fraction' of the Saudi army had 'any real degree of military professionalism and only two comparatively small mechanized infantry brigades had any real combat power'.[18] The Saudi Arabian National Guard, a smaller praetorian force designed to balance the army, played only a small role in the conflict. Much like the army, it mostly failed to cover itself in glory in the 1991 Battle of Khafji, the key engagement often used by Saudi Arabia and Qatar to highlight their battle-proven skills.[19] The Saudi Air Force's role in the operations was significant – clocking nearly 7,000 sorties, second only to the US in number – but pilots lacked suitable equipment and training for an offensive role, ultimately hampering their efficacy.[20]

In the 1990s and early 2000s, Saudi Arabia spent significant sums on military procurement and training, but the 2009 border war with the Houthis strongly suggested that Saudi forces continued to suffer from ingrained organisational, doctrinal and operational problems. Despite its vast technological superiority and its alliance with the Yemeni government, Riyadh suffered significant setbacks and combat casualties against relatively poorly equipped but battle-hardened insurgents. Ultimately, the kingdom agreed to an unsatisfactory truce after the Houthis resisted months of Saudi airstrikes and land incursions, and infiltrated to the Saudi side of the border.[21] In turn, the Yemeni government was unable to impose its control over the northern Saada province, the location of most of the fighting, or to reach a sustainable political solution, allowing the Houthi movement to grow even stronger in the following years. Saudi Arabia's poor performance contributed to the sidelining of Prince Khaled bin Sultan al-Saud, son of defence minister Prince Sultan, who oversaw the campaign as assistant minister of defence.

The silver lining to the 2009 Yemeni debacle was that it galvanised momentum behind a major modernisation project for the Saudi military that had long been held up by weak leadership within the ministry of defence, allegations of corruption and a lack of vision. In 2010, Riyadh embarked on one of the largest military procurements in history, opening discussions on up to $90 billion-worth of new kit and upgrades.[22] In addition, 2010 saw the replacement of the long-serving royal heads of the Navy and Air Force with non-royals, a positive sign that meritocratic values were gaining ground, at least at the top.[23] Multinational exercises for all services were also increased to build up and harden Saudi forces.[24]

The road to Yemen

Even before the 2009 border war and the 2015 intervention, Saudi Arabia had historically seen Yemen as a source of threat.[25] The kingdom has repeatedly alternated between engagement, containment and intervention as means of dealing with (and, at times, unwittingly exacerbating) ideological, territorial and other menaces presented by its southern neighbour, whether real or imagined. Yemen is seen as intimately connected to the security of the Arabian Peninsula, in part because of the dense transnational and tribal links among the various countries, and in part because Yemen is resource-poor, populous and politically different as the sole non-monarchy on the peninsula. It is prone to exporting its own instability, much to the fear of its neighbours.

Because of these problems, the Gulf states relied for many years on Ali Abdallah Saleh, president of North Yemen from 1978 and later of a unified Yemen from 1990 until 2012, to maintain stability. Yet relations with Saleh became increasingly problematic in the face of his corrupt and divisive governance. His ambivalent campaign against the Yemen-based al-Qaeda in the Arabian Peninsula (AQAP) – which Saudi Arabia and the UAE have long seen as a key security threat – worsened Yemen's already considerable economic and social challenges.

The Houthis pursued an ambitious path

Fears over Yemen's stability peaked with the appearance of Ansar Allah, a movement headed by the Houthi family that has challenged Yemen's central government since the mid-2000s, and that fought the 2009 border war which humiliated the Saudi armed forces. Containing Houthi power became a driver of Gulf engagement in Yemen: the GCC designed and brokered the 2011–12 transition from the Saleh administration to that of his vice-president, Abd Rabbo Mansour Hadi, hoping that other Yemeni factions, and a complex political process, would keep the Houthis in check. The Houthi ascendancy is key to understanding Saudi and Emirati threat perceptions: for Riyadh and Abu Dhabi, regional and local threats are interconnected and mutually reinforcing. Thus, the concomitant rise and exertion of regional influence by Ansar Allah and Iran in the past decade has particularly unnerved Gulf leaders, who simplistically but nevertheless inextricably link them to one another.

Emboldened by rhetorical, as well as some material, Iranian support; frustrated by what it perceived to be limited political gains made during talks among Yemeni factions; and distrustful of Gulf intentions, the Houthis pursued an ambitious path. They allied with their former foe Ali Abdallah Saleh, seized the capital Sana'a in September 2014 and proceeded to venture into often hostile territory, capturing the strategically important Red Sea city of Hudeida, the country's second-largest port. In early 2015, the group took parts of the key port city of Aden. Within days of the Houthi takeover of the capital in September 2014, Iranian flights began to land in Sana'a, allegedly carrying Iranian advisers and weaponry.[26] Bombastic declarations from Tehran that Iran now controlled four Arab capitals (Baghdad, Damascus, Beirut and now Sana'a) were taken as literal policy statements, causing powerful shock waves in Gulf capitals.[27]

Nevertheless, although the UN found in 2015 that Iran had been supplying weapons and materiel to Ansar Allah since 2009, overall, the group does not fit the profile of an Iranian-controlled non-state actor.[28] The Zaydi Islam professed by Houthis differs in significant ways from Iran's Twelver Shi'ism. Tehran has no decisive say over Houthi decision-making, and the relationship between them is recent and opportunistic.[29] It is doubtful that Iran ordered the Houthi power grab.[30] Instead, it is probable that, once it happened, Tehran began to see Yemen as a battlefield where it could, with little effort, pin down and bleed Saudi Arabia as it focused on Iraq and Syria.

The Houthis' southward expansion alienated significant segments of the Yemeni population beyond the weak and battered government of President Mansour Hadi, including urban elites in Sana'a and Taizz, tribes in central Yemen, the tribal–Islamist coalition known as Islah, southern secessionists and Saudi-allied Salafists. It also revitalised AQAP, which the Houthis had fought intensely even before they took over Sana'a in 2014. AQAP benefited from the security vacuum as pro-Hadi forces battled the Houthis, as well as from the disbanding of US-backed counter-terrorism units, popular anti-Houthi sentiments among the tribes from which AQAP recruits and the initial Saudi–Emirati prioritisation of the Houthi threat.

The Houthis' territorial expansion, attempted institutional takeover of the state and rallying of significant, well-armed units of the military loyal to Saleh precipitated the joint Saudi–Emirati operation. Concerned by the collapse of the Arab order since 2011 and the perceived lack of any will in Washington to preserve it or to counter perceived Iranian bellicosity, Saudi Arabia and the UAE became more aggressive in their foreign policies. Neither state was prepared to allow a group they both consider a

Yemeni Hizbullah-in-the-making to institutionalise its power, dominate Yemeni politics, control vast swathes of strategic territory (including the Bab Al-Mandeb Strait) or acquire long-range missiles and an (arguably antiquated) air force. The apprehension in Riyadh and Abu Dhabi that Ansar Allah would eventually morph into a Hizbullah on the southeastern tip of the Arabian Peninsula, inviting ever-greater Iranian support and posing an ever-increasing threat to the kingdom and beyond, was not unreasonable. Nevertheless, in their haste to counter this perceived, latent threat and to mobilise domestic and regional support, the Gulf states overemphasised the Iranian role, thereby removing almost all agency from the Houthis themselves and oversimplifying the dynamics of domestic Yemeni politics. The policies that flowed from this assessment and the corresponding rules of engagement would serve to aggravate and entrench the conflict.

The Gulf-led intervention in Yemen occurred only a couple of months after King Salman ascended to the Saudi throne, at which time his hitherto untested son, Prince Mohammed, landed the defence-ministry portfolio (among others). Given the importance of individual decision-makers in Gulf politics, and the fact that the intervention represented such a profound break from the past in terms of ambition, risk and forces committed, it has understandably become associated with King Salman and is something that he, and his son, are likely to be remembered for. However, the idea of and planning for an intervention in Yemen arose from the Houthi seizure of Sana'a, and therefore predated Salman's reign. Saudi Arabia suspended its financial aid to Yemen as soon as the Houthis took over Sana'a, turning its attention to contingency planning instead. UAE leaders were from early on full partners in this effort, which gathered significant support within Gulf ruling circles. Indeed, for many Gulf officials, it was regrettable not that the intervention took place, but that it had not started earlier, before the Houthis expanded south towards Aden.

Though the nature and scale of the intervention may well reflect the thinking and appetite for risk of particular leaders, the decision to intervene was more than simply the product of rash decision-making by young, capricious leaders. Indeed, it was an almost inevitable structural reaction to events occurring within a volatile regional context that had sharpened threat perceptions. Of particular importance was the nascent Saudi–Emirati axis in the Gulf region. Although the two countries had long been at odds on key matters, they were brought closer by the erosion of the regional order, an overly eager Qatar, a rising Iran and their common enmity toward certain forms of populist Islamism. As the two largest economies and militaries of the Gulf, they possessed an unmatched ability to set the regional agenda and to pursue policies in tandem, making Yemen a test case.

The war in Yemen

Examining the actions of the GCC states in Yemen is challenging because of the opacity of Gulf military decision-making and operations, as well as the scarcity of independent sources within Yemen. However, a critical mass of information can be gathered from a range of sources, including UN reports, sporadic but detailed reportage from independent journalists, interviews with policymakers and advisers in the region, and informed commentary by experts with apparent access to government sources in the Gulf, the United Kingdom, France and the United States.

Stand-off warfare

The Houthis marched on Aden on 22 March 2015, seizing the international airport and several outer neighbourhoods. By this stage, *Decisive Storm* had been in the planning stages for some months.[31] The operation was launched on 25 March, when the Houthis assaulted Taizz, Yemen's third-largest city. This allowed the group to capture Al Anad Air Base in the neighbouring Lahij province, the (now former) headquarters for US special operations combating al-Qaeda. The next day, Adel al-Jubeir, then-Saudi ambassador to the US and soon to become foreign minister, announced the start of the bombing campaign from Washington. The choice of Washington foreshadowed the logistical support, expedited weapons and ammunition deliveries, intelligence sharing and targeting assistance that the US, along with the UK and France, would quickly provide to the coalition.

The stated objectives of the operation were to recapture the entirety of Yemen and destroy the Houthi movement, thus denying Iran a presence on the Arabian Peninsula. As the fighting unfolded, the Gulf states quietly formulated ambitions that were more realistic, though still difficult to meet. They sought to defend Aden, roll back the Houthi expansion in southern and central areas (and eventually put pressure on Sana'a), and neutralise the high-end military capabilities of Houthi-allied military units loyal to Saleh. Politically, the goal was to extend Mansour Hadi's authority beyond Aden's immediate environs, break the Saleh–Houthi alliance and force the Houthis to return to the negotiating table in a weaker position. It quickly became clear that neither country would mount a massive ground invasion as each relied instead on overwhelming airpower, special forces, units from allied nations and local partners.

The first phase of the campaign included comprehensive air and naval blockades, ostensibly to prevent weapons supplies from reaching the Houthis, as well as airstrikes to destroy Yemen's air and coastal defences, air force and ballistic-missile capabilities. The latter were seen as direct threats to Saudi territory and coalition assets.[32] The meagre air and naval capabilities of Houthi–Saleh forces could not compete with the clear superiority of the coalition (backed by US, UK and French vessels enforcing a UN arms embargo on the Houthis). Tellingly, there was no direct Iranian challenge to this blockade. Instead, Iran sent in May 2015 a ship supposedly carrying humanitarian supplies, which was peacefully – and unsurprisingly – prevented from reaching Yemeni shores. Such theatrics allowed Iran to appear to be taking the high ground while embarrassing Saudi Arabia at a time when the humanitarian consequences of the blockade were beginning to take hold.

Within 24 hours of the launch of *Decisive Storm*, Saudi military spokesman Brigadier-General Ahmed al-Assiri provided optimistic assessments of the campaign's progress, claiming that coalition forces controlled the skies and had 'devastated' the Houthis' ballistic missiles and command-and-control centres.[33] In reality, satellite imagery showed that much of Yemen's air force and air defences remained untouched, while key runways remained usable. Of far greater concern was the enduring Houthi–Saleh capability to launch ballistic missiles mounted on mobile launchers known for being difficult to hunt down, a fact that became egregiously apparent in subsequent months, when pro-Houthi military units fired ballistic missiles in a humiliating reminder of Houthi resilience, forcing Saudi civilians along the border to seek shelter and triggering the deployment of Saudi *Patriot* missile-defence systems.

After destroying its initial list of military targets relatively quickly, the coalition widened its targeting scope by the second month of the operation, striking roads and fuel infrastructure to limit Houthi mobility.[34] Despite the announcement in late April of an end to *Decisive Storm*, and a proclamation of completed objectives, bombing continued and even intensified.

According to Michael Knights and Alexandre Mello, coalition targeting followed three patterns: coercive attacks against Houthi allies to compel them to separate from Ansar Allah, retaliatory attacks against Houthis, and continued *Scud* hunting.[35] Though the air war was a key component in the coalition's standoff approach, it came with serious costs. Figures and estimates of the collateral damage inflicted on Yemen vary, but the number of civilian casualties is certainly in the thousands. Meanwhile, the wider humanitarian impact of accompanying food, water and medicine shortages was acute. This led to widespread condemnation of the operation in international forums. Most sorties were flown by Saudi pilots, which worsened collateral damage because they reportedly dropped bombs from a high altitude compared to more experienced Emirati pilots, who conducted lower-altitude bombings.[36] While both Saudi Arabia and the UAE used precision weapons and benefited from US and UK targeting support, there are also reports of the use of cluster bombs and the targeting of civilian areas and medical infrastructure, which the coalition has either denied or blamed on Saleh and the Houthis.[37]

> *The wider humanitarian impact was acute*

Coordination of airpower was difficult, with nine states operating eight different classes of fast jets (F/A-18, F-15s, F-15c, F-16, *Mirage* 2000, *Tornado* IDS, *Typhoon* Eurofighter and SU-24), all based in Saudi Arabia. This posed unparalleled logistical and operational challenges. An additional complication came in the form of UK and US advisers present in the coalition operation room to advise in some oblique way on the targeting process. In addition, the US flew more than 700 air-to-air refuelling sorties, providing a capability that Arab states lack.[38] The US has also been involved in search-and-rescue operations.[39] The coordination of these multifarious, pan-national elements was technically impressive at times. Analysts and foreign military commanders alike may need to recalibrate their expectations of the level of technical expertise that key states, such as the UAE, can demonstrate in difficult, hostile circumstances.

On the ground, the advance of the coalition presented new problems. The deeper its troops advanced into Yemeni territory, the more exposed they and their supply lines became to attacks by Houthis and allied forces. Accordingly, September 2015 saw the worst loss of life in the Emirates' military history. More than 45 Emiratis, 33 Yemenis and five Bahrainis were killed when a missile reportedly struck an arms cache stored in a coalition base. The UAE responded with three days of national mourning, and with a prolonged series of air raids on targets around Yemen. Missile attacks continue sporadically to kill coalition troops. Incidents include a strike that killed up to a dozen troops on 14 December, and another that killed one Emirati soldier in early February 2016. Nevertheless, the campaign progressed and began to focus on reconquering central areas (notably in the provinces of Maarib and Taizz) so that coalition forces can eventually close in on Sana'a.

The coalition advance presented new problems

Along the Saudi–Yemeni border, *Scud* missiles, rockets and artillery shells have continued to test Saudi defences.[40] As in 2009, the Houthis mounted incursions from their heartland of Saada province, attacking Saudi border posts and posting footage online featuring provocative statements such as 'the Houthis are taking over Saudi Arabia'.[41] Saudi soldiers have been killed in clashes near the Saudi city of Najran – a city of 1.6 million just 15 kilometres from the Yemeni border. Embarrassingly, this temporarily forced the Saudi national airline to suspend flights to the city and local schools to close.[42] By December 2015 more than 80 people had been killed in cross-border skirmishes, and by February 375 Saudi civilians had been killed by Houthi rocket attacks in Najran.[43] The symbolism of such strikes on Saudi territory is worth highlighting. Hitting inside Saudi Arabia is a sign of military resilience and commitment, as well as a galvanising tactic for the Houthis and many Yemenis who resent the Saudi intervention. And while the mountainous territory in the affected areas favours the Houthis and their guerrilla-style attacks, it is still a source of embarrassment for Saudi Arabia that the country has suffered quite so badly from such attacks.

Despite such setbacks, both Saudi Arabia and the UAE have registered significant tactical and operational successes during the intervention. *Operation Golden Arrow*, which wrested Aden from Houthi control, demonstrated operational skill and audacity. A team of around 50 ship-deployed special forces composed of Yemenis serving in the UAE and Saudi forces alongside UAE Presidential Guard special forces landed in Crater, one of the coalition-controlled areas in Aden.[44] The UAE's request for US transportation support to land materiel in Aden had been rebuffed, according to the *New York Times*, in part because the US did not think that the UAE possessed the capability to undertake the planned amphibious landing.[45] The UAE responded by purchasing its own transportation craft from an Australian company and proceeding to successfully deploy approximately 25% of the UAE's *Leclerc* tanks and other armoured vehicles.[46] This success secured the port and airport of Aden, facilitating logistics and allowing the Hadi government to have an in-country base.

The aftermath of the Aden operation also illustrated the coalition's limitations. The low numbers of Saudi and Emirati troops, and their reliance on local allies, meant the crucial element of post-conflict stabilisation was missing. Consequently, competition among the disparate local Yemeni factions escalated, and security dramatically worsened in late 2015 and early 2016. This created a security vacuum that AQAP and ISIS sought to fill, which in turn complicated the goal of turning Aden into the base of the Hadi government. Indeed, the hotel at which government officials were staying was bombed. The coalition's headquarters in Aden was also attacked in October 2015, forcing further retrenchment among coalition troops.

Moreover, in October 2016, the Houthis, or possibly units loyal to Saleh, attacked the UAE's key supply ship, disabling it in international waters and dramatically reducing the state's ability to ferry both kit and people. This showcased the threat the Houthis posed to international shipping, legitimating one of the reasons why the coalition went to war in the first place. But it also brutally exposed the UAE's decision to forgo the kind of drawn-out procurement process that states normally endure in favour of a quick-fix solution: the US had rejected using this kind of ship precisely because of its vulnerability to missiles.[47]

Back on land, the coalition struggled to help break the Houthi siege of Taizz. A city largely hostile to the Houthis, Taizz sits on the route between Aden and Sana'a. A failure to free Taizz would augur badly for a possible attack on the capital.

Coalition warfare

From the beginning, Saudi Arabia and the UAE were eager to obtain international support for the intervention, which was couched in the language and theatre of international legitimacy. They sought to restore the internationally recognised government and worked to secure UN Security Council Resolution 2216 that banned arms supplies to the Houthis and Saleh. Just as importantly, they sought Sunni cover through the formation of a symbolic coalition of Sunni countries against a backdrop of heightened sectarianism in the region.

The coalition was made up of an impressive range of regional states, some of which contributed much-needed forces, valuable support and political cover. With the notable exception of Oman, which, to the irritation of Saudi Arabia and the UAE, chose to play the role of a neutral mediator, support from fellow Gulf states was forthcoming and highly publicised for local and international consumption. Al-Jazeera reported that Qatar sent as many as 1,000 of its troops, though the accuracy of this report is questionable. Not only would 1,000 troops comprise approximately 10% of the state's entire army – an unfeasibly large proportion of troops to send abroad – but the report intimated that they were supported by 200 Qatari armoured vehicles and 30 *Apache* attack helicopters.[48] Qatar did not possess any *Apaches* when the report appeared, and would likely have struggled to deploy 200 armoured vehicles in one go.[49] Bahrain and Kuwait have also deployed smaller numbers of troops to Yemen and to the Saudi side of the Yemeni border, respectively.[50] Gulf participation served to sustain a narrative of solidarity and steadfastness, which helped to counter international scepticism and criticism of the operation.

Riyadh and Abu Dhabi also enrolled support from other Sunni countries, which contributed manpower. Some interpreted this support as payback for years of GCC financial aid and a bid to guarantee future assistance.[51] On 4 May 2015, the Senegalese foreign minister announced that his country would contribute 2,100 soldiers, for which Saudi Arabia would 'pay Senegal a substantial sum'.[52] Sudan deployed hundreds of special-forces soldiers to work with the coalition, most of whom were deployed to secure Aden and its vital infrastructure as Emirati special forces moved deeper into the country. Estimates of the Sudanese contribution range from 4,000 to 10,000 men.[53] Eritrea leased its Hanish Islands (strategically located only 29km from Yemen) and its port city of Assab to the UAE for 30 years for use against the Houthis, as well as signing wider security and defence agreements. A UN monitoring mission later found that Eritrea had embedded 400 troops within Emirati forces – in contravention of existing UN resolutions on Eritrea – in return for financial compensation and oil.[54] As of spring 2016, Djibouti was also negotiating the leasing of a military base to Saudi Arabia to further enable the encirclement of Yemen.[55]

But there were notable absentees, too. Egypt provided ships for the naval blockade, but not the ground force that many in Saudi Arabia expected. This was a surprising rebuff for Saudi Arabia and the UAE given their staunch diplomatic and financial support of President Abdel Fattah Al-Sisi since 2013. More surprising still was Pakistan's refusal. Saudi–Pakistani relations have been close for decades.[56] Not only has Riyadh provided billions of dollars of aid to Pakistan, but a very close security arrangement ties the countries together. Pakistan had deployed 10,000 troops to staff the Saudi 10th Armoured Brigade after the seizure by fundamentalists of the mosque in Mecca in 1979 highlighted chronic weaknesses in Saudi capabilities.[57] There was, from the Saudi side at least, an expectation that Pakistan would repay decades of Saudi support by deploying troops in this instance too. However, when Pakistani Prime Minister Nawaz Sharif took the Saudi request to parliament in April 2015, it was rejected.[58] This rebuff provoked anger and embarrassment in Riyadh, and exposed Saudi diplomatic limitations.

Even so, the coalition provided welcome capabilities. It managed to assemble approximately 170 aircraft, the largest such force ever gathered in

Arab history.[59] These included F-16s from Jordan (6), Egypt (4), Bahrain (4), Morocco (6), and the UAE (12), which were based at Taif near Mecca; and Kuwaiti F/A-18 *Hornets* (15), Qatari *Mirage* 2000s (10) and Sudanese Su-24s (3), which were based at King Khalid Air Base in southwest Saudi Arabia.[60] The UAE also deployed around 30 fast jets (F-16e and *Mirage* 2000), as well as a range of helicopters. Saudi Arabia itself contributed approximately 100 planes (F-15c, F-15s, *Tornado* IDS, *Typhoon* and support aircraft).

From the very beginning, the coalition's strategy emphasised the role of local allies in ground operations, a reflection of its reluctance to conduct a massive ground operation itself. A vast but diverse array of anti-Houthi local forces existed throughout southern Yemen, but securing their loyalty and aligning their interests and operations with those of the coalition (including the formal recognition of Hadi's authority) proved arduous. Neither Saudi Arabia nor the UAE had the experience and expertise of Iran in overseeing and directing the operations of local militias with a small cadre of highly skilled personnel.

Saudi Arabia adopted a pragmatic approach to alliances

Operating in Yemen exposed the two countries to difficult decisions about whom to partner with. The risks of entanglement with unsavoury or unreliable partners were substantial given the wide variety of Yemeni forces and the nature of the tribal and political terrain. The spectrum of possible partners ranged from secular secessionists from the south and tribal elements to the Muslim Brotherhood-aligned Islah and Salafist forces. A momentary convergence of interests even existed with AQAP, though both Riyadh and Abu Dhabi viewed the movement as a threat to be addressed once the Houthis were rolled back. Nevertheless, while there is no evidence that Saudi Arabia or the UAE actively conspired with AQAP, the latter benefited from the chaos of the war, which left vast swathes of southeast Yemen ungoverned for months on end.[61]

Saudi Arabia adopted a pragmatic approach to alliances. Until early 2015, the country had demonstrated a strong antipathy towards the Muslim Brotherhood, culminating with Saudi backing for the 2013 coup in Egypt and the denunciation of the movement as a terrorist group in March 2014. In 2015, King Salman toned down this uncompromising approach, allowing Riyadh to selectively engage Muslim Brotherhood affiliates on a local basis, notably in Yemen. Given that Yemenis often sustain multiple affiliations, such flexibility was essential to build partnerships, as with Ali Mohsen Al-Ahmar, a former military chief and a tribal leader with close links to Islah.[62] Prompted by Saudi insistence, Mohsen provided political and military support to Hadi, and was rewarded by becoming Hadi's vice-president in early 2016.

In contrast, UAE policy remained considerably more guarded and conditional toward potential Islamist allies in the region.[63] In an August 2015 tweet, Anwar Gargash, the minister of state for foreign affairs, best reflected the UAE's antipathy towards Islah by describing it as 'an opportunistic group … waiting for the chance to steal the achievements and lead the scene in Yemen'.[64] Emirati dilemmas came into focus during the battle over Taizz, where the UAE, in line with its stringent anti-Brotherhood worldview, originally demanded that local partners renounce their Islamist and al-Qaeda affiliations in return for support.[65] This stance was eventually tempered, and for good reason. Taizz is strategically located between Aden and Sana'a, and is also well placed as the gateway to the Bab al-Mandeb, one of the world's key sea-lane choke points. It is thus critical to any plan to control Yemen's key cities. Moreover, Hammoud Saeed al-Mikhlafi, one of the strongest militia leaders in Yemen, was based in Taizz and, like other local commanders, was resolutely focused on his own city rather than on any plan to advance a pan-regional Islamist alliance. He was also relatively moderate and could offer some assurances as to the limited nature of his political and military aspirations. Some reports suggest that the UAE eventually agreed to join Riyadh in supporting Mikhlafi.[66] Another example of an important UAE- and Saudi-backed tribal leader is Shaikh Mansour al-Khanqu, who is also affiliated to Islah.[67] The UN found that Salafi groups opposed to the Houthis also grew in Taizz around this time, receiving some support from the coalition.[68]

In the belated fight against al-Qaeda's gains in the Hadhramaut region, the UAE strove to recruit, train and deploy local forces formed into first and second Military Regional Commands; co-opt existing fighting groups such as the Hadhramaut Tribal Confederation; and forge an alliance with what Michael Knights described as 'a patchwork of nearly 4,000 tribal rebels'.[69] This was different to the approach adopted in Aden, where fighters were added to regular Yemeni Army units. In both of these instances, the UAE mobilised Yemeni tribes that had moved to the Gulf states in the 1960s and 1970s, some of which obtained Gulf nationalities and joined the armed forces while retaining links to Yemen.[70] The UAE also sought to quickly train up local forces, which included an army- and police-led focus on training with Yemeni ground forces, and the training of Yemeni pilots at Al Anad Air Base. The latter were furnished with IOMAX AT-802 light strike aircraft ideal for close air support of ground troops.[71] Hundreds of South American mercenaries were also deployed to Yemen from their base in Abu Dhabi.[72]

UAE forces worked alongside these forces as well as directing them. The Emirati Presidential Guard played a conspicuous role in *Operation Golden Arrow* alongside Yemenis trained in the UAE and the Saudi armed forces.[73] Nor was this modus operandi isolated to the battle for Aden. The presence of special forces (usually Emirati) or Yemeni troops at moments of direct contact with the Houthis has been a pattern in evidence throughout the conflict, as opposed to wider 'front lines' of regular coalition troops facing up to the Houthis. For example, the battle for Al Anad Air Base was led by a 1,500-man, UAE-trained and -equipped Yemeni force.[74]

Assessments and implications

Saudi Arabia and the UAE have built and led a large and complex coalition to prosecute a far-reaching war with ambitious objectives, and in so doing have challenged existing ideas of the utility of Gulf-state military force. Equally, some of the operational vignettes that have emerged from the war – the amphibious landing at Aden; some of the logistical work supporting the air war; the Emirati-led effort to expel AQAP from the port city of Mukalla in the southeastern province of Hadhramaut – have also contradicted conventional assessments of the competence of the region's military forces. Nevertheless, the evidence suggests that the paradigm has not shifted, but rather has been slightly nudged.

Adjusting to the war

The initial grandiose tasks that the coalition set for itself, including rolling back Houthi influence across the country, recovering the capital city and restoring the Hadi government, were wildly implausible and remain so. Even the subsequently more limited aims to undercut Houthi power and create rifts in the Houthi–Saleh alliance in order to force them to the negotiating table in a weaker position proved difficult to achieve.

Indeed, Saudi Arabia and the UAE struggled to translate military gains into actionable political leverage during the talks convened by the UN in spring and summer 2016, in part because the political and military tracks appeared disconnected, and in part because of the complexity of the Yemeni situation, which at times seemed to bedazzle the negotiators.

Whether prompted by the US or the UN, or driven by its own considerations, the coalition sought to create political momentum for talks, announcing military and political de-escalation measures including ceasefires. For example, in what was widely interpreted as a conciliatory gesture, Saudi Foreign Minister Adel al-Jubeir tweeted in May 2016:

> Al-Qaeda and ISIS are terrorist organizations. However, the Houthis are Yemenis and are our neighbors with whom one can hold talks. Whether we disagree or agree with the Houthis, they remain a part of the social fabric of Yemen.[75]

Privately, Saudi officials also recognised the need to compromise (including on the departure of Hadi during the transition), but seemed unable to induce their Yemeni allies to align and organise themselves accordingly.

Embarrassingly, the coalition's relative successes did not induce greater cohesion or encourage a sense of purpose among the array of anti-Houthi Yemeni actors. The enduring insecurity in Aden meant that President Hadi chose to stay in a safe palace in Saudi Arabia, paying sparse visits to liberated areas in Yemen. This undermined his already-dented credibility and authority. Political infighting between Hadi and other Saudi- and Emirati-backed politicians was also problematic: resenting then-vice-president Khaled Bahah's popularity and fearing that Bahah could supplant him as part of a settlement, Hadi unexpectedly replaced him with Ali Mohsen Al-Ahmar in April 2016. Such competing aims and loyalties among Yemenis fuelled brinksmanship and intransigence, especially on the part of Hadi, and undermined his claim to be able to reach and implement a settlement.

In contrast, the Houthi–Saleh axis proved solid and coherent. Existing tensions between Ansar Allah and Saleh, long sworn enemies, remained contained, and while the Saleh camp suffered from some defections, his tribal allies and many of the military units loyal to him resisted coalition entreaties and absorbed the burdens of war. Despite discontent over the conflict's humanitarian toll and the leaders' own abuses, there was no discernible loss of popular support for either Ansar Allah or Saleh. Public rallies in Sana'a and elsewhere continued to draw large crowds.

Facing a serious military challenge, Saudi Arabia and the UAE realised that they could not hope to achieve their stated aims on their own. Rosy military assessments and repeated announcements of a coming final push toward Sana'a were belied by the coalition's travails in Taizz and elsewhere. The growth of ISIS – and, more importantly, AQAP – was both a threat and an embarrassment, forcing the two governments to divert attention and resources to counter them.

Coalition and strategy

Assembling the coalition of the willing proved relatively successful, notwithstanding the disappointments of Pakistan and Egypt. The airpower coalition in particular required that the participating states overcome chronic logistical difficulties in Saudi Arabia to organise and sustain their bombing campaign.

Despite the ramshackle and ad hoc way in which the coalition was put together, with vanishingly little coordination or discussion in terms of its plans, it suffered no defection over the conduct of the war, as Saudi Arabia in particular absorbed the reputational and associated costs. There were few public signs of discontent among core coalition members, and while countries did adjust their deployments, this cannot necessarily be blamed on inter-coalition tensions, as operational requirements were often the decisive factor.

Although the Houthi problem was viewed as pressing, it was not grave enough to compel the coalition to engage in 'total war'. The habitual Gulf intolerance for casualties remained intact. The September 2015 missile strike that killed dozens of Emiratis was, after all, a simple case of a missile hitting its mark, and not the product of any overly risky tactical venture by the coalition. In the aftermath of the strike, Emirati leaders paid visits to each grieving family in part to contain public shock and discontent.

This concern about casualties shaped rules of engagement and underpinned the coalition's wider strategy, which was, firstly, to conduct the war through proxy forces as much as possible, and, secondly, to conduct the war from afar, limiting the manifest dangers from the Houthis to a minimum. However, it is likely that the Saudis expected to rely heavily on Pakistani ground troops. Their absence forced the coalition to look for replacement troops, finding them in Sudan and other countries. This search was made easier because of the relatively low quality and cost of such troops, and the minimal political costs for contributing nations. At the same time, it demonstrated the coalition's haphazard approach to military strategy once its basic preferences were articulated.

Operations

Within the coalition, the key dynamic was evidently between Saudi Arabia and the UAE. However strategically close the two had become, they had different military cultures. Importantly, there was a gap in expeditionary experience, capability and combat-readiness. The UAE deployed considerably better trained and nimble forces, and possessed superior logistical capabilities that had a quick enabling effect on Yemeni partners. However, whatever Saudi Arabia lacked militarily, it made up for in terms of its size, influence and seniority. While operational and political differences certainly existed, UAE deference to the Saudi leadership was the norm publicly. On the ground, each maintained considerable autonomy.

However capable the UAE in particular proved to be, sustaining the deployment quickly became an issue. The UAE struggled to maintain a sufficient level of force and the associated pace of troop rotations as missions accumulated. Soldiers were soon rotated out of Yemen without being replaced, a sign not just of fatigue or the paucity of suitable troops but possibly also misgivings among the leadership.

Another source of frustration for the coalition was the underdevelopment of unified GCC military structures despite decades of rhetorical support for GCC military integration. While Kuwait, Bahrain and Qatar all contributed troops, it was up to the coalition to organise its deployments on a largely ad hoc basis.

Operationally, Saudi Arabia and the UAE found themselves facing a chronic shortage of infantry. They used their special forces and mercenaries sparingly, and typically only in stand-alone, choreographed operations rather than as part of continuous ground operations or in front-line fighting. In lieu of a cohesive coalition, Saudi and UAE forces had to do most of the heavy lifting themselves. This highlighted traditional weaknesses in the Saudi military.

A particular Saudi weakness was revealed by the intensity of the cross-border fighting. Saudi border defence was, once again, sorely lacking. The inhospitable, mountainous terrain along the border allowed the low-tech, insurgent approach adopted by the Houthis to negate the advantages of the more technologically advanced Saudi military. Judging by Saudi military and civilian casualties, the lessons of 2009 had not been learned.

Sudanese soldiers helped to guard the airport in Aden, which was useful, but still the coalition lacked offensive soldiers to take the battle to the Houthis. Instead, it was forced to rely on hastily assembled, locally recruited and trained partners (as in Aden), or on the temporary 'leasing' of fighting groups to support the coalition's aims (as in Mukalla). Ultimately, this approach proved to be costly and unsustainable.

Local knowledge

Saudi Arabia's weak performance was due, in part, to declining knowledge among its officials about Yemen. For years, the Saudi point man on Yemen was Prince Sultan, who oversaw Saudi activities and patronage there. His declining health and eventual death in 2011 meant the Saudi system lacked a unified, comprehensive and hands-on approach to Yemen. The threat of AQAP compelled the intelligence branch of the Ministry of

Interior (Mabahith) to take action, elevating Prince Mohammed bin Naef to interior minister, but the ministry's focus was limited to AQAP. When protests shook Sana'a in 2011, Saudi Arabia championed the role of the GCC instead of intervening directly in the crisis. Prince Mohammed bin Naef, who has since become the Crown Prince, is rumoured to be sceptical about the Yemen operation.

As the war unfolded, the coalition's frustration grew with the realisation that muscle and cash do not necessarily translate into sustainable leverage over individual partners and do not override the preferences of local actors. It would be easy to conclude that Saudi Arabia and the UAE have much to learn from Iran in terms of the remote control of proxy forces in foreign lands. However, and for a host of reasons, Gulf countries lack a defence doctrine that prioritises asymmetric warfare and investment in proxies.

International support

US support for the coalition, while ambivalent, played an enabling role in the whole venture. Without it, the entire campaign would have necessarily been smaller in scale. A reluctant US administration had consented to the operation in support of its complex regional commitments. US President Barack Obama had prioritised a nuclear agreement with Tehran and publicly pledged to contain Iran's actions in the region. Winning Saudi and Emirati consent for, or at least their agreement not to interfere with, the deal meant accepting an operation widely viewed as unwise or even unnecessary in Washington.

As a result, the US provided intelligence, targeting advice, logistical support, air-to-air refuelling, expedited munitions resupply and maintenance that were key to the coalition's operations. While Washington saw this assistance as necessary to maintain the relationship and to influence the coalition's military behaviour, it made the US a de facto partner in the war effort, leaving it liable for any resulting collateral damage and other abuses, and thus vulnerable to public criticism.

The subsequent outcry on Capitol Hill, in the European Parliament and elsewhere over American (and British) logistical support and arms deliveries to countries accused of deliberately targeting civilians and ignoring international humanitarian law could have long-term consequences for the capacity of the Gulf states to resource operations. Calls in the US and the EU to stop arms sales to Saudi Arabia have intensified, illustrating the Gulf's dependency on Western military suppliers. These concerns have only grown after the passage in late September of the Justice Against Sponsors of Terrorism Act by the US Congress, which allows Americans harmed by the 9/11 attacks to bring a civil lawsuit against the Saudi government. This is seen across the Gulf as a deeply hostile move by Congress, which plays a critical role in approving US arms sales.

* * *

Ultimately, the coalition's way of war has proven to be flawed. While the participants have demonstrated their will to intervene, it is still too soon to determine whether they will be equally willing to sustain the operation to a successful end. Importantly, the coalition has not found a way to achieve its operational aims while minimising its losses. By mid-2016, force had compelled the Houthis to sit at the negotiating table, but not to agree on a political settlement. In the meantime, the costs of the operation continue to mount, not just in terms of massive financial outlays (believed to run into the billions of dollars every month),[76] but of the suffering of the Yemeni people, including the Houthis, their supporters and opponents. The coalition's overreliance on airstrikes has led to an egregious number of civilian deaths and the widespread destruction of Yemen's infrastructure as the number of military targets has diminished. Nevertheless, the coalition has pressed on with its air war. A functioning post-conflict Yemeni state is probably unattainable now, regardless of the levels of financial support for reconstruction.

For Saudi Arabia and the UAE, a plausible outcome of the intervention is a failed state at their border, in which the Houthis survive as a key military actor dominating a vast territory, and in which the conditions for radicalisation and jihadi recruitment are ideal. If nothing else, both countries face complex decisions and uncomfortable entanglements with opportunistic and unreliable local factions and politicians. While they have demonstrated their readiness to deploy force against perceived threats in proximate territories, the conclusions that other states draw from the campaign will be strongly influenced by its still-uncertain outcome. The Yemen campaign is at most a model for limited intervention in weak countries, not a template for strategic self-sufficiency or for future inter-state wars in the Gulf region. It remains to be seen whether this war will serve as the impetus for a rethink of Gulf defence or compel the Gulf states to embrace a more inclusive and better calibrated approach to the perennially weak state of their southern neighbour.

Notes

1 Salman Al-Dossary, 'Iran Finally Admits to Regional Interference', *Asharq Al-Awsat*, 17 April 2015, http://english.aawsat.com/2015/04/article55342976/opinion-iran-finally-admits-to-regional-interference.

2 Ian Black, 'Saudi King's Son Drives Reforms and War in a Year of Anxiety and Change', *Guardian*, 20 January 2016.

3 Kenneth M. Pollack, *Arabs at War: Military Effectiveness, 1948–1991* (Lincoln, NE: University of Nebraska Press, 2004), p. 3.

4 *Ibid.*, p. 574.

5 Norvell B. De Atkine, 'Western Influence on Arab Militaries: Pounding Square Pegs into Round Holes', *Middle East Review of International Affairs*, vol. 17, no. 1, Spring 2013; Norvell B. De Atkine, 'Why Arabs Lose Wars', *Middle East Quarterly*, vol. 6, no. 4, December 1999.

6 See Barry Rubin, 'The Military in Contemporary Middle East Politics', *Middle East Review of International Affairs*, vol. 5, no. 1, March 2001, pp. 58–61; William C. Taylor, *Military Responses to the Arab Uprisings and the Future of Civil–Military Relations in the Middle East* (New York: Palgrave Macmillan, 2014), pp. 75, 129; and Stephanie Cronin, *Armies and State Building in the Modern Middle East* (New York: I.B. Tauris, 2014), especially Chapter 5, 'Tribes, Coups and Princes: Building a Modern Army in Saudi Arabia'.

7 See, for example, Steffen Hertog, 'Rentier Militaries in the Gulf States: The Price of Coup-Proofing', *International Journal of Middle East Studies*, vol. 43, no. 3, 2011; Rubin, 'The Military in Contemporary Middle East Politics', pp. 49–50; and James T. Quinlivan, 'Coup-Proofing: Its Practice and Consequences in the Middle East', *International Security*, vol. 24, no. 2, 1999, pp. 131–65.

8 For a case study of this approach focusing on Saudi Arabia, see Cronin, *Armies and State Building in the Modern Middle East*, Chapter 5. For a broader discussion of militaries in the Middle East and their professionalisation, see Mehran Kamrava, 'Military Professionalization and Civil–Military Relations in the Middle East', *Political Science Quarterly*, vol. 115, no. 1, 2000.

9 Colum Lynch, 'This Is Not How a Protection Racket Is Supposed to Work', *Foreign Policy*, 22 October 2013, http://foreignpolicy.com/2013/10/22/this-is-not-how-a-protection-racket-is-supposed-to-work/; Anthony H. Cordesman and Bryan Gold, *The Gulf Military Balance*, Volume 1: *The Conventional and Asymmetric Dimension* (Washington DC: Center for Strategic and International Studies, January 2014), pp. 50, 217; Rubin, 'The Military in Contemporary Middle East Politics', p. 49.

10 The Yemen intervention reflects a wider evolution in the approach of key GCC states to regional security issues prompted by the Arab Spring. See Karen E. Young, 'The Emerging Interventionists of the GCC', LSE Middle East Centre Paper Series, December 2013, http://eprints.lse.ac.uk/55079/1/__libfile_REPOSITORY_Content_LSE%20Middle%20East%20Centre%20Papers_The%20Emerging%20Interventionists%20of%20the%20GCC.pdf.

11 See Daniel P. Brown and Ariel I. Ahram, 'Jordan and the United Arab Emirates: Arab Partners in Afghanistan', in Gale A. Mattox and Stephen M. Grenier (eds), *Coalition Challenges in Afghanistan: The Politics of Alliance* (Stanford, CA: Stanford University Press, 2015).

12 See *ibid.* and Loveday Morris, 'UK Attache Says UAE Plays Crucial Role in Afghanistan', *National*, 20 January 2010.

13 'Top Falcons: The UAE's F-16 Block 60/61', *Defense Industry Daily*, 26 January 2014; Josh Rogin, 'Petraeus: The UAE's Air Force Could Take Out Iran's', *Foreign Policy*, 17 December 2009, http://thecable.foreignpolicy.com/posts/2009/12/17/petraeus_the_uaes_air_force_could_take_out_irans.

14 Rajiv Chandrasekaran, 'In the UAE, the United States Has a Quiet, Potent Ally Nicknamed "Little Sparta"', *Washington Post*, 9 November 2014.

15 'Islamic State Crisis: UAE Sends F-16 Squadron to Jordan', BBC, 7 February 2015, http://www.bbc.co.uk/news/world-middle-east-31202878.

16 David Kirkpatrick and Eric Schmitt, 'Arab Nations Strike in Libya, Surprising U.S.', *New York Times*, 25 August 2014.

17 Anthony H. Cordesman and Abraham R. Wagner, *The Lessons of Modern War*, Volume IV: *The Gulf War* (Boulder, CO: Westview Press, 1994), p. 193.

18 *Ibid.*, p. 197.

19 *Ibid.*, pp. 201–4.

20 *Ibid.*, pp. 211–14.

21 Lucas Winter, 'Riyadh Enters the Yemen–Huthi Fray', *Middle East Quarterly*, vol. 19, no. 1, Winter 2012.

22 Adam Entous, 'Saudi Arms Deal Advances', *Wall Street Journal*, 12 September 2010, http://www.wsj.com/articles/SB10001424052748704621204575488361149625050.

23 IISS, *The Military Balance 2012* (Abingdon: Routledge for the IISS, 2012), p. 311.

24 *Ibid.*, p. 313.

25 Joseph A Kechichian, 'Trends in Saudi National Security', *Middle East Journal*, vol. 53, no. 2, Spring 1999, pp. 243–7.

26 Yara Bayoumy and Mohammed Ghobari, 'Iranian Support Seen Crucial for Yemen's Houthis', Reuters, 15 December 2014, http://uk.reuters.com/article/us-yemen-houthis-iran-insight-idUSKBN0JT17A20141215.

27 Samia Nakhoul, 'Iran Expands Regional "Empire" Ahead of Nuclear Deal', Reuters, 23 March 2015, http://www.reuters.com/article/us-mideast-iran-region-insight-idUSKBN0MJ1G520150323.

28 'Iran Arming Yemen's Houthi Rebels Since 2009: UN Report', *Middle East Eye*, 1 May 2015.

29 Thomas Juneau, 'Iran's Policy Towards the Houthis in Yemen: A Limited Return on a Modest Investment', *International Affairs*, vol. 92, no. 3, 2016, p. 647.

30 Ali Watkins, Ryan Grim and Akbar Shahid Ahmed, 'Iran Warned Houthis against Yemen Takeover', *Huffington Post*, 20 April 2015.

31 International Crisis Group, 'Yemen at War', Crisis Group Middle East Briefing No. 45, 27 March 2015, p. 1.

32 Jeremy Binnie and Sean O'Connor, 'Indecisive Storm', *Jane's Defence Weekly*, 8 July 2015, p. 25.

33 'Brig. Gen Ahmed Asiri in His First Daily Briefing Talks for the "Decisive Storm" Operation, That the Goals of Phase 1 of the Operation Were Achieved', Saudi Press Agency, 28 March 2015, http://susris.com/2015/03/27/saudi-general-says-operation-decisive-storm-phase-1-goals-achieved/.

34 Michael Knights and Alexandre Mello, 'The Saudi–UAE War Effort in Yemen (Part 2): The Air Campaign', Washington Institute for Near East Policy, 11 August 2015.

35 *Ibid.*

36 Mark Mazzetti and Eric Schmitt, 'Quiet Support for Saudis Entangles U.S. In Yemen', *New York Times*, 13 March 2016.

37 Rick Gladstone, 'New Report of U.S.-Made Cluster Bomb Use by Saudis in Yemen', *New York Times*, 14 February 2016. For a hard-hitting critique of the humanitarian cost of the war, see Ben Anderson, Samuel Oakford and Peter Salisbury, 'Dead Civilians, Uneasy Alliances, and the Fog of Yemen's War', Vice News, 11 March 2016.

38 Oriana Pawlyk, 'Remember the War in Yemen? The US Air Force Is There', *Air Force Times*, 25 February 2016, http://www.airforcetimes.com/story/military/2016/02/25/remember-war-yemen-us-air-force-still-there/80935524/.

39 Barbara Starr and Ben Brumfield, 'US Navy Rescues 2 Saudi Pilots Who Ejected from F-15 Aircraft', CNN, 28 March 2016, http://edition.cnn.com/2015/03/28/middleeast/saudi-arabia-pilots-rescued/.

40 'UAE "Preparing" Troops for Anti-IS Ground Force in Syria', *New Arab*, 7 February 2016, http://www.alaraby.co.uk/english/news/2016/2/7/uae-preparing-troops-for-anti-is-ground-force-in-syria; Jeremy Binnie, 'Arab Coalition in Yemen Reportedly Hit by Second Tochka Missile Attack', *Jane's Defence Weekly*, 23 December 2015, p. 18.

41 'Yemen – Houthis Ambush Saudi Army Convoy in Jazan Region, Saudi Arabia', https://youtu.be/W1_KeMSIRtQ.

42 'Houthis Launch Rocket Attacks on Saudi City', Economist Intelligence Unit, June 2015, pp. 18–20.

43 *Ibid.*, p. 20; William MacLean and Angus McDowell, 'Saudi Arabia Says 375 Civilians Killed on its Border in Yemen War', Reuters, 1 February

2016, http://www.reuters.com/article/us-yemen-security-saudi-idUSKCN0VA36T.

44 Michael Knights and Alexandre Mello, 'The Saudi–UAE War Effort in Yemen (Part 1): Operation Golden Arrow in Aden', Washington Institute for Near East Policy, 10 August 2015.

45 Mazzetti and Schmitt, 'Quiet Support for Saudis Entangles US in Yemen'.

46 *Ibid.*; Jeremy Binnie, 'HSV-2 Turns Up Off Aden', *IHS Jane's Defence Weekly*, 28 July 2015; Jeremy Binnie, 'Analysis: Emirati Armoured Brigade Spearheads Aden Breakout', *IHS Jane's Defence Weekly*, http://www.janes.com/article/53503/analysis-emirati-armoured-brigade-spearheads-aden-breakout.

47 David Des Roches, 'Making Sense of the Naval Missile Exchanges in Yemen', The Arab Gulf States Institute in Washington, 17 October 2016, http://www.agsiw.org/making-sense-naval-missile-exchanges-yemen/.

48 'Qatar Deploys 1,000 Ground Troops to Fight in Yemen', Al-Jazeera, 7 September 2015, http://www.aljazeera.com/news/2015/09/qatar-deploys-1000-ground-troops-fight-yemen-150907043020594.html.

49 IISS, *The Military Balance 2016* (Abingdon: Routledge for the IISS, 2016), pp. 315, 350.

50 'Kuwait to Send Troops to Saudi Arabia to Fight Yemen Rebels – Newspaper', Reuters, 29 December 2015, http://uk.reuters.com/article/uk-kuwait-yemen-security-idUKKBN0UC0I520151229.

51 Tom Hussain, 'Once Iran's Ally, Sudan Sends Advisers for Yemeni Offensive Iran Opposes', McClatchyDC, 5 May 2015, http://www.mcclatchydc.com/news/nation-world/world/article24784117.html.

52 'Senegalese Government to Send Troops to Yemeni Border', Economist Intelligence Unit, June 2015, p. 24.

53 'Sudan to Send 10,000 troops to Join Arab Forces in Yemen: Report', *Sudan Tribune*, 20 October 2015.

54 'Report of the Monitoring Group on Somalia and Eritrea Pursuant to Security Council Resolution 2182 (2014): Eritrea', United Nations Security Council Monitoring Report (S/2015/802), pp. 11–15; 'Saudi Arabia Mobilises Eritrean Support for Yemen', Economist Intelligence Unit, December 2015, p. 18.

55 Habib Toumi, 'Saudi Arabia "To Open Military Base in Djibouti"', *Gulf News*, 8 March 2016, http://m.gulfnews.com/news/gulf/saudi-arabia-to-open-military-base-in-djibouti-1.1686291.

56 Though Saudi–Pakistani relations have vacillated over certain issues, the countries' bilateral relationship since the 1960s has been, overall, particularly close. See Safdar Sial, 'Emerging Dynamics in Pakistani–Saudi Relations', Norwegian Peacebuilding Resource Centre Report, October 2015, https://www.files.ethz.ch/isn/195227/202d14d49238cab72b99e625383101d3.pdf.

57 Cronin, *Armies and State Building in the Modern Middle East*, p. 247. Such weaknesses were, for example, cruelly demonstrated by Saudi Arabia's inability to retake the mosque from the terrorists for more than two weeks.

58 Simeon Kerr and Farhan Bokhari, 'Pakistan Turns Down Saudi Request for Military Role in Yemen', *Financial Times*, 10 April 2015.

59 The number of aircraft deployed varies from report to report and over time. Knights and Mello, 'The Saudi–UAE War Effort in Yemen (Part 2)'.

60 Different reports give different numbers of aircraft from each coalition partner. See Jeremy Binnie and Sean O'Connor, 'Indecisive Storm', *Jane's Defence Weekly*, 8 July 2015, p. 29.

61 Yara Bayoumy, Noah Browning and Mohammed Ghobari, 'How Saudi Arabia's War in Yemen Has Made Al Qaeda Stronger – and Richer', Reuters, 8 April 2016, http://www.reuters.com/investigates/special-report/yemen-aqap/.

62 Neil Partrick, 'Saudi Arabia's Problematic Allies Against the Houthis', Carnegie Endowment for International Peace, 12 February 2016, http://carnegieendowment.org/sada/?fa=62753; 'Saudi Changes Stance Towards Yemen's Islah: Egyptian Diplomat', Middle East Eye, 24 March 2015, http://www.middleeasteye.net/news/saudi-changed-stance-towards-yemens-islah-egyptian-diplomat-759641844.

63 David B. Roberts, 'The United Arab Emirates' Secular Foreign Policy', *Foreign Affairs*, 18 March 2016, https://www.foreignaffairs.com/articles/united-arab-emirates/2016-03-18/mosque-and-state.

64 Quoted in 'Yemen Engagement Forces Hard Choices on UAE Leadership', Economist Intelligence Unit, November 2015, p. 24.

65 'Rifts Among Anti-Houthi Forces Will Complicate Taiz Campaign', Economist Intelligence Unit, 4th Quarter 2015, p. 34.

66 Mohammed al-Qalisi, 'Yemeni Resistance Commander Gives Inside Story of Taez Fight Against Rebels', *National*, 3 January 2016; Laura Kasinof, 'A Voice of Authority Emerges from the Opposition in Yemen', *New York Times*, 21 July 2012; Nicholas A. Heras, 'Hammous Saeed al-Mikhlafi Leads the Fight Against the Houthis in Taiz', Jamestown Foundation, *Militant Leadership Monitor*, vol. 8, no. 8, 31 August 2015, http://www.jamestown.org/single/?tx_ttnews%5Btt_news%5D=44312&no_cache=1#.VsMAMfmLSVM.

67 Nicholas A. Heras, 'Shaykh Mansour: North Yemen's Influential Powerbroker', Jamestown Foundation, *Militant Leadership Monitor*, vol. 6, no. 12, 31 December 2015, http://www.jamestown.org/regions/middleeast/single/?tx_ttnews%5Btt_news%5D=44931&tx_ttnews%5BbackPid%5D=49&cHash=5dec84d287d129063608b12b03e718d2#.VsMN6vmLSVM; Ahmed Himmiche, Dapena Fernandez, Virginia Hill, Lucy Mathieson and Joel Salek, 'Letter Dated 22 January 2016 from the Panel of Experts on Yemen Established Pursuant to Security Council Resolution 2140 (2014) Addressed to the President of the Security Council', United Nations Security Council, 26 January 2016, p. 21, http://www.securitycouncilreport.org/atf/cf/%7B65BFCF9B-6D27-4E9C-8CD3-CF6E4FF96FF9%7D/s_2016_73.pdf.

68 Himmiche et al., 'Letter Dated 22 January 2016 from the Panel of Experts on Yemen', pp. 2–3, 21.

69 Michael Knights, 'The UAE Approach to Counterinsurgency in Yemen', *War on the Rocks*, 23

May 2016, http://warontherocks.com/2016/05/the-u-a-e-approach-to-counterinsurgency-in-yemen/.

70 The existence of these links were suggested by a scholar who undertook significant on-the-ground research, particularly in eastern Yemen, in 2015, and who gave a talk under Chatham House rules in London in June 2015. See also Kristin Smith Diwan and Fatima Abo Alsrar, 'Gulf States Struggle to Achieve Goals in Yemen's War', Arab Gulf States Institute in Washington (AGSIW), 10 March 2016, http://www.agsiw.org/gulf-states-struggle-to-achieve-goals-in-yemens-war/.

71 Jeremy Binnie, 'Yemeni Pilots Carry Out Airstrikes with IOMAX AT-802 Turboprops', *Jane's Defence Weekly*, 4 November 2015; 'UAE Armed Forces Concludes Training of New Batch of Members of Yemeni Resistance', WAM, 24 November 2015, https://www.wam.ae/en/news/emirates/1395288404514.html; 'Yemen Engagement Forces Hard Choices on UAE Leadership', Economist Intelligence Unit, November 2015, p. 24.

72 Emily B. Hager and Mark Mazzetti, 'Emirates Secretly Sends Colombian Mercenaries to Yemen Fight', *New York Times*, 25 November 2015.

73 Knights and Mello, 'The Saudi–UAE War Effort in Yemen (Part 1)'.

74 *Ibid*.

75 'Saudi FM: Fighting al-Qaeda Now a Priority in Yemen', Al Arabiya, 14 May 2016, http://english.alarabiya.net/en/News/middle-east/2016/05/14/Saudi-FM-Fighting-al-Qaeda-a-priority-in-Yemen.html.

76 Author discussions with Western officials and Gulf-based diplomats.

Review Essay

The Eurafrican Idea

Mark Gilbert

Eurafrica: The Untold History of European Integration and Colonialism
Peo Hansen and Stefan Jonsson. London: Bloomsbury, 2016.
£21.99/$29.95. 344 pp.

It is not often that one reads a work of academic history that has both interpretative value and policy relevance, as Peo Hansen and Stefan Jonsson's *Eurafrica* does. For scholars of European integration, the book's value lies in underlining how central the concept of 'Eurafrica' was during the negotiations that led to the founding of the European Economic Community in March 1957. For policy analysts, its worth lies in showing how European policymakers long saw the fates of Western Europe and Africa as being intricately interwoven. From the vantage point of 2016, as hundreds of thousands of desperate migrants gamble their lives on voyages towards the Mediterranean's inhospitable northern shores, one finds oneself wondering why European leaders so quickly jettisoned the Eurafrica idea in the aftermath of decolonisation, and why the concept has not been revived in recent times. Hansen and Jonsson argue that the concept is ultimately a product of colonial attitudes, but it surely could be appropriated for more progressive ends.

After the First World War, numerous intellectuals and politicians across Western Europe began to argue that Africa was, in geopolitical terms,

Mark Gilbert is Resident Professor of History at SAIS Europe. He recently co-authored, with P.M.H. Bell, *The World Since 1945: An International History* (Bloomsbury, 2016).

 DOI 10.1080/00396338.2016.1257203

Europe's heartland and principal resource. Africa's exploitation and development would be a way both of revitalising war-torn Europe and – for some early proponents of a European political unity – of building a pan-European identity. Africa would provide Europe with *Lebensraum*, as well as with raw materials. It would become – in a phrase used entirely without irony – 'Europe's plantation', growing crops for the benefit of European consumers.

All in all, the cooperative exploitation of Africa by Europeans would be 'a new and higher form of colonialism' (p. 33) that, supposedly, would lead in the long term to improvements in the African condition. Hansen and Jonsson are at pains to point out that even the most progressive of the Eurafricanists (and there were many, especially among Italian fascists, who were anything but progressive) tended to regard Africa, in patronising, racialist terms, as a 'dark continent' that needed European know-how and culture to emerge from poverty. The authors quote Count Richard Coudenhove-Kalergi, the founder of the Pan-Europe movement, as saying that as long as 'the black race is unable to develop and civilize its part of the world, the white race must do it' (p. 38). Many histories of European integration begin with Pan-Europe; Coudenhove-Kalergi himself is often depicted as a precursor to the 'founding fathers' of the European Union. In a way he was. Not the least of the services done by this book is to anchor the early European movement in the geopolitical thought of the interwar years.

In fact, the more cracked Eurafricanists unconsciously reflected the totalitarian mood of the time. In 1932, Herman Sörgel, a German architect, envisaged damming the Mediterranean at Gibraltar, as well as the leading rivers that empty into the Mediterranean, with the objective of significantly lowering the water level, generating electricity and building a 'land bridge' to Africa. A new European man would be forged, Sörgel believed, from the colossal efforts envisaged by his plan – although it is not hard to imagine who would have provided the grunt labour if such an insane scheme had ever been implemented. In any event, nothing came of this 'outrageous blueprint'. As Hansen and Jonsson ironically remark, 'Mussolini was not enthusiastic about the idea of having Italy's ports dried up' (p. 63), although the fascist dictatorship was otherwise one of the biggest supporters of Eurafrica.

Europe's 'last chance'

The political impracticality of the pre-1945 versions of Eurafrica should not disguise their psychological appeal. As E.H. Carr pointed out during the Second World War, the experience of total war provided 'a sense of meaning and purpose widely felt to be lacking in modern life'.[1] The totalitarian regimes of Hitler and Stalin, as Carr shrewdly discerned, drew much of their capacity to move the masses by carefully inculcating the perception that they were harnessing the will and energies of entire populations in pursuit of titanic collective tasks. In its wilder manifestations, the notion of Eurafrica was plainly tapping into this desire on the part of European peoples to build on a gigantic scale. The European project itself was rooted in a similar rejection of the essential pettiness of bourgeois liberalism (look at some of the earliest statements of European federalists), although the practice of European integration has often seemed to be the embodiment of liberal commercialism.

Hansen and Jonsson have correctly ascertained that the desire of leaders to remain great, and to stand tall in the world, was at least as much at the heart of the European project as the more commonly evoked need to achieve a stable basis for peace in Europe. The premise of the 'progressive', or standard, narrative of European integration is that it is a story of how the elites of a war-shattered continent consciously cooperated to establish, over time, a unique polity that has eschewed the traditional power politics of nation-states and sought to prize collective decision-making, through supranational institutions, for the common good. This story comes replete with heroes and villains, the heroes being the visionary statesmen – Jean Monnet, Guy Mollet, Paul-Henri Spaak, Konrad Adenauer, Robert Schuman, Alcide De Gasperi and, in later days, Jacques Delors and Helmut Kohl – who grasped the nettle of national sovereignty, and the villains being the diehards who persisted in thinking that nationhood was something to be preserved and even enhanced. The progressive narrative is hence pervaded by what the authors call 'intra-European concerns' (p. 108) – by a marked Brussels-centric emphasis, in short, on the 'construction' of Europe's institutions.

In fact, as Hansen and Jonsson point out, Europe's founding fathers were all acutely conscious that Europe's best hope of being counted as an independent power in a world dominated by the United States and the Soviet Union was to increase its landmass, population, material wealth and raw materials (and acquire nuclear weapons). Developing Africa offered West European nations a 'great opportunity to reinvigorate their respective colonial enterprises and hence their status as great powers' (p. 80).

Hansen and Jonsson show that Spaak, Schuman, Adenauer and Mollet were all advocates of Eurafrica, with the French, unsurprisingly, being especially gung-ho. Eirik Labonne, a French technocrat who had been ambassador to Moscow, proposed highly detailed plans for the economic exploitation of Africa to a ministerial committee of the French government. His view was that 'the Atlas Mountains should be our Urals and Africa our Siberia' (p. 98). The Schuman Declaration of 9 May 1950, which makes explicit reference to the planned development of Africa as one of the great objectives of the nascent European community, reflected the climate of the times – though, as Hansen and Jonsson remind us, this aspect of the Schuman Plan is often squeamishly excised from the text (p. 123). As late as the mid-1950s, there was no thought of relinquishing the African colonies; rather, their territories were meant to serve as a boundless reservoir of resources that would give Western Europe what Pierre Nord, a French advocate of Eurafrica, described as 'a last chance' to remake itself as a geopolitical entity able to exercise independent action (pp. 145–6).

The Treaties of Rome (1955–57) were negotiated with this Euro-colonial mindset at the fore – or so Hansen and Jonsson contend. The French were predictably determined to obtain access for their colonies to the Common Market, but so were the Germans, who fought the French over the costs of the investment fund established by the European Economic Community (EEC) Treaty for economic infrastructure in the colonial territories, but who nevertheless saw the exploitation of Africa's wealth in raw materials as an essential part of the project. Only the Dutch had doubts. Especially after the Suez debacle (November 1956), Guy Mollet pressed for the construction of a European bloc that included the African colonies of the six founding members as the only way to achieve European freedom of action and maintain European prestige. Eurafrica was a sovereign remedy that would strengthen Europe's standing in the world, allow the colonial territories to transition more securely to independence and, incidentally, permit the Algerian conflict to end in compromise. In January 1957, Mollet told the United Nations that 'Eurafrica may become one of the principal factors of world history' by enabling Algeria to avoid the 'social and economic regression as well as political regression towards dictatorship or the quasi-feudal regime of certain Arab states' which was the 'inevitable' outcome of independence under the National Liberation Front (p. 184). Mollet and French foreign minister Christian Pineau were indefatigable in proclaiming that Eurafrica, now defined as a broad Euro-African community based upon common economic, cultural and strategic interests, was the future for Africa in the medium term, with independence being postponed for a couple of decades at least.

The final text of the EEC Treaty, which confirmed that the colonial territories were to have privileged access to the Common Market for their exports, were to be gradually opened to exports from the member states, and were to be the beneficiaries of $511 million of EEC investment over five years, reflected this French position, as did the fact that Algeria was recognised as an integral part of France (although it was to benefit from the EEC's investment fund). Mollet, Adenauer and Spaak all interpreted these decisions as the 'boldest part' of the Treaties of Rome. 'Would it not be a success', asked Spaak during a press conference, 'if we could realise the dream of Eurafrica?' Guy Mollet told the US Congress on 27 February 1957 that Eurafrica was the ultimate goal of the EEC project. Speaking in Canada a few days later, he proclaimed that France's immediate 'exalting tasks' were 'to construct Europe, to develop Sahara, to build Africa' (pp. 236–7). To some extent, the historiography of European integration has reiterated these somewhat self-satisfied claims. Hansen and Jonsson are quite clear that, to the contrary, the EEC Treaty had resulted not in a 'partnership of equality' but in 'a licensed patronage in which the superior partner would continue overseeing and developing the inferior one' (p. 254).

Development without colonialism

The trouble was that the Africans did not want to go along with this convenient (for Europeans) arrangement. They wanted national independence, and wanted it immediately. Within six years of the signature of the Treaties of Rome, most of Africa had acquired sovereign status. Hansen and Jonsson argue that the special relationship with the EEC enshrined in the EEC Treaty, and renewed at Yaoundé in 1963, diluted the idealism of the independence movement and diverted its plans for economic development away from the creation of pan-African structures into pathways more acceptable to the former colonial powers. With obvious sympathy, the authors quote (among others) Kwame Nkrumah describing the EEC's role as a 'system of collective colonialism which will be stronger and more dangerous than the old evils we are trying to liquidate' (p. 270). Following the historian and theorist of globalisation Immanuel Wallerstein, Hansen and Jonsson contend that the association of the African former colonies with the EEC was an

> arrangement that allowed the political elites of what subsequently became (nominally) independent states to posit themselves as partners in a world of 'interdependent' states and regional formations, while at the same time accommodating the economic demands and policies of their former colonial masters. (p. 272)

In short, Africa's elites consciously shirked the task of developing the continent, preferring to manage power and profit from it, while acquiescing to the subordinate role that the latest form of European colonialism ascribed to them. With a touch of polemic, Hansen and Jonsson state that the 'Eurafrican project conceived between 1920 and 1960 was strongly complicit in seeing Africa off to an ill-fated beginning on its journey to independence' (p. 275). Maybe, but it might also have been that African elites distrusted the grand schemes being proclaimed by men as unstable as Nkrumah and were acutely conscious that self-development would likely require the regimentation of society. Contemporary alternative models, such as Mao Zedong's bloodthirsty 'Great Leap Forward', South Korea's industrialisation through military despotism or even Jawaharlal Nehru's bureaucratic brand of democratic socialism can hardly have been inspiring to the more conservative (or thoughtful) of Africa's new leaders. It would have been interesting, in fact, in the last quarter of this book to have heard more about what the Africans themselves thought of the pros and cons of the Eurafrica project. There is a paradoxical sense in which this book, which in many ways is a model of revisionist thinking about the history of European integration, is more Eurocentric than it might (and perhaps should) have been.

Hansen and Jonsson open their book with a heartfelt and unashamedly political attack on what they regard as the fundamental hypocrisy of EU foreign policy towards its 'neighbourhood' in Africa (and elsewhere). In short, they believe that the EU stealthily pursues its own interests while cynically claiming to be exporting its values and model of peaceful development. More subtly, at the end of the book the authors briefly address Nicolas Sarkozy's July 2007 exhumation of the Eurafrica idea and the language of the December 2007 Strategic Partnership between Africa and the EU, which advocated a 'partnership between equals' to develop Africa's material wealth, but also to promote 'democratic governance, human rights and peace and prosperity on the African continent' (p. 276). Hansen and Jonsson plainly believe that the history of the Eurafrica concept ought to induce profound scepticism about the likelihood of Europe paying more than lip service to 'soft' goals such as human rights and democracy in Africa. If history is any guide, Europeans will likely collude with African elites to grab as much as they can in the ongoing 'new scramble for Africa'.

The moral bankruptcy of treating Africa as a resource to be exploited is a key motif of this book: unusually for academic historians, the authors leave no doubt about their political convictions. Since the refugee crisis began, however, it has become obvious that a more positive policy towards Africa simply makes good political sense. Whereas in the 1950s, and even more so before the Second World War, Africa was sparsely inhabited and undeveloped in the literal sense that large parts of its territory were still untouched by human hands, today its population has long since overtaken Europe's, and has probably surpassed its capacity ever to provide its own peoples with a decent, dignified life. As Nigeria alone approaches the point at which it will have as many citizens as the combined populations of Britain, France and Italy (before its population peaks it will have half as many people as the whole of Europe), the choices facing policymakers in both Europe and Africa are stark. Either Africa's peoples obtain a higher standard of living (which will require investment) or they will move northwards in search of the security from disease, hunger and political oppression that the United Nations solemnly declares to be the birthright of all human beings. Africa and Europe share a common interest, therefore, in promoting a genuine, coordinated development of the African continent that puts people first.

There have been moments in the EU's history at which its leaders would have grasped this fact – indeed, celebrated the opportunity that it offers. Hansen and Jonsson unquestionably make their case that colonialist ideology was lurking beneath the surface of the Eurafrica concept, but it is nevertheless impossible to read their book without marvelling at the self-confidence with which Europe's founding fathers talked airily of 'making Europe in Africa'. The contrast with the inward-looking, provincial, penny-pinching EU of the last decade is both striking and depressing. Is it completely fanciful to hope that the EU might make a foray from its fortress by developing a generously funded Marshall Plan (Mollet Plan?) for northern Africa – an aid programme that would be conditional upon the creation of joint African–European intergovernmental institutions able to negotiate and implement common proposals for economic betterment? Such a task might cleanse the Eurafrica concept of the taint of colonialism, and, more importantly, might enable more Africans to live a better life. Hansen and Jonsson's splendid book rightly dwells upon the ambiguous legacy of the concept of Eurafrica for the process of European integration. It is not always an edifying story. The notion, however, that Europe might find moral purpose in assisting the development of its southern neighbour is not an unworthy one – and is increasingly becoming a geopolitical necessity.

Notes

1 Edward Hallett Carr, *Conditions of Peace* (New York: Macmillan, 1942), p. 119.

Review Essay

Raiders in Kashmir: India's Pakistan Problem

Shashank Joshi

Not War, Not Peace: Motivating Pakistan to Prevent Cross-Border Terrorism
George Perkovich and Toby Dalton. New Delhi: Oxford University Press, 2016. £19.99/Rs695.00. 297 pp.

There have been small, revisionist powers with a penchant for asymmetric warfare.[1] And there have been small, nuclear-armed powers.[2] But until Pakistan became nuclear-armed in the late 1980s, inching its way, one cold test at a time, to an air-delivered device a few steps ahead of its larger neighbour, there was no small, revisionist, nuclear-armed state in the world.[3] Perhaps North Korea has since travelled a similar path, but its external provocations have had considerably less impact outside its borders than those of Pakistan.[4]

Pakistan's army has created, encouraged and sheltered non-state armed groups as instruments of war from the very first days of the nation's existence.[5] It has supported violent separatist movements, militant Islamist guerrillas and urban terrorist attacks in both Afghanistan and India, ramping up involvement as its nuclear shield matured through the 1990s.[6] These proxies have failed to wrest Kashmir from India or guarantee a pliant Kabul, and have resulted in drastic blowback within Pakistan itself, in the form of more than 20,000 civilian deaths in the past decade alone.[7] But they have kept India off balance, forcing it to divert defensive resources away from China and highlighting the shortcomings of the state.

Shashank Joshi is a Senior Research Fellow at the Royal United Services Institute (RUSI) in London. His most recent book is *Indian Power Projection: Ambition, Arms and Influence*, published as part of the RUSI Whitehall Paper series.

Survival | vol. 58 no. 6 | December 2016–January 2017 | pp. 195–208 DOI 10.1080/00396338.2016.1257204

'It's a Rubik cube – dealing with Pakistan', laments a former Indian national security adviser. 'You keep fiddling with the squares, and as you move one set others are affected or become problems. You don't have a solution' (p. 38). Is this a counsel of despair, or obliquely hopeful imagery? After all, Rubik's cubes can be solved, at least until jumbled once more.

Not War, Not Peace: Motivating Pakistan to Prevent Cross-Border Terrorism is an effort to think through possible solutions with a level of care and rigour that is unsurpassed either in the published literature or, one suspects, in the corridors of power in New Delhi. George Perkovich is the author of an acclaimed history of India's nuclear-weapons programme, *India's Nuclear Bomb*, published in 1999.[8] His co-author on *Not War, Not Peace*, Toby Dalton, was a senior policy adviser in the US Department of Energy with service in Pakistan. Both work at the Carnegie Endowment for International Peace in Washington. Writing for Oxford University Press, India, they are sensitive to the emotional edge that the subject carries there, without losing the strategist's eye for the second- and third-order effects of any given policy choice.

Their book has been lent extraordinary timeliness and importance by the course of events through summer and autumn 2016, with India–Pakistan relations tumbling, violently, to their lowest ebb in a decade. In June, Indian-administered Kashmir erupted in the largest popular protests since the 1990s. India cracked down harshly, blaming Pakistani interference.[9] It also retaliated by highlighting unrest within its neighbour. Indian Prime Minister Narendra Modi gave prominent mention to the restive Pakistani province of Balochistan in his Independence Day speech on 15 August, followed by All India Radio intensifying its Balochi-language programming, and New Delhi pointedly granting asylum to Baloch leaders.[10]

It was in this febrile atmosphere that militants entered an Indian Army camp near the Kashmiri town of Uri on 18 September, killing 19 soldiers in the deadliest such attack for 20 years. As with an earlier assault on an air base in nearby Pathankot in January, and despite the Pakistani defence minister's grotesque allegation that India had mounted a false-flag attack on itself, the Uri attackers were almost certainly members of one of two groups, Jaish-e-Mohammed (JeM) or Lashkar-e-Taiba (LeT), each with long-standing and extensive ties to Inter-Services Intelligence (ISI), the Pakistan Army's spy agency.[11]

India's politicians, press and analysts responded with fury, demanding what they saw as long-overdue military retaliation. 'For one tooth, the complete jaw', wrote Ram Madhav, the influential general secretary of the ruling Bharatiya Janata Party (BJP). 'Every Pakistan post through which infiltration takes place should be reduced to rubble', demanded Gurmeet Kanwal, a retired brigadier who is a prominent voice in Indian defence debates.[12] These views reflected pent-up frustration with what has been described as 'strategic restraint', India having abjured military retaliation after large-scale attacks in Kashmir and New Delhi in 2001–02 and in Mumbai in 2008.[13] It looked briefly as though Modi, who once mocked his predecessors for their pusillanimity on Pakistan, would follow this pattern and stick to a diplomatic response.[14] But on 29 September, Indian officials dramatically announced that special forces had, the previous night, crossed the Line of Control (LoC) which divides Indian from Pakistani Kashmir and conducted what were described as 'surgical strikes' on Pakistani militants.[15]

Previous governments had conducted small reprisal raids in the 1990s and 2000s, so the operation was not as radical as the government and its supporters claimed.[16] But it was a rupture with the past in several ways. The apparent geographic scope was larger, with the targets spanning 200 kilometres across the LoC. There was a high degree of inter-agency coordination, with India's foreign-intelligence organisation and its Earth-observation satellites pressed into service. Above all, the decision to go public was a major departure from the private signalling of the past. So too was the tacit approval of the United States; White House National Security Advisor Susan Rice spoke to her Indian counterpart by phone shortly before the attack. Pakistan, ordinarily eager to point out Indian aggression, flatly denied that anything untoward had taken place, though promptly activated forward air bases and beefed up border defences.

In India, the meaning of the strikes continues to be debated. 'Indian troops were like Hanuman who did not quite know their prowess before the surgical strikes', boasted India's defence minister, alluding to the monkey god of Hindu mythology who was cursed to forget that he possessed supernatural powers.[17] Indian news anchors donned flak jackets and celebrated an act of military redemption. In truth, the raid is unlikely to have penetrated more than a few kilometres into Pakistan-controlled territory, and inflicted relatively small numbers of casualties. But it successfully probed Pakistan's red lines and thereby established a public precedent for crossing the LoC in response to major provocations – something that India's cautious leaders adamantly refused to do even during the Kargil War in 1999, at the cost of greater Indian casualties.[18]

Perkovich and Dalton, whose book was published on 30 June, could not have imagined better publicity. 'Indian leaders', they had written in *Not War, Not Peace*, 'are most likely to respond to another major terrorist attack by conducting largely symbolic airborne attacks on terrorist-related targets in Pakistan-administered Kashmir' (p. 22). September's raids were not airborne, but this was otherwise prescient. India deliberately signalled restraint by manipulating what Thomas Schelling called 'cartographic psychology'.[19] It confined its raid to the (provisional) LoC in Kashmir rather than the (permanent) international border to the south, allowing New Delhi to claim it was only intruding on territory it claimed as its own rather than into Pakistan proper. 'Like virginity, the homeland wants an absolute definition', Schelling had noted. 'This character the Soviet bloc has been losing and may lose even more if it acquires a graduated structure like the old British Empire.'[20] The territory between India and Pakistan is similarly graduated, allowing each to probe the gaps. Indeed, Pakistan's narrative of Kashmir obliges it to maintain the appearance that 'Azad Kashmir', though under its control, is politically distinct from the heartland.[21]

Home truths

Not War, Not Peace deftly sets out the military, intelligence and political demands of such special-forces raids and other Indian options. The authors examine India's ability to prosecute a limited ground war (pp. 73–103), airstrikes (pp. 104–34), targeted assassinations and broader covert warfare aimed at destabilising Pakistan's army or the country at large (pp. 135–79), and the nuclear capabilities and doctrines that would come into play should the use of these options spiral into a larger conflict (pp. 180–225). They are at pains to explain the difficulties involved. In this, they are helped by a revealing set of interviews with retired and serving diplomatic, intelligence and military officials from both India and Pakistan. Extended quotations are sprinkled liberally throughout the text, and they serve an important function. While Indians often chafe at foreigners talking down their armed forces or urging restraint, here we have knowledgeable Indians themselves delivering home truths.

A three-star military officer laments the 'complete lack of understanding between civilian and military leaderships', describing the situation as a 'disaster' (p. 33). 'We might have acquired precision munitions', admits a former intelligence officer, 'but the data we have on [Pakistani] camps and infrastructure is not so accurate' (p. 46). 'You need constant intelligence with high accuracy, which we don't have', agrees a retired high-ranking air-force officer (p. 125). 'Our capacity to act covertly has atrophied over the years', complains another intelligence officer (p. 167). These details, though anecdotal and partial, and perhaps exaggerated in places, are important. In India as in the West, political leaders' willingness to talk about and urge military options, without ever understanding their operational prerequisites and implications, encourages a sort of naive militarism. Consider how the idea of the no-fly zone has been propounded in recent debates over Libya and Syria. We also see implausible extrapolations from permissive scenarios to far more contested ones. Shallow cross-border raids against lightly defended targets away from population centres, such as the September strikes or a raid into Myanmar in 2015 (pp. 137–9), may tell us relatively little about India's ability to hit LeT's sprawling headquarters just 30km from the city of Lahore. And while Pakistan was able to deny India's September strikes, limiting the pressure for escalation, it would not be able to explain away larger, deeper, more visible raids.

But capabilities are less than half the story. *Not War, Not Peace*'s real achievement is to inject strategic thinking into a debate that focuses on means, rather than their connection to ends. If the aim is to push Pakistan's army to pacify terrorist groups in its patronage (pp. 40–3), then how do ground wars, or airstrikes, or covert warfare achieve this end? 'Can we hit Pakistan?' one retired Indian national security adviser recalls being asked in a cabinet meeting. 'Yes', he answered, 'but for what result?' (p. 4).

The cynics' answer is 'votes'. One former Indian national security adviser, Shiv Shankar Menon, has noted, tartly, that past 'covert operations were not announced to the country because the primary goal was to pacify the LoC', and 'not to manage public opinion at home'.[22] But as September's strikes demonstrated, the domestic political rewards can be substantial. The opposition Congress Party, normally loath to offer even a hint of praise for the government, quickly offered its congratulations, and rushed to publish details of raids that it had authorised while in government, complete with dates. India has forthcoming local elections in February 2017 in the massive state of Uttar Pradesh. The BJP is open about campaigning on the back of the strikes, with its election posters featuring prominent references to them alongside photographs of Modi.[23] Such appeals fall on fertile ground. A recent Pew survey shows that a large majority (62%) of Indians believe that using overwhelming military force is the best way to defeat terrorism, in contrast to less than half of Europeans and Americans.[24]

But domestic plaudits have no bearing on India's true target, the calculations of Pakistan's army. India can shape those calculations, but it faces an unavoidable trade-off between impact and escalation (pp. 268–9). Modest strikes can easily avoid escalation, but they offer no serious disincentive to Pakistan. Larger strikes may threaten something of value to the Pakistani army, but they would almost certainly prompt a broader war in which India's advantage would be slender and nuclear risks would quickly rise. Another former national security adviser, M.K. Narayanan, who was in office during the Mumbai attacks, has written that New Delhi forwent military action in 2008 'not due to any fears of a possible nuclear conflict', but because 'it was likely to be indeterminate'.[25] Moreover, the adverse impact on India's economy and diplomatic standing could outweigh the original cost of terrorism. And both Indian occupation of Pakistani territory and the perception of heavy civilian casualties would catalyse support for Pakistan's army and jihadists (p. 84).

So while India can safely escalate beyond raids of a few kilometres, there is no plausible sweet spot at which Pakistan's generals would unwind decades of policy on an issue – Kashmir, and the broader Indian threat – that they see as fundamental not just to their own corporate existence but to the nation's survival, the two being much the same thing in their eyes.[26] In October, Modi proudly boasted that the strikes proved India's army was 'no less' than Israel's, but Perkovich and Dalton argue that the comparison may be less than encouraging (p. 10).[27] Neither highly proficient assassinations of Hizbullah commanders, nor frequent retaliatory airstrikes, nor even the full-fledged air and ground war which battered Beirut and southern Lebanon in 2006 have seriously weakened the group, nor Iranian support for it.[28] Hizbullah has ten times as many rockets today as it did a decade ago, and Iran and Hizbullah work in lockstep in Syria in support of the Assad regime.[29] Indeed, the combined might of the United States, Israel and Saudi Arabia has not proven sufficient to limit Iran's state sponsorship of armed militant groups of every ethnic and religious stripe.[30] That sponsorship is too disaggregated to target cleanly, too focused on Arab and Israeli interests to incur global outrage, and ultimately too important to abandon because of foreign pressure alone.

How to win friends and compel people

'A nuclear state', noted Michael Quinlan, 'is a state that no one can afford to make desperate'.[31] Pakistan must therefore be induced to change tack out of rational calculation, not desperation. That requires continued control over territory. Much as Israel relies on Hamas to control other groups' rocket strikes from Gaza, or the United States required regime support to disarm Syria of chemical weapons, India is in the paradoxical situation of requiring its neighbour's army to be weak enough to pose a diminished threat, but strong enough to influence and eventually demobilise its proxies. 'The Pakistan Army and the ISI would seem to be necessary instruments in dismantling or at least compelling militant groups to abandon terrorism', suggest the authors (p. 86). While right-wing Hindu nationalists sometimes express a desire to see Pakistan break up, most serious officials understand that such an outcome would not be as benign as the transformation of East

Pakistan into Bangladesh in 1971 (p. 232). 'The minute anyone says Pakistan might break up', confesses a high-ranking Indian intelligence official, 'that scares the shit out of me' (p. 162).

Perkovich and Dalton do not spurn the threat or use of force. But they do argue that it is best pursued alongside 'non-violent compellence', particularly economic sanctions and diplomatic isolation (p. 280). This is difficult, because it cannot be pursued unilaterally. Pakistan's relationship with the United States may have frayed, perhaps beyond repair, in the past five years. But Pakistan's territory and ports, and the forces that guard them, play an important role in China's flagship Belt and Road Initiative, and Beijing continues to shelter its junior ally in the United Nations, most recently blocking efforts to add JeM leader Masood Azhar to the UN's list of proscribed terrorists.[32] Russia, a historic ally of India, is also moving closer to Pakistan, holding unprecedented joint exercises immediately after the Uri attack in September.[33]

On the other hand, India's new clout is yielding results. Writing pre-Uri, the authors had warned, reasonably, that 'other states within the South Asian Association for Regional Cooperation (SAARC) would be reluctant to act against fellow member Pakistan' (p. 247). But within weeks of the attacks, India succeeded in sabotaging the organisation's forthcoming summit in Islamabad by peeling away Bangladesh, Bhutan and Afghanistan. Just as important was Abu Dhabi Crown Prince Sheikh Mohamed bin Zayed Al Nahyan's acceptance of an invitation to be the chief guest at the India's Republic Day celebrations in 2017, despite the UAE's close defence ties to Pakistan. In October 2016, a highly controversial report in Pakistan's *Dawn* newspaper suggested that even China was privately indicating to Islamabad that it would not shield Pakistan from international censure indefinitely.[34] India's own deepening defence ties to Washington, marked by a significant logistics agreement in August 2016, have also boosted India's diplomatic efforts.[35] It is clear, for instance, that American signals intelligence has played a role in helping India to attribute more than one terrorist attack to Pakistan-backed groups.[36] Such attribution is crucial to India's efforts to persuade third parties to apply pressure on Pakistan.

Even so, isolation is no panacea.[37] Pakistan's period of greatest isolation, in the 1990s, coincided with a surge in its support for regional militancy (pp. 140–2). Pakistan fuelled and transformed the Kashmiri uprising after 1987, instigated a mass-casualty bombing in Mumbai in 1993, nurtured the Taliban from 1994, and in 1999 used non-uniformed personnel to seize Indian outposts, provoking the Kargil War. Arguably, India was itself isolated in the early part of this period, facing nuclear sanctions, denunciation of its repression in Kashmir and the loss of its Soviet partner. This brings us to what may be the most important aspect of non-violent pressure: international cooperation. Such cooperation may come at a price.

Perkovich and Dalton emphasise that India's ability to fashion an anti-Pakistan coalition depends not only on persuading others of Pakistani malfeasance, but also on Indian willingness to negotiate with Pakistan, including on the vexed question of Kashmir. 'International actors become reluctant to apply pressure on one set of parties to a dispute if they do not believe that the other party is demonstrably committed to reach equitable outcomes too' (p. 256). It is certainly possible to find examples of this: the international coalition against Iran fashioned between 2003 and 2015, for instance, would likely have weakened and ultimately collapsed had the United States or another member of the six-power negotiating bloc persisted with hardline positions, such as refusing Iran the right to enrich uranium.[38] But in some ways, Perkovich and Dalton under-sell the case for talks, which they frame largely as signals of goodwill intended to secure international support in the event of their probable collapse. Yet the most important India–Pakistan dialogue of recent years, a back channel initiated just five years after the Kargil War and continued until 2007, nearly producing a historic agreement over Kashmir, was almost entirely secret.[39] Talks intended solely as public gestures of flexibility, to be cashed in at a later date, will never achieve the discretion and seriousness necessary for resolving highly sensitive issues.[40]

Some Indians would argue that their country can simply outgrow the problem. Others are less sanguine. 'The state of our relationship with Pakistan', writes Shiv Shankar Menon in his 2016 book *Choices: Inside the Making of India's Foreign Policy*, 'has been an albatross that has hobbled Indian diplomacy and enabled other powers to gain leverage in India's and the subcontinent's affairs'.[41] 'India has the power and habits of mind and institutions to win on its own a 100-year war of attrition with Pakistan', concede the authors. 'But India cannot achieve its ambitions to be a global power if it remains bogged down in such a war' (p. 279). India's present government agrees with the first of these statements, but seeks to refute the second. New Delhi's new gamble is that calibrated punishment places the onus for escalation – and so the risk of further isolation – onto Pakistan. The best-case scenario is a return to the detente of the mid-2000s, but no less likely is a new, more violent equilibrium.

Notes

1 See Rod Thornton, *Asymmetric Warfare: Threat and Response in the 21st Century*, 1st ed. (Cambridge: Polity, 2007).

2 Avner Cohen, *Israel and the Bomb* (New York: Columbia University Press, 1998).

3 See Feroz Khan, *Eating Grass: The Making of the Pakistani Bomb* (Stanford, CA: Stanford University Press, 2012).

4 Vipin Narang, 'Nuclear Strategies of Emerging Nuclear Powers: North Korea and Iran', *Washington Quarterly*, vol. 38, no. 1, 2 January 2015, pp. 73–91, doi:10.1080/0163660X.2015.1038175.

5 See Husain Haqqani, *Pakistan: Between Mosque and Military* (Washington DC: Carnegie Endowment for International Peace, 2005); Shuja Nawaz, 'The First Kashmir War Revisited', *India Review*, vol. 7, no. 2, 26 May 2008, pp. 115–54; Praveen Swami, *India, Pakistan and the Secret Jihad: The Covert War in Kashmir, 1947–2004*, 1st ed. (London: Routledge, 2007); C. Christine Fair, *Fighting to the End: The Pakistan Army's Way of War* (Oxford: Oxford University Press, 2014); Christopher Jaffrelot, *The Pakistan Paradox: Instability and Resilience* (Oxford: Oxford University Press, 2015), pp. 481–528.

6 For an excellent summary of India–Pakistan competition since the late 1990s, see Myra MacDonald's forthcoming *Defeat Is an Orphan: How Pakistan Lost the Great South Asian War* (London: C. Hurst & Co., 2016).

7 'Fatalities in Terrorist Violence in Pakistan 2003–2016', South Asia Terrorism Portal (SATP), 2 October 2016, http://www.satp.org/satporgtp/countries/india/states/andhra/data_sheets/annual_casualties.asp; Neta C. Crawford, 'Update on the Human Costs of War for Afghanistan and Pakistan, 2001 to Mid-2016', Costs of War Project, Brown University, August 2016, http://watson.brown.edu/costsofwar/files/cow/imce/papers/2016/War%20in%20Afghanistan%20and%20Pakistan%20UPDATE_FINAL_corrected%20date.pdf.

8 George Perkovich, *India's Nuclear Bomb* (Berkeley, CA: University of California Press, 2002).

9 Ipsita Chakravarty, 'Inside South Kashmir: Weeks After Burhan Wani's Death, Anantnag Remains Protest

Country', Scroll.in, 16 September 2016, http://scroll.in/article/816582/inside-south-kashmir-where-protests-change-shape-from-town-chowk-to-bylane-to-village-field.

10 Gaurav Vivek Bhatnagar, 'Modi Steps Up India's Baloch Outreach Programme', *Wire*, 17 September 2016, http://thewire.in/66619/india-radio-programming-balochi-language-get-interactive-todays-launch-website-mobile-app/; ANI, 'After Bugti, Another Baloch Nationalist Hyrbyair Marri May Seek Asylum in India', *Indian Express*, 9 October 2016, http://indianexpress.com/article/india/india-news-india/after-bugti-another-baloch-nationalist-hyrbyair-marri-may-seek-asylum-in-india-3073883/.

11 Stephen Tankel, 'Beyond the Double Game: Lessons from Pakistan's Approach to Islamist Militancy', *Journal of Strategic Studies*, 16 June 2016, pp. 1–31, doi:10.1080/01402390.2016.1174114; C. Christine Fair, 'Lashkar-E-Tayiba and the Pakistani State', *Survival*, vol. 53, no. 4, August–September 2011, pp. 29–52, doi:10.1080/00396338.2011.603561; Praveen Swami, 'Behind Terror Attack, a Reborn Jihad Empire', *Indian Express*, 3 January 2016, http://indianexpress.com/article/india/india-news-india/behind-terror-attack-a- reborn-jihad-empire/.

12 Gurmeet Kanwal, 'Time to Hit and Hurt the Pakistan Army!', *Rediff*, 18 September 2016, http://www.rediff.com/news/column/time-to-hit-and-hurt-the-pakistan-army/20160918.htm.

13 Sunil Dasgupta and Stephen P. Cohen, 'Is India Ending Its Strategic Restraint Doctrine?', *Washington Quarterly*, vol. 34, no. 2, Spring 2011, pp. 163–77.

14 Biju Govind, 'Your Leaders Are Making a Fool of You in the Name of Kashmir: Modi Tells Pakistanis', *Hindu*, 24 September 2016, http://www.thehindu.com/news/cities/kozhikode/modi-addresses-rally-in-kozhikode/article9142853.ece.

15 The best accounts of the raid, all drawing heavily on sometimes divergent and therefore unreliable anonymous sources, are Praveen Swami, 'Surgical Strikes: Bodies Taken Away on Trucks, Loud Explosions, Eyewitnesses Give Graphic Details', *Indian Express*, 5 October 2016, http://indianexpress.com/article/india/india-news-india/pakistan-border-terror-camps-surgical-strikes-kashmir-loc-indian-army-jihadist-3065975/; Saikat Datta, 'Behind the Scenes: How India Went about Planning "Surgical Strikes" after the Uri Attack', Scroll.in, 29 September 2016, http://scroll.in/article/817807/behind-the-scenes-how-india-went-about-planning-surgical-strikes-after-the-uri-attack; Sandeep Unnithan, 'Crossing a Red Line', *India Today*, 6 October 2016, http://indiatoday.intoday.in/story/surgical-strike-indian-army-loc-uri-attack-pakistan/1/781369.html; Sushant K. Singh, 'Inside the Surgical Strike: Choppers on Standby, 70–80 Soldiers', *Indian Express*, 1 October 2016, http://indianexpress.com/article/india/india-news-india/surgical-strikes-india-pakistan-loc-jammu-and-kashmir-indian-army-3059059/; and M. Ilyas Khan, 'India's "Surgical Strikes" in Kashmir: Truth or Illusion?', BBC, 23 October

2016, http://www.bbc.co.uk/news/world-asia-india-37702790.

16 Shashank Joshi, 'Everything That We Know about India's Cross-LoC Strikes before Uri', Scroll.in, 5 October 2016, http://scroll.in/article/818324/everything-that-we-know-about-indias-cross-loc-strikes-before-uri.

17 PTI, 'Pakistan's Condition Is Like Anaesthetised Patient after Surgery: Manohar Parrikar', *Indian Express*, 1 October 2016, http://indianexpress.com/article/india/india-news-india/pakistans-condition-is-like-anaesthetised-patient-after-surgery-manohar-parrikar-3059986/.

18 Peter R. Lavoy, 'Introduction: The Importance of the Kargil Conflict', in Peter R. Lavoy (ed.), *Asymmetric Warfare in South Asia: The Causes and Consequences of the Kargil Conflict* (Cambridge and New York: Cambridge University Press, 2009), pp. 12–13.

19 Thomas C. Schelling, *Arms and Influence* (New Haven, CT: Yale University Press, 1966), p. 61.

20 *Ibid*., p. 62. See also Thomas C. Schelling, *The Strategy of Conflict* (Cambridge, MA: Harvard University Press, 1960), p. 169.

21 Christopher Snedden, *Understanding Kashmir and Kashmiris* (Oxford: Oxford University Press, 2015), pp. 208–9.

22 Suhasini Haidar, 'Earlier Cross-LoC Strikes Had Different Goals: Former NSA', *Hindu*, 12 October 2016, http://www.thehindu.com/news/national/former-national-security-adviser-shiv-shankar-menon-on-crossloc-strikes/article9208838.ece?homepage=true.

23 Suhas Munshi, 'Amit Shah Lays Out BJP Logic: Nobody Can Politicise Surgical Strikes, Except BJP in UP', Catch News, 7 October 2016, http://www.catchnews.com/politics-news/amit-shah-lays-out-bjp-logic-nobody-can-politicise-surgical-strikes-except-bjp-in-up-1475856582.html.

24 'India and Modi: The Honeymoon Continues', Pew Research Center, 19 September 2016, http://www.pewglobal.org/2016/09/19/india-and-modi-the-honeymoon-continues/.

25 M.K. Narayanan, 'The Best Among Limited Options', *Hindu*, 21 September 2016, www.thehindu.com/opinion/lead/m-k-narayanan-on-indiapakistan-diplomacy-and-terrorism/article9128770.ece.

26 Fair, *Fighting to the End*, p. 173.

27 Dhrubo Jyoti, 'Modi Praises Indian Army for Surgical Strikes, Compares it to Israel', *Hindustan Times*, 18 October 2016, http://www.hindustantimes.com/india-news/modi-praises-indian-army-for-surgical-strikes-compares-it-to-israel/story-eTqN4s5a3Y70KVv4DRMfWM.html.

28 Shashank Joshi, 'Is India's Israel Envy Misplaced?', Live Mint, 25 September 2016, http://www.livemint.com/Opinion/uyJOfREeXcteX07QEyp2ZM/Is-Indias-Israel-envy-misplaced.html.

29 Amos Harel and Gili Cohen, 'Hezbollah: From Terror Group to Army', 12 July 2016, http://www.haaretz.com/st/c/prod/eng/2016/07/lebanon2/.

30 Afshon Ostovar, *Vanguard of the Imam: Religion, Politics, and Iran's Revolutionary Guards* (Oxford: Oxford University Press, 2016), pp. 102–20, 159–78, 204–29.

31 Michael Quinlan, *Thinking About*

Nuclear Weapons: Principles, Problems, Prospects (New York: Oxford University Press, 2009), p. 30.

32 'China Extends Hold on Indian Bid to Ban Jaish Chief Masood Azhar at UN', *Dawn*, 2 October 2016, //www.dawn.com/news/1287545. See also Andrew Small, *The China–Pakistan Axis: Asia's New Geopolitics* (London: C. Hurst & Co., 2015).

33 Indrani Bagchi, 'Will Russia–Pakistan Joint Drill Alter Moscow–Delhi Ties?', *Times of India*, 25 September 2016, http://timesofindia.indiatimes.com/india/Will-Russia-Pakistan-joint-drill-alter-Moscow-Delhi-ties/articleshow/54503220.cms.

34 Cyril Almeida, 'Exclusive: Act Against Militants or Face International Isolation, Civilians Tell Military', *Dawn*, 7 October 2016, http://www.dawn.com/news/1288350/exclusive-act-against-militants-or-face-international-isolation-civilians-tell-military.

35 Varghese K. George, 'India, US Sign Military Logistics Pact', *Hindu*, 30 August 2016, http://www.thehindu.com/news/international/india-us-sign-logistics-pact/article9049583.ece.

36 James Glanz, Rotella Sebastian and David E. Sanger, 'In 2008 Mumbai Attacks, Piles of Spy Data, but an Uncompleted Puzzle', *New York Times*, 21 December 2014, http://www.nytimes.com/2014/12/22/world/asia/in-2008-mumbai-attacks-piles-of-spy-data-but-an-uncompleted-puzzle.html; Josy Joseph, 'Spy Games: Is India Too Dependent on US Inputs?', *Times of India*, 25 January 2015, http://timesofindia.indiatimes.com/india/Spy-games-Is-India-too-dependent-on-US-inputs/articleshow/46007743.cms; Rahul Tripathi, 'Pathankot Terror Attack: US Alerted India on Infiltration', *Economic Times*, 9 January 2016, http://economictimes.indiatimes.com/news/defence/pathankot-terror-attack-us-alerted-india-on-infiltration/articleshow/50505309.cms.

37 On the challenges of isolating state sponsors of terrorism, see Daniel Byman, *Deadly Connections: States That Sponsor Terrorism* (Cambridge: Cambridge University Press, 2005), p. 280.

38 Dalia Dassa Kaye, 'The Middle East After Vienna', *Foreign Affairs*, 7 July 2015, https://www.foreignaffairs.com/articles/iran/2015-07-07/middle-east-after-vienna.

39 Steve Coll, 'The Back Channel', *New Yorker*, 2 March 2009, http://www.newyorker.com/magazine/2009/03/02/the-back-channel; Sanjaya Baru, *The Accidental Prime Minister: The Making and Unmaking of Manmohan Singh* (London: Penguin, 2015), pp. 188–95; Khurshid Mahmud Kasuri, *Neither a Hawk Nor a Dove: An Insider's Account of Pakistan's Foreign Relations Including Details of the Kashmir Framework* (Oxford: Oxford University Press, 2015), *passim*.

40 Jonathan Powell, *Terrorists at the Table: Why Negotiating Is the Only Way to Peace* (New York: St Martin's Press, 2015), pp. 99–100, 180.

41 Shiv Shankar Menon, *Choices: Inside the Making of India's Foreign Policy* (Washington DC: Brookings Institution Press, 2016), p. 74.

Book Reviews

Environment and Resources

Jeffrey Mazo

Why Are We Waiting? The Logic, Urgency, and Promise of Tackling Climate Change
Nicholas Stern. Cambridge, MA: The MIT Press, 2015.
£19.95/$28.95. 406 pp.

Nicholas Stern's 2006 review for the British government of the economics of climate change was a landmark in the recognition that warming is a global problem that requires a global solution. A decade on, in *Why Are We Waiting?*, he brings his case up to date. While the risks and cost of climate change are likely to be greater than he estimated in *The Stern Review*, the solutions are also clearer, and there has been more progress on low-carbon energy than anticipated. The next two decades will see a remarkable coincidence of two vital historical transformations: a fundamental structural change to the global economy, and a window of opportunity to keep global warming below dangerous levels. 'That these two periods coincide presents both opportunity and time for decision' (p. xiv), but the window is closing rapidly.

In the first two chapters, Stern offers a 'proof of concept' for the needed transition to a low-carbon economy, pointing out pathways involving energy efficiency, renewables, unconventional hydrocarbons, carbon capture and storage, and changes in transportation and land-use policy, spread across every country and every sector. The investment necessary to drive the transition would be on the order of 1–3% of GDP per year. But taking into account the co-benefits of a green economy, strong emissions reduction might even be cheaper than business as usual, even without considering the long-term costs of climate change. The wave of innovation, invention and creativity generated

 DOI 10.1080/00396338.2016.1257205

by a new global energy–industrial revolution could, according to Stern, have 'greater potential than previous technological revolutions to improve world living standards and quality of life' (p. 37).

Proof of concept is one thing; practical policy is another. In Part II, Stern discusses the usefulness of economic history and theory in guiding climate policy, and suggests specific policies and institutions for reducing emissions. But standard economic approaches can be misleading or misguided when faced with the science of climate change. In particular, Chapter 4 focuses on the critical and neglected (from a policy perspective) role of the 'integrated assessment models' used to project the economic impact of climate change. He argues that these models underestimate the potential damage, fail to capture the overall scale of risks and ignore negative feedback from climate impacts. Even more important is the question of discounting, or how we value the present compared to the future. Stern spends two full chapters exploring this issue. This synthesis of technically detailed economic analysis with moral and ethical philosophy is a hidden gem.

The final part of the book, exploring the international framework for climate action, has already to some extent been overtaken by events. In part, this is an inevitable hazard of working in a fast-moving field, but in part it is by design. *Why Are We Waiting?* is the second update to the 2006 *Stern Review*; the author's 2009 *A Blueprint for a Safer Planet* was timed to influence the Copenhagen Climate Summit, which failed to reach a comprehensive global agreement. This latest work was similarly timed around the more successful 2015 Paris Climate Summit. The Paris Agreement, which came into effect in November 2016, met most of the criteria Stern laid out for success (pp. 270–1). Yet Stern also points out that this is only a start. 'While an international agreement is ... crucial to accelerating action to the pace and scale required' (p. 212), bottom-up approaches appear to be as or more effective than those imposed from the top, across all scales. The two approaches can be mutually reinforcing, and international climate governance must be consciously shaped to foster this interplay. This is still a work in progress. In *Why Are We Waiting?*, Stern shows us not just the why, but the how.

The Mushroom at the End of the World: On the Possibility of Life in Capitalist Ruins
Anna Lowenhaupt Tsing. Princeton, NJ: Princeton University Press, 2015. £22.95/$29.95. 331 pp.

According to some, the first living thing to emerge on the site of the Hiroshima atomic-bomb explosion in 1945 was a matsutake mushroom. (Anna Lowenhaupt Tsing records this belief among both Chinese mushroom traders and Japanese scientists, but is unable to confirm the story.) The matsutake mushroom (*Tricholoma matsutake*) is a gourmet delicacy in Japan, where it commands high prices. It grows wild, thriving in pine forests across the northern hemisphere. Changes in land use since the 1950s, however, along with the spread of pine wilt, made it rare in Japan, at the same time that economic growth caused a significant increase in demand. A global trade sprang up, with foragers, many of them displaced or disenfranchised cultural minorities, eking out a precarious living supplying Japanese gourmets.

Tsing, a University of California anthropologist, draws on her field experiences, notably among the foraging communities in Oregon, in the US Pacific Northwest, to turn matsutake and its discontents into both an example of and metaphor for modernity, colonialism, nationalism, global and local capitalism, and their consequences. She travels among Mien, Hmong, Khmer, Mexicans and Anglos living in Oregonian forest camps and explores their histories, interactions and relations with other groups acting as links in the global commodity chain. Her delicate prose draws the reader into a complex world that resists reduction to essentials.

The book is not without its flaws, particularly some of Tsing's underlying and unexpressed assumptions. She puts too much emphasis on the idea that matsutake relies on disturbed ecosystems, and strains the simile with regard to economic and cultural disturbances. In several places she describes what are still magnificent and majestic landscapes as 'ruined industrial forests' (such as on p. 205). She decries frontier romanticism while indulging in her own Rousseauian reveries. And while eschewing reductionism can offer new insights, reductionism isn't an evil per se. By trying to see both the forest and the trees, Tsing sometimes loses sight of both.

The Mushroom at the End of the World is, in the words of the author, 'unlike most scholarly books ... a riot of short chapters' (p. viii). The structure of the book is a metaphor: 'I wanted them to be like the flushes of mushrooms that come up after the rain: an over-the-top bounty; a temptation to explore; and always too many'. Extending this trope, one could point out that the book embodies tenuous, hidden threads connecting widely dispersed and apparently unrelated trends and concepts, whose links only become apparent under the right conditions. Despite a disclaimer that 'this book is not a critique of the dreams of modernization and progress' (p. 2), such a critique forms one of these threads. Tsing suggests that 'my experiment in form and my argument follow each other' (p. viii), and contends that the concepts and connections she explores are 'recalcitrant to the kind of "summing up" that has become the hallmark of modern knowledge' (p. 33). *The Mushroom at the End of the World* is a scholarly work, inside a meditation, wrapped in poetry. It is difficult to come to grips with, especially if the reader doesn't share Tsing's assumptions, but it is well worth the effort.

Dodging Extinction: Power, Food, Money, and the Future of Life on Earth
Anthony D. Barnosky. Oakland, CA: University of California Press, 2014. £22.95/$29.95. 256 pp.

Around 440 million years ago, a global extinction event saw the disappearance of nearly 86% of living species. Since then, there have been four other mass extinctions, most recently at the end of the Cretaceous Period some 65 million years ago. Over the last few decades, biologists have increasingly warned that we are facing – may even be in the midst of – a sixth. And as palaeontologist Anthony Barnosky puts it in *Dodging Extinction*, this time is different for two reasons: 'unlike the dinosaurs, we can see what's coming ... [and] this time it's not something that's being done to us; it is something we are doing to ourselves' (p. 29). If we continue the path we are now on, ignoring the evidence that things are in fact getting even worse and setting aside any population or consumption increases (let alone climate change), we could see comparable species loss in as little as three centuries (p. 32).

The drivers of this extinction are power, food and money. Before technology gave us access to energy sources other than photosynthesis, the planet supported a large-animal biomass of about 200m tons. At the end of the last Ice Age, about 10,000 years ago, the number fell by half as many large species went extinct. By 300 years ago, the total had recovered – but was made up mostly by humans and our livestock. By now the number has shot up by a factor of seven, powered by fossil fuels. Barnosky calculates that humanity needs more energy just for itself than has normally been available to power the entire terrestrial ecosystem (p. 59). The story is similar for food: we now use more than a third of available land worldwide simply to feed ourselves. There is no need to dive into the ecological weeds to see why humans are driving other species to extinction.

Barnosky treats money from a similar global and abstract perspective, as a shorthand for ecosystem services. This key concept needs to be more widely understood by policymakers: species and ecosystems make up the 'natural capital' that provides direct benefits – ecosystem services – to individuals and society. And this is why extinction matters: it destroys natural capital, with long-term macroeconomic effects. Yet natural capital is all too often treated as free and unbounded. We find ourselves facing the tragedy of the commons on a global scale.

Perhaps it takes a palaeontologist's long perspective, but this is one of the best summaries of the global energy–water–food nexus published in the last ten years. Barnosky approaches his subject as an ecologist rather than an environmentalist. His case is all the more frightening because it is presented as dispassionate science, although there are enough emotive examples to drive the point home. Most importantly, Barnosky is able to find reason for optimism. 'Up for grabs in the scientific community is whether or not we can do anything to stop the Sixth Mass Extinction', he writes. 'After researching and writing this book, I think we can' (p. xii). Wider awareness of the issue is a necessary first step.

Let There Be Water: Israel's Solution for a Water-Starved World
Seth M. Siegel. New York: Thomas Dunne Books, 2015. $27.99. 337 pp.

One of the most important ecosystem services is the provision of clean water. In *Let There Be Water*, Seth Siegel touches only briefly on the now-familiar threat of an imminent global water crisis and its drivers. His interest is rather in how such a crisis can be avoided or ameliorated, and specifically how Israel's experience can serve as a model for the nations of the world, developed and developing alike. Israel has faced many of the drivers of a water crisis: limited supply, a rising population and standard of living, climate change. But Siegel points out that water crises are almost always avoidable, and Israel is a now a net exporter of water. This is the story of Israel's success.

The main constraints on clean water are not so much physical scarcity as they are underinvestment, underdevelopment and insufficient or inappropriate management. Siegel's book is partly a history – cultural, political and technical – and partly a story of how Israel leveraged its successful water policy into a political tool. Israel's ability to provide water to its Arab neighbours, and its technology and skills more widely, is not just a source of income; it has promoted better relations and engagement throughout the world. The stories of Iran and China are particularly interesting. But even California, with the world's sixth-largest economy and now in its fifth year of drought, has turned to Israel for help.

What sets Israel apart from other countries in terms of water, Siegel says, is not its technology but the extent to which it has promoted and adopted it. His final chapter identifies a dozen elements of Israel's water philosophy that together explain its success: 'The Water Belongs to the Nation', 'Cheap Water Is Expensive', 'Use Water to Unify the Country', 'Regulators, Not Politicians', 'Create a Water-Respecting Culture', 'All of the Above', 'Use Water Fees for Water', 'Innovation Wanted', 'Measure and Monitor', 'Plan Today for Long into the Future', 'Advocates Needed' and 'The Time to Act Is Now'. No other country is likely to be able to entirely replicate Israel's approach; many of these elements have difficult or intractable cultural aspects. But Siegel offers a comprehensive blueprint for those who are willing to try.

The Rightful Place of Science: Disasters & Climate Change
Roger Pielke, Jr. Tempe, AZ and Washington DC: Consortium for Science, Policy & Outcomes, 2014. $8.99. 114 pp.

The Collapse of Western Civilization: A View from the Future
Naomi Oreskes and Erik M. Conway. New York: Columbia University Press, 2014. $9.95. 89 pp.

There is often a tension in scholarly writing on contentious issues between the demands of academic objectivity and the desire to persuade. These two short books, from scholars on opposite sides of the climate-policy debate, offer examples of how, in different ways, prioritising the latter at the expense of the former risks undermining both.

Roger Pielke, Jr, is a political scientist at the University of Colorado who has written extensively on climate policy. He is a controversial figure, often labelled a sceptic or denier (despite his unqualified acceptance of the reality of climate change), simply because his positions on the degree of risk, and the appropriate response, are more nuanced than many. The most prominent example was his ouster as a writer for the statistics-driven website FiveThirtyEight.com in 2014, over a post arguing that the rising cost of natural disasters was not driven by climate change.

That question forms the core of his short book. It is an important one – perhaps one of the most important – for driving climate policy. There is nothing new in this book that has not already been hashed out in the peer-reviewed literature and the academic blogosphere. Yet therein lies the rub. The back-and-forth, although mired in statistical theory, is not difficult for the layman to follow. Pielke is well aware of the (in this writer's view, well-founded) criticisms of his methods, yet there is no sign of these criticisms in his book. The uninformed reader might be forgiven for concluding that no scientific controversy exists, when in fact Pielke is in the minority. This is not helped by the fact that the remainder of the book is a response to critics, but based on attributions of motive rather than assessments of merit.

The Collapse of Western Civilization, in contrast, makes no claim to be scientifically detached. Written by two historians of science (whose *Merchants of Doubt* is the go-to book on commercially driven science denial), it is presented as a history written in 2393, three centuries after 'the great collapse'. Such a 'future history' conceit has been used many times before to good effect, for example Whitley Strieber and James Kunetka's 1984 *Warday*, an account of America five years after a limited nuclear attack. When it comes to climate change, however, especially projected more than a century into the future, uncertainty is the name of the game. By fixing on one of an essentially infinite set of scenarios, the book tries to highlight the urgency of the threat. But the chosen scenario, while plausible, is an extreme case and is no more plausible than many other less compelling ones. As a result, it is diverting, but not persuasive and perhaps even counterproductive.

There is nevertheless value in both books, if read in conjunction with the right foils. In Pielke's case, these would be the critiques offered on such websites as Skeptical Science and Realclimate, and Pielke's replies. In the case of Oreskes and Conway, they might be something like Kurt Campbell et al.'s (slightly dated) *The Age of Consequences* (2007), which offers three future histories of varying severity. (For readers of *Survival*, the volume has the added merit of focusing on foreign policy and national security.) *Disasters and Climate Change* and *The Collapse of Western Civilization* are both welcome returns to the tradition of pamphleteering, but reflect the bad as well as the good of that tradition.

United States
David C. Unger

The Great Exception: The New Deal and the Limits of American Politics
Jefferson Cowie. Princeton, NJ: Princeton University Press, 2016. £19.95/$27.95. 273 pp.

Bernie Sanders take note: there will likely never be a return to the politics of the New Deal in the United States, and American liberals would do themselves and their causes a huge favour by recognising that. That is the pessimistic, powerful and well-documented case that Jefferson Cowie makes in *The Great Exception*.

Countless books have been written about the New Deal, from the magisterial celebrations of Arthur Schlesinger, Jr, to more critical studies by later historians. Rather than write another detailed history of the Franklin Roosevelt years, Cowie mines the longer sweep of American social, economic and political history to make a bold and generally heterodox argument. The New Deal, he argues, did not so much build on earlier progressive movements such as populism, progressivism and traditional craft unionism, as turn away from all of them to briefly follow a radically different course, one largely without precedent and, as it turned out, largely without sequel. The New Deal, as he sees it, was the product of very special circumstances that allowed Franklin Roosevelt to wrench American politics, and hence social and economic policy, away from its normal patterns of individualism, an ethnically and racially divided working class, and laissez-faire economic governance to create, for a time, a new electoral coalition, new government institutions and a new set of popular expectations and beliefs.

One of those special circumstances was the unintended result of a decade of restricted immigration under the Johnson–Reed Immigration Act of 1924, which helped transform an ethnically divided white working class into a more cohesive one. Another was, by the time of Roosevelt's inauguration, two-and-a-half years' experience of deep depression without an effective safety net, which helped create a desperate demand for federal action, shredding earlier taboos. Complementing this was growing frustration at the prolonged inaction of the Hoover administration in the face of spreading suffering, which gave Roosevelt ample political space to experiment and act, even when his actions and experiments produced little tangible relief.

Operating in these special circumstances, the New Deal distinguished itself by appeals to collective feeling and promotion of corporatist solutions. That is what made it the great exception in a country that long worshipped individual identities and success stories. It was also a great exception for the Democratic Party, which until then had typically been the champion of Jeffersonian individualism, states' rights and anti-bigness remedies such as anti-trust. Even Progressive Era Democrats, who, like Progressive Republicans, were more activist in temperament and less wary of strong governance than their Gilded Age predecessors, had sought, in Cowie's account, to champion individual more than collective goals. That difference ultimately split the ranks of former progressives initially attracted to the New Deal.

Post-New Deal decades saw a reversion to longer-running American norms. With the Depression's desperation gone, mass immigration resuming after 1965, a more individualistic New Left and the religious revival of recent decades, some of Cowie's special circumstances started running in reverse, with predictable political and cultural results. Outsourcing, the decline of unions and the expanding role of big money in politics reinforced these trends. Despite growing inequality and the Great Recession beginning in 2008, the twenty-first century saw not a return to the New Deal but something like a return to the post-Civil War Gilded Age, when money ruled and those without it were politically and economically powerless.

Cowie, who teaches labour history at Cornell University's School of Industrial and Labor Relations, is not ready to give up in despair. His prescription is to rebuild a more typically American left, based more on individual identities and agendas, though to some that might seem a contradiction in terms. He also calls for the drawing of practical lessons from Progressive Era successes rather than New Deal anomalies. That, too, may prove ahistorical or utopian. But Cowie makes a convincing case that the alternative cannot be simply waiting, like Samuel Beckett's characters, not for Godot, but for the New Deal's return.

A Sense of Power: The Roots of America's Global Role
John A. Thompson. Ithaca, NY: Cornell University Press, 2016.
$29.95. 343 pp.

John A. Thompson has written an ambitious and useful book challenging two familiar explanatory theories about what drove the United States to push beyond the traditional hemispheric horizons of its nineteenth-century foreign policy and embrace the global aspirations that have characterised it at least since the end of the Second World War. Neither the widening economic interests of a globally trading, globally investing economy, nor increasing military threats to North American security from a world made smaller by airpower, seem to him sufficient explanations in light of the economic statistics and military planning documents he has closely examined.

Thompson's own explanation is somewhat more diffuse. He points instead to a sense among elites and ordinary citizens alike of America's growing power in the world, which fed a corresponding sense of responsibility to influence distant events. Because we could, we should. Discounting any coherent necessity or deliberate strategy to create an America-friendly world order, Thompson sees a more ad hoc process unfolding case by case.

As a result, his narrative sometimes wavers between proposing a new theoretical construct – ambition driven by a sense of power – and mere empiricism: things happening because they happened. Are we really forced to choose between the monocausal determinism of economic or security motives and the illusive psychological constructs of intellectual history? Deterministic theories are easy enough to refute, especially when they are expected to bear the entire burden of explanation. International life is far too complex for such vulgar reductionism. But might not either of the two explanations Thompson disparages sometimes have been at play, along with others? Why must finding that some elites were driven by a sense of power mean that economic and security motives were not also powerful factors in decision-making?

The evidence Thompson brings to bear for his model is not always conclusive. Noting the relatively small ratios of America's trade or investment to its gross output does not exclude the possibility of these playing a much more decisive role in the economic activities or net profits of key policymaking elites. International investment houses were over-represented in the foreign-policy establishment from the Second World War onwards. Another peril lies in knowing when the public declarations of policymakers should be taken as reflective of their real motives and beliefs. Thompson fairly criticises William Appleman Williams, one of the most influential theorists adducing economic motives, for taking at face value words that might have been part of an effort to sell the public on policies whose real motives lay elsewhere. Yet he sometimes risks falling into the same trap himself when it supports his own sense-of-power argument, for example in citing bipartisan endorsements of more active internationalism during the Truman years. Thompson may be unerring in his own sense of when remarks should be taken at face value and when not. But the inconsistent application of such metrics tends to undermine what might otherwise be rock-solid evidence.

Still, Thompson, who is Emeritus Reader in American History at Cambridge, has made a major theoretical contribution to American diplomatic history by adding his sense-of-power theory to the mixture. Moreover, he has produced a valuable, and often persuasive, new narrative that will leave readers better equipped to make their own judgements about the underlying drivers at play.

Why America Misunderstands the World: National Experience and Roots of Misperception
Paul R. Pillar. New York: Columbia University Press, 2016.
£21.95/$29.95. 211 pp.

Paul R. Pillar raises interesting and important questions about the preconceptions drawn from America's own national experience that tend to shape the way most Americans see the world and the likely effects of US policy. Every country has such preconceptions, but Pillar argues, mostly persuasively, that America's are particularly potent, deep-rooted and misleading.

Among the reasons he cites for this are America's relatively secure geographic position; its dominant military and economic power; its mostly successful domestic experience of building a diverse, multi-ethnic society; its stable, functioning democracy; and its Revolution-born belief in its own international benevolence. Most Americans see these features as merits, not flaws. But that is just Pillar's point, since many Americans seem to believe that people in other lands should be able to easily achieve, with just a little help, what Americans have achieved for themselves at home. More challenging circumstances or different aspirations in other countries are too readily shoved aside as irrelevant. Likewise, America's ability to transform other countries is overestimated, and domestic popular impatience quickly manifests itself when foreign ventures do not meet America's unrealistic goals or timetables.

Pillar, who had a long career as a top analyst and administrator at the Central Intelligence Agency (CIA) before moving on to academia, acknowledges and builds on the pioneering research of Robert Jervis and others into the psychological dimensions of foreign policy. Pillar argues that psychology and predispositions play a crucial role in shaping policies and must be taken into account in analysing them.

Pillar reaches back into early American history for his analysis of national traits and preconceptions, showing how these played out in earlier centuries. His efforts to correlate background preconceptions with foreground decision-making sometimes seems strained, vague or overly abstract. Such are the hazards of theory, especially theories rooted in psychology. But the narrative quickens and tightens once Pillar gets to the 1990s, the period during which he served as chief of analysis and then deputy director of the CIA's counter-terrorism centre, and the following decade, when, after a falling out with the centre's director, Cofer Black, Pillar moved on to become a leading critic of George W. Bush's handling of the response to 9/11 and the ensuing 'war on terror'.

Pillar makes an impassioned case that, during those two decades, the nation's top political leadership brushed aside expert analysis from the intelligence community with disastrous consequences. He argues that, in part due to some of the preconceptions he describes in this book, most politicians get things generally wrong most of the time, as does much of the electorate, while those like himself, who are professionally trained to be objective, generally get it right, but are not listened to. To which one might reply, welcome to the messiness of democratic government, in which the people – and the leaders they elect – are meant to be the ultimate decision-makers.

Still, given the unhappy record of recent years, we should hope future leaders can learn something about the dangers of bending to (or orchestrating) the country's political winds, drawing on historical preconceptions rather than fresh intelligence, and ignoring the input of the professional analysts the government expensively trains and maintains to provide its policymakers with informed guidance.

Trouble in the Tribe: The American Jewish Conflict over Israel
Dov Waxman. Princeton, NJ: Princeton University Press, 2016.
£22.95/$29.95. 316 pp.

It would be difficult to imagine a book like this being written ten or even five years ago. Its central premise is that the American Jewish community, long famed for its legendary ability to mobilise the virtually homogeneous views of its members into fearsomely effective political pressure in support of Israeli governments of whatever political colouration, is now a house divided against itself. So much so, argues Dov Waxman, that Israel, once the symbol and focus of Jewish unity, is now a key factor splitting American Jews into warring camps.

Is this really true? The answer depends on the metrics for unity/disunity one chooses to apply. According to Waxman, who teaches political science, international relations and Israel studies at Northeastern University, American Jews remain overwhelmingly committed to Israel's survival and to its military success in wars, regardless of the origin and nature of those wars. What they argue about, vociferously and often abusively, are Israel's relations with Palestinians in the occupied territories: chiefly, the two interrelated issues of policies toward Jewish settlers there and the desirability of a two-state solution. And while relatively small numbers take absolute positions on these issues, most, according to the polling data Waxman presents, fall into a middle ground that sees a two-state solution as desirable in principle, but blocked more by Palestinian tactics and attitudes than by those of the Israeli government.

In some ways, the discord is driven by the struggle of a generally liberal American Jewish community to adjust to the increasingly right-wing policies of recent Israeli governments. But the overall picture is not quite so simple, with serious questions emerging about who exactly will constitute the American Jewish community over the next few decades. The Orthodox, who tend to take more right-wing, pro-Likud positions than the non-Orthodox, also tend to have much larger families and many fewer mixed marriages than more liberal non-Orthodox and secular Jews. And affiliation rates with Jewish organisations tend to be much lower among the young, especially the non-Orthodox young, than among their parents.

So one version of the future could be a newly reunified, mainly Orthodox, organised Jewish community rallying behind Likud policies in Israel and Republican policies in the US. Or not. Demography is not destiny, and future developments in Israel could produce a very different picture.

While today's relative disunity is unsettling to the establishment leaders of Jewish organisations that derive much of their clout from politicians' perceptions of a unified Jewish community, it should not be so surprising. The political and religious identities of American Jews have been continually evolving with their changing experiences in the United States and the world. From the comfortably assimilated German Jews who, at the turn of the twentieth century, shunned pre-state utopian Zionism as potentially undermining their hard-won acceptance as unhyphenated Americans, to the more nationally diverse post-Holocaust, post-Israeli-statehood mainstream who embraced (Labor) Zionism as a central part of Jewish-American identity, change, not stasis, has been the norm. Today, with old-style Labor Zionism out of electoral favour in Israel and the Orthodox and Ultra-Orthodox Haredim becoming a larger and more visible presence in the American Jewish community, the picture is changing once again. This book offers a useful grounding for thinking about the changes already taking place, and what may lie ahead.

Liberalism's Last Hurrah: The Presidential Campaign of 1964
Gary A. Donaldson. New York: Skyhorse Publishing, 2002.
$14.99. 376 pp.

Skyhorse, an independent, New York-based publisher, has done students of American politics a service by reissuing Gary A. Donaldson's 2002 classic account of the 1964 campaign. (That service is somewhat diminished, however, by an apparent lack of careful proofreading that let too many incorrect first names and other minor errors slip through.) Donaldson traces the historic roots of all the major-party contenders and the surprising sequels to that November Democratic landside.

There are several possible candidates for the first recognisable forerunner of the 2016 US presidential elections, but 1964 is surely one of them. That year's Republican presidential nominee, Barry Goldwater, split his party even more than Donald Trump has done this time, with moderate Republicans such as Nelson Rockefeller, George Romney and Jacob Javits shouted down by Goldwater delegates at the party's raucous San Francisco convention. Other leading Republican moderates kept their distance from Goldwater's campaign, while the candidate entrusted his run to enthusiastic but clumsy amateurs.

Goldwater, a decent man and a patriot, deliberately avoided racially inflammatory remarks and Trump-style attacks on minorities in that riot-scarred year. White southern opponents of civil rights flocked to his banner anyway. Not only had Goldwater been one of only six Republicans to vote against the landmark 1964 Civil Rights Act, his constant invocation of states' rights echoed the slogans of generations of southern segregationist politicians.

In the south at least, Goldwater inherited the backlash vote stirred up and mobilised in the primary season by the genuine demagogue George Wallace.

Wallace ran surprisingly well in that spring's Democratic primaries, even in northern states such as Wisconsin, Indiana and Maryland (all states where Trump did well in 2016). Wallace's northern successes were concentrated among the white working class in the not-yet-rustbelt factory regions of those states. He drew voters anxious that civil-rights gains would threaten their tenuous grasp on upward mobility by increasing competition for their jobs and creating white flight and lowered property values in their neighbourhoods. These voters swung back to Lyndon Johnson and the Democrats in November. But as we can see today, their flirtation with Wallace was not a one-time fluke but a portent of future realignment.

Goldwater went down to a landslide defeat, with Johnson winning a record 61% of the popular vote and 486 out of 538 electoral votes. But in hindsight we can see that Goldwater's failure helped pave the way for Ronald Reagan's success 16 years later. Reagan's nationally broadcast television speech for Goldwater in the closing weeks of the 1964 campaign helped establish him as the leading national conservative champion in the wake of Goldwater's humiliating loss, and launched Reagan's own post-Hollywood career in electoral politics (he successfully ran for governor of California in 1966). 1964 also saw the Republicans widen their Eisenhower-era beachhead in the once-solid Democratic South.

But the parallels go only so far. Industrial America was not yet a rustbelt in 1964. The nationwide unemployment rate that November was a low 4.8%, and would continue to fall into the next year. Lyndon Johnson was running as an incumbent who, though not personally popular, basked in the glow of his martyred predecessor, assassinated just the year before. American combat involvement in Vietnam had barely begun. These circumstances combined to assure the kind of resounding across-the-board Democratic victory few have predicted for this year. Hence the title *Liberalism's Last Hurrah*, a seemingly epochal triumph that turned out to be more of a swan song, at least for New Deal-style liberalism. Later Democratic victors from Carter to Obama ran on very different political platforms and won their victories with very different electoral coalitions.

Donaldson, who teaches American History at Xavier University of Louisiana, reaches the conclusion, justifiable in 2002, that with Johnson's disappointing and erratic performance in office during the two years following his election, the Democrats effectively vacated the political centre, opening the way to a long era of conservative Republican ascendancy. The story of this year's surprising presidential campaign scarcely reflects that pattern. If nothing else, we can look forward to a spate of interesting books describing the new political realities revealed by the presidential campaign of 2016.

Europe

Hanns W. Maull

Slippery Slope: Europe's Troubled Future
Giles Merritt. Oxford: Oxford University Press, 2016.
£16.99/$29.95. 270 pp.

In this extended essay about the state of the European Union, Giles Merritt, a veteran Brussels watcher first for the *Financial Times* and then with *Europe's World*, recalls an interview with Jacques Delors in 1984, before he formally assumed the presidency of the European Commission. Then, as now, there was, as Merritt puts it, 'a palpable sense of drift in Europe' (p. 231). Asked for his priorities for the job that awaited him, Delors responded that he wanted to complete the single market. At the time, this was widely seen as Mission Impossible. Yet with this project, Delors succeeded in galvanising a fundamental change in the European mood. Who and what could pull the European Union out of its present morass, as Delors did then? Merritt does not pretend to have the answers, but he persuasively warns how dangerous that morass has become – not only for the EU, but for Europeans. If they are to get out of it, Merritt suggests, they must let go, as an essential first step, of a number of dangerous myths, including the beliefs that 'Europe is strong' (his Myth No. 3), 'Europe is technologically advanced' (Myth No. 4) and 'Europe's voice is heard around the world' (Myth No. 8). They must also recognise Europe's vulnerability in a world of rapid and far-reaching change.

Merritt pinpoints Europe's dangerous deficiencies – its mismatched human resources, which foretell a future of both mass unemployment and severe shortages of skilled people; its rapidly declining technological prowess; and its lack of clout in international politics. ('The vaunted "soft power" of the European Union is really no power at all', he writes on p. 181.) Above all, Europe is plagued by the largely dysfunctional system of European governance that has evolved over the last two decades. The EU, says Merritt, has become ineffective, inefficient and opaque. Yet he also sees tantalising opportunities for Europe as a model and laboratory for international cooperation and multilateral solutions to shared problems on a global scale. For that, however, Europe would need to develop the kind of unity of purpose and action that 'irresistible external and internal pressures are demanding' (p. 180). To help Europe's politicians 'rise to the occasion' (p. 205), Merritt concludes with a ten-point 'To do' list, arranged by rising order of difficulty. It ends with a plea for political union, to save the euro and to retain a seat for Europe at the global top table.

The EU: An Obituary
John R. Gillingham. London: Verso, 2016. £12.99/$19.95. 281 pp.

There is no shortage of books deconstructing the European Union, but this one is unusually knowledgeable, insightful and acerbic. Its dramatic subtitle exaggerates its conclusion, but only a little: in his 'postscript 2016', the author notes, 'The EU may not disappear altogether but survive in vestigial form, yet it will no longer be central to the conduct of European affairs' (p. 245). In fact, European institutions were never as important to European governance as people believed them to be, except during the period that Jacques Delors was at the helm of the European Commission (1985–95). Gillingham presents a history of European integration driven by external developments instead, firstly by America's grand design of 'containment' and the Cold War in Europe; then, from the early 1970s onward, by the breakdown of the Bretton Woods system of fixed exchange rates and the triumph of neoliberalism; and finally by the end of the Cold War, which led to the unification of Germany, the construction of the European Union by means of the Maastricht Treaty, and 'the fatal decision to adopt the euro as a single currency' (p. 4). Today, the external factors that, in Gillingham's view, challenge the very survival of the EU include the cyber revolution, the wave of migrants flooding Europe, and the rise of China and India. In Gillingham's narrative, there are heroes (Margaret Thatcher, Ronald Reagan) and villains (Jean Monnet, Walter Hallstein and, above all, Jacques Delors); the latter were responsible for pushing European integration down the path towards a democratically deficient, technocratic super-state by propagating 'an ideology of Europeanism' (p. 1).

Curiously, Gillingham concentrates all his erudite ire on the European Union, while simultaneously arguing that the EU (and its predecessors) were largely irrelevant. This would logically suggest that it was Jacques Delors, during his ten years at the helm of the European Commission, who wrought all the damage, something Gillingham indeed seems to believe. This conclusion sits uneasily, however, with his belief that it is the nation-states that constitute Europe: the European Union, he holds, far from being a polity *sui generis*, as the Europeanists would have it, is just another international organisation (p. 5). Surely, then, the member-state governments must have had something to do with the perilous path the EU has taken since the early 1970s? It is also somewhat irritating to the European reader that Gillingham, while relentlessly dissecting the EU's flaws and criticising its flabbiness, holds up the United States as a paragon of democratic virtue and economic success. The notion that not only the EU, but also its member states and even the US, might experience episodes of political malfunction does not seem to resonate with the author.

Yet, despite these misgivings, and the author's sometimes obsessive inclination to find fault with the EU (the generous remuneration and perks enjoyed by EU civil servants, for instance, are the subject of extensive discussion not once, but twice, on pages 125f. and 165f.), Gillingham's indictment of the union deserves to be read carefully. The author's knowledge of his subject is impressive, and the evidence he marshals to support his argument that European integration since the 1970s has pushed the continent into an existential crisis is extensive and troubling. It would be great – and probably cheer the author – if the EU could undermine his case through successful actions and policies.

The Euro: And its Threat to the Future of Europe
Joseph E. Stiglitz. London: Allen Lane, 2016. £20.00/$28.95. 496 pp.

Europe's Orphan: The Future of the Euro and the Politics of Debt
Martin Sandbu. Princeton, NJ: Princeton University Press, 2015. £22.95/$29.95. 313 pp.

The Future of the Euro
Matthias Matthijs and Mark Blyth, eds. New York: Oxford University Press, 2015. $29.95. 368 pp.

On 12 February 2009 – in the midst of the worldwide financial storm unleashed by the collapse of the US investment bank Lehman Brothers half a year earlier – Jean Claude Trichet, then the president of the European Central Bank, celebrated the tenth anniversary of the euro. 'The euro is a historic achievement', he said in Osnabrück, Germany. 'Its first ten years have been a success.' A few months later, the euro crisis broke out when a new Greek government drastically revised upward its estimate of Greece's public debt.

The crisis triggered expensive collective rescue efforts for several eurozone economies by the EU member states, the European Central Bank (ECB) and the IMF. Its results have been economic stagnation, a drastic increase in unemployment in the southern parts of Europe, particularly among the young, and what many see as increasing German hegemony in Europe. Deep cleavages have reopened between the wealthy North and the poorer South. In response to the crisis, populist movements have emerged to challenge existing parties across Europe. In autumn 2016, the travails of one of Europe's most important private financial institutions, Deutsche Bank, were a reminder that none of the problems underlying the crisis had been resolved: public-debt levels continued to be high, growth was mostly anaemic, austerity policies were robbing people of their futures, and the pernicious links between private banks and government debt were still in operation. All this threatened to undermine not only the eurozone, but also the European Union as a whole, and its national democratic foundations. In Angela Merkel's frequently repeated words, 'If the euro fails, Europe fails.'

So far, the eurozone has held together, and the crisis has receded, at least for now. Yet the price paid by Europeans has been steep. Among the less obvious collateral damage was Europe's actual and potential influence as a global actor. Not only are the material foundations on which the EU might have built such a role weakening, but, more importantly, the credibility of the European Union as a role model, and its effectiveness as a new kind of global power, have taken a huge hit. Consequently, Europe's ability to hold its own and exercise some influence amid the turbulence of a globalising world looks more precarious by the day.

How did this all come about? And how might Europe escape from its present conundrum? Books addressing these questions are now appearing by the dozen. Most of them see the eurozone as deeply flawed from the beginning, and from there draw a straight line to the unhappy experiences of the last few years. Their conclusion is that the EU's Economic and Monetary Union (EMU) needs to be either fundamentally rebuilt or dissolved. Among the books considered here, Stiglitz makes that case in particularly eloquent detail. The most important of the books, however, offers a rather different perspective. In *Europe's Orphan: The Future of the Euro and the Politics of Debt*, Martin Sandbu launches a carefully argued and refreshingly comprehensive attack on the conventional wisdom about the euro crisis. To Sandbu, the euro has been unfairly maligned and disowned by its parents, the eurozone member governments. The problems experienced by eurozone countries since 2010, he argues, were caused not by any flaws in the architecture of the EMU, but by a glut of capital worldwide and bad policy choices among member governments. Managing the debt crisis required neither the extensive rescue efforts undertaken, nor the austerity measures imposed in their aftermath. The euro itself was never in danger, nor was its membership. As long as a country did not choose to leave the eurozone, only the ECB could force its departure. Nothing about the euro makes it incompatible with national democratic governance – though, as all three books point out, there is much in the policies that surround the euro that is incompatible with, or at least rather toxic for, democracy. In fact, Sandbu provocatively argues that the euro still offers important opportunities to Europe, and that the UK should therefore adopt it (an option that no longer exists, alas, now that the UK has voted for Brexit). Summing up his diagnosis, Sandbu concludes that 'the Eurozone's crisis is a result of ideological resistance to writing down debts – whether those of banks or those of sovereigns' (p. 266).

How well do his arguments hold up against those of the euro's critics? The first challenge to Sandbu's case concerns the EMU's original design. In their important volume on *The Future of the Euro*, Matthias Matthijs and Mark Blyth (with their collaborators) hold that the euro was, politically speaking, insufficiently embedded from the very start. They are surely correct to observe that markets function well only in the context of a political framework that provides certain essential requirements that markets cannot provide by themselves, such as the security of market participants or the protection of their property rights. The book's first section (with chapters by Kathleen R. McNamara, Erik Jones, Nicolas Jabko and Vivien A. Schmidt) vividly describes how the EMU's governance arrangements were tested, found wanting and then modified under the impact of the crisis.

Similarly, but more conventionally, Joseph Stiglitz, in his *The Euro*, also blames the EMU's inherent flaws for the crisis. In his view, a single currency for a heterogeneous group of countries is feasible but very demanding: 'If different countries are in different situations, they ideally want different interest rates to maintain macroeconomic balance and different exchange rates to attain a balance of trade' (p. 93). A single currency seemingly takes away both these options, and the members therefore need other mechanisms to compensate. The Maastricht Treaty failed to set these up, however, demonstrating, as Stiglitz sees it, a serious lack of economic understanding among its drafters. His extensive proposals for ways the EMU could be restructured to make the single currency sustainable (pp. 239–71) have, as the author himself concludes, close to zero chance of being effected by governments.

Yet does it follow, as the critics of the single currency argue, that the euro needed a fully fledged financial and banking union, as well as genuinely supranational economic and political institutions, to work? Sandbu says no, presenting a plausible case against this conclusion. The issue here is not whether the euro needs supranational arrangements, but what form these should take and, perhaps even more importantly, how they should be used by those in key decision-making positions. As Sandbu tells it, it was not the governance arrangements of the euro that caused the damage, but the way in which governments made use of them. There is plenty of evidence to support this view, starting with the very composition of the eurozone. It was obvious from its beginning that the EMU was a project of economic convergence based on the German socio-economic model. Yet, as Matthijs and Blyth observe, 'flexible interpretation and canny massaging of the rules' (p. 4) allowed 11 of the then-15 member states of the EU to apply, even though only Luxembourg fully met the defined criteria. In other words, member governments made it clear from the beginning that this was not to be a rules-based order, but rather a political undertaking. When not only France, but also Germany, the chief architect of the EMU, broke through the annual public-debt ceiling with impunity, it was evident that the system did not function the way it was designed to because those in charge of the project – the member governments – did not really want it to.

The second line of attack against Sandbu's case concerns crisis management. Would the crisis and its results have been different if governments had pursued different policies within the existing EMU framework? The position of most governments, starting with Berlin, has been that there was no alternative to their actions. Yet Sandbu suggests that governments could and should have forced write-offs of both bank and sovereign debts; Germany was, as he sees it, too lenient with Greece in the first phase of the crisis, rather than too harsh. The approach that Sandbu would have liked to see pursued from the beginning was indeed the approach taken by the eurozone from 2012 onward – but even then, after much damage had been done, it was pursued only timidly and inconsistently. The fact that the haircuts administered by the Troika of the EU, the ECB and the IMF to the private creditors of both the Greek government and Cypriot banks proceeded smoothly, among other examples, supports Sandbu's case that this could have been done earlier and more decisively.

All the books reviewed here severely criticise the way Europe has dealt with the consequences of the crisis in the weaker member states. Stiglitz, drawing on his experience as a former chief economist at the World Bank, is particularly eloquent on the failure of the Troika's prescriptions. Stiglitz and Sandbu, as well as Matthijs and Blyth, all offer detailed accounts of the profound flaws and pernicious consequences of the EU's chosen approach, not least for the democratic foundations of Europe and its member states. In fact, probably the only people who still (pretend to) believe in the validity of the prevailing approach, built around austerity and structural reforms, can be found in Berlin and Brussels. The evidence that those policies are not working as intended is overwhelming – yet only the IMF has had the courage to admit as much publicly.

Overall, Sandbu is probably right: the problems underpinning the euro crisis were not design flaws so much as bad decisions and bad policies, adopted in Berlin, Brussels and elsewhere. A crisis may well have been inevitable under the adverse circumstances of the world financial crisis, but there was nothing inevitable about the enormous damage wrought, both materially and ideationally. The single currency and its architecture is not the source of Europe's present troubles; the crisis is but a symptom of deeper problems. All three books address the puzzle of why the EU has clung to policies that have little evidence to support them and patently have not worked in practice. All arrive at the same conclusion: Europe's decision-makers are hampered by ideological blinkers. For Sandbu, this can be seen in their reflexive rejection of debt write-downs; for Matthijs and Blyth, in their belief in markets; for Stiglitz, in their neoliberal thinking. Yet all three books also point to processes of erosion and even decay, not only in the European project but also – more fundamentally – in Western European democracies. This has resulted in a dearth of political courage, creativity and innovation in addressing the admittedly ever more difficult challenges thrown up by deepening interdependence, breeding a loss of legitimacy, solidarity and trust among political elites across Europe.

All three books help us better understand the European conundrum, and all three agree that the disastrous implications of the euro crisis for Europe stem from misguided ideological preconceptions and political irresponsibility at both the national and European levels. European interdependence requires that leaders be responsible to actors beyond their own national constituencies; at the same time, however, the form this responsibility takes will be different depending on the constituency in question. The ongoing crisis of Europe reflects a failure of member governments to live up to their responsibilities both at home and within Europe. What the continent needs now is above all a new approach to European integration that reconstructs the relationship between Europe, its member countries and their citizens in ways that restore legitimacy and trust.

Counter-terrorism and Intelligence

Jonathan Stevenson

Dheepan (film)
Jacques Audiard, director and screenwriter.
Distributed by UGC Distribution, 2015.

Les Cowboys (film)
Thomas Bidegain, director and screenwriter.
Distributed by Pathé, 2015.

Eye in the Sky (film)
Gavin Hood, director. Guy Hibbert, screenwriter.
Distributed by Entertainment One, 2015.

In Jacques Audiard's brilliantly gritty and seamlessly shot *Dheepan*, which won the Palme d'Or at Cannes last year, the title character is a former Tamil Tiger commander who, in the wake of the government slaughter that quelled the Sri Lankan insurgency in 2009, poses as the husband of a woman and the father of a girl who have lost their respective families so that the three of them can escape to France as war refugees. He ends up as a caretaker in an anarchical, Mogadishu-like *banlieue*, quietly supporting his notional family until his warrior (and chivalric) compulsions get the better of him and he challenges local thugs. Oblique camera angles, artful sound and lightning-quick jump-cuts exude perpetual threat, and the acting is naturalistic in the best sense: unpretentious but crafted. Although the film is leavened by tentative notes of repose, the bigger story – about the proliferation of irregular warfare from the battlefield to the suburb and potentially back again – is sadly a major narrative of the early twenty-first century.

Les Cowboys, a French–Belgian production, insightfully channels the plot and concept of John Ford's classic western *The Searchers* through a story about a Christian girl's decision to leave her rural French family for a Pakistani man and live as a Muslim. The screenplay by Thomas Bidegain (who also directed) is notably elegant, spare and skilful, imparting a great deal through visual juxtaposition. The movie also features American character actor John C. Reilly in a fine turn as a cynical CIA officer (or facsimile thereof). Bidegain's take is hard-nosed – the two cultures are profoundly different and inevitably clash – but not without hope.

The British-made *Eye in the Sky*, which dramatises events inside the kill chain of a drone strike on high-value al-Shabaab targets in the heavily Somali Nairobi suburb of Eastleigh, is earnest, clichéd and unsubtle, and takes quite a bit of dramatic licence. But relative to most films about post-9/11 counter-terrorism – which are generally poor – it is not a bad film, with a strong cast serving a rather didactic script as best it can. Helen Mirren and the late Alan Rickman play UK-based British officers intent on proceeding with a combined US–UK–Kenyan operation despite a palpable prospect of collateral damage in the form of a little girl selling bread near ground zero. The conscientious US Air Force drone pilot (Aaron Paul) situated in Nevada resists. The most evocative, if not terribly well integrated, role belongs to Somali-American actor Barkhad Abdi as a Kenyan special-forces undercover spotter. He does not say much, and most of what he does say is in Somali, but the fear and anguish on his face, and the courage of his actions, are eloquent.

The New Spymasters: Inside Espionage from the Cold War to Global Terror
Stephen Grey. London and New York: Viking, 2015.
£20.00/$27.99. 368 pp.

When the Cold War ended and transnational Islamist terrorism perpetrated by non-state actors emerged as the most immediate threat to the United States and Europe, the practice of human intelligence (known as HUMINT) changed. The choreographed spy-versus-spy contests that Graham Greene and John le Carré had canonised, with implied rules and their own kind of etiquette, would not occur between Western intelligence officers and their new, more culturally alien quarries. Wider ethnic and cultural differences between intelligence adversaries made clandestine infiltration and recruitment, as well as effective counter-intelligence, more difficult, as did religiously motivated foes' fanatical dedication to their cause and relative insusceptibility to monetary inducement, moral blackmail or political suasion.

As investigative reporter Stephen Grey observes in his insightful, literate, historically anchored and endearingly anecdotal book on the transition of HUMINT work from the Cold War to the age of terror, these realities were driven home at a CIA base in Khost, Afghanistan, on the last day of 2009. On that day, Humam al-Balawi, a Jordanian doctor the CIA prized as a recruited infiltrator of al-Qaeda, detonated a suicide vest and killed himself and seven of his putative colleagues before they had a chance to present him with the birthday cake the CIA base chief had baked for him. She was among the dead. 'The operation had been the CIA's best shot in the spying game and the White House had been watching. It failed in spectacular fashion' (p. 15). Grey argues vigorously that, although that failure and other less dramatic ones established a premium on technical intelligence (which is generally more reliable if less probative than the human variety), the role of the classical secret agent remains important.

The author notes that while the bad information supplied by Iraqi German agent Rafid Ahmed Alwan (code-named *Curveball*) served to falsely entrench ambiguous technical data as evidence of Iraqi weapons of mass destruction, that very example also shows how important HUMINT can be in verifying, contextualising and focusing other raw, unsifted intelligence. This function is especially important as technical collection becomes 'overwhelmed by its own capabilities' (p. 259). The main problem with *Curveball* was that the requisite 'healthy and professional relationship between an agent and his handler' (p. 151) did not exist. For Grey, the upshot is not to give up in the face of stiffer challenges but to try harder by exploiting jihadist groups' particular weaknesses. One of them is the constant need for recruits. Thus, he points to Danish ex-convict and biker Morten Storm, who turned to Islam as a kind of purgatory; travelled discreetly in radical circles; balked at his prospective jihadism; helped the Danish and British intelligence services identify, arrest and convict two jihadist bomb-makers; and was arguably key to locating American jihadist Anwar al-Awlaki for the drone strike that killed him in Yemen. Grey's ethical commentary and policy prescriptions are boilerplate, if broadly sound. But his central point about 'the human factor' in intelligence operations is plain and notable: 'spies are not just another "ear" at the table, a stealer of secrets, but sentient beings who convey understanding' (p. 287).

Islamist Terrorism in Europe: A History
Petter Nesser. London: C. Hurst & Co., 2015. £20.00. 371 pp.

The New Threat from Islamic Militancy
Jason Burke. London: The Bodley Head, 2015. £9.99. 290 pp.

Norwegian analyst Petter Nesser's book is a meticulous, fact-rich and straightforward survey of Islamist terrorism in Europe, the importance of which recent mass-casualty terrorist attacks in France and Belgium staged by the Islamic State (also known as ISIS or ISIL) have highlighted. After examining trends and methods, Nesser undertakes an incisive chronological analysis, starting with a well-aimed and useful look at the Islamist terrorist activity in Europe that predated and immediately followed 9/11. As he notes, the extant networks were rooted in the al-Qaeda-assisted Algerian Groupe Islamique Armé's campaign in France in the 1990s, which had been incited by France's support – regarded as echoing its past colonial biases and brutality – for Algeria's anti-Islamist government in the civil war that began in 1991. This helps explain why jihadist infrastructure in Europe is so difficult to dismantle, though most of the operations in 2000–03 did not target European countries as such and instead focused on US, NATO and Israeli marks. It was the US-led invasion and occupation of Iraq that triggered a 'shift from Europe functioning primarily as a support base, to a situation where European countries became targets of strategic and retaliatory attacks' (p. 127) so as to deter their further involvement in Iraq.

Accordingly, the Iraq War 'breathed new life into European jihadism' (p. 129), fuelling al-Qaeda's recruitment and operations in Europe – just as the war in Syria has done for ISIS. Nesser goes on to portray Europe as an increasingly powerful vortex for transnational jihadist efforts, describing successive epochs of Pakistani infiltration, the northward spread of terrorist activity in Europe, the decentralisation and proliferation of smaller operations, and finally the present heterogeneous threat that materialised with the rise of ISIS and its competition with al-Qaeda. Thus, in addition to being extraordinarily thorough, Nesser's book is unprecedentedly systematic. His prose also has an objective, professional tone that is refreshing, and to some extent reassuring. These qualities have yielded a singularly valuable contribution to the literature on jihadist terrorism.

In contrast to Nesser, Jason Burke can occasionally be a bit breathless and sanctimonious in explaining the rise of ISIS and assessing its ramifications. He starts his book by saying that 'we owe it to' the victims to 'make the effort it takes to find the answer' to the question of why terrorism occurs (p. 13). He closes with the admonition that terrorism should be apprehended 'in measure and in reason, not in panicked ignorance' (p. 245). Few who are serious about counter-terrorism are either intellectually lethargic or traumatised into senselessness. That aside, Burke's account of ISIS's ascendancy is duly appreciative of the historical context and enlivened by his journalistic approach. He is also admirably candid – in particular, about his and other analysts' misreading of the Arab Spring as a development that would discourage Sunni militancy, when in fact it left jihadists 'perfectly poised to exploit the chaos' (p. 23). The author is often insightful as well. In particular, he probes what Marc Sageman has called 'leaderless jihad', and the related – and increasing – social-media-fuelled prevalence of lone-wolf attacks inspired by ISIS or al-Qaeda, with impressive curiosity. What has evolved, he suggests, is a larger 'movement without organisation but held together instead by commonly understood guidelines' (p. 206). More conventional analysts may dispute the level of threat posed by this phenomenon, but there now seems to be little doubt about its salience.

Guantánamo Diary
Mohamedou Ould Slahi. Larry Siems, ed. Edinburgh:
Canongate Books, 2015. £12.99. 372 pp.

Among President Barack Obama's great frustrations has been his inability to close the prison for al-Qaeda suspects at the US Marine base at Guantanamo Bay, Cuba. The reasons are bureaucratic, political and diplomatic: the Pentagon and CIA have registered security concerns about releasing some of the inmates; many in Congress have opposed closing the prison; and the United States has had difficulty finding willing host countries for those deemed releasable. However practically insurmountable these reasons may have been, the sheer injustice of detaining suspects without trial on the basis of a nebulous war with no definable end is clear – all the more so for those who are substantially innocent. One such person appears to be Mohamedou Ould Slahi, a Mauritanian who willingly turned himself in to local authorities eight days after 9/11, expecting to be cleared quickly. He was in US custody from November 2001 until October 2016. The US government held up his diary's redacted publication, ultimately made possible by the efforts of Slahi's lawyers and other supporters, for eight years.

Perhaps titled in sardonic assonance to war correspondent Richard Tregaskis's *Guadalcanal Diary*, a heroic account of the marines' gruelling battle on the eponymous Pacific island during the Second World War, *Guantanamo*

Diary covers roughly the first four years of Slahi's imprisonment. As an engineering student in Germany, he was inspired by the insurgency against the communist Afghan government. He trained with and swore allegiance to al-Qaeda in the early 1990s, and briefly fought with the group before losing interest as al-Qaeda shifted its focus to the United States. He eventually returned to Germany to complete his degree. He remained an observant Muslim and maintained contact with some of his friends in al-Qaeda. For practical reasons he moved to Canada shortly before Montreal resident and al-Qaeda member Ahmed Ressam was arrested in connection with the 'Millennium Plot' to bomb Los Angeles International Airport, but in January 2000 returned to his home country of Mauritania. After 9/11, those circumstances got him arrested, 'rendered' to Jordan and then to Afghanistan, and finally imprisoned at Gitmo for 15 years (pp. xxiii–xxx).

The general substance of much of Slahi's diary is now publicly known, but his personal voice drives home fear, anxiety and physical pain amounting to 'living literally in terror' (p. 218) – he was subjected to 'enhanced interrogation' – that objective descriptions by third parties cannot fully impart. He also expresses some of the odd but familiar Stockholm Syndrome-like psychological accommodations a prisoner makes to his captors, who are 'a family all the same, whether you like it or not' (p. 315). One guard, who seems to have become a genuine friend, told him in a note: 'it is impossible not to like a character like yourself' (p. 369). At the same time, however, Slahi conveys disdain and ridicule. Of one interrogator who threatened to have his family raped if he didn't talk, and promised he would be released if he did, Slahi writes: 'I was old enough to know that he was a rotten liar and a man with no honor, but he was in charge, so I had to listen to his bullshit again and again. I just wished the agencies would start to hire smart people' (p. 18). Later, he denigrates the interrogators' ingratiating ruse of passing him a letter purportedly from a family member that was obviously 'a cheap forgery' (p. 195). Eventually his captors resorted to raw brutality that made him willing to tell them whatever they wanted to hear. As he put it, '"If you're ready to buy, I'm selling"' (p. 291). Thus, Slahi's most noteworthy revelation may be not that the Guantanamo programme reflected the United States' panicked ethical self-abasement – that is by now widely accepted – but that the programme also embodied the US government's systematic incompetence.

The Bad-Ass Librarians of Timbuktu: And Their Race to Save the World's Most Precious Manuscripts
Joshua Hammer. New York: Simon & Schuster, 2016. $26.00.
278 pp.

Joshua Hammer, a veteran conflict journalist with deep knowledge of and affection for Africa, has written a jaunty gem of a book that looks behind the terror of jihadism to the grinding joylessness of Islamism and the smug banality of al-Qaeda's institutionalised oppressiveness. He tells mainly the story of Abdel Kader Haidara, a government librarian in Timbuktu who collected thousands of Islamic and other manuscripts and then saved them from al-Qaeda's scorched-earth destructiveness. He accomplished this feat by pulling together a team of librarians who spirited the volumes to secure locations in southern Mali in footlockers and mule carts as al-Qaeda in the Islamic Maghreb (AQIM) combined forces with pro-independence Tuareg rebels and occupied Timbuktu in April 2012.

Hammer is centrally concerned not with the headline drama of suicide attacks and mass killing, but rather with the deadening effect that jihadism has had on local cultures and societies. To be sure, there was in Timbuktu a long-standing tension between tolerant, scholarly strains of Islam and censorious, anti-intellectual Salafism, as well as a record of covetous French colonialism, both of which gave rise to the protective sequestration of manuscripts by educated elites. But AQIM visited a new level of cultural stricture and threat on the city. In addition to looting houses, shops and government offices, gun-toting AQIM militants forced women to wear veils, made men grow beards, obliterated ancient Sufi shrines and replaced Timbuktu radio's eclectic selection with non-stop Koranic recitation. Beyond that, they imposed corporal punishments (such as spontaneous floggings and public amputations) on those who violated sharia law, severely interpreted. And, just before fleeing the city as French forces and Malian government troops closed in, they burned 4,202 manuscripts at the Ahmed Baba Institute of Higher Learning and Islamic Research 'in an act of nihilistic vindictiveness' (p. 209). By then, however, Haidara and his team had put most of the valuable documents beyond reach.

Like the excellent French–Mauritanian film *Timbuktu* (2014), the book forcefully registers the jihadist modus operandi of elevating corruptible, compliant outcasts into sullen, self-aggrandising enforcers. The greatest merit of *The Bad-Ass Librarians of Timbuktu* is that it convincingly repudiates extremist Islamism at the quotidian level, at which it does not pose a global threat: it is objectionable not just because it imperils Westerners, their friends and the existing political order, but also because it is socially and intellectually retrograde, and abusive of the people it purports to protect. Hammer also chronicles the often brave resistance of Timbuktu's Muslim citizenry to AQIM's wantonness. He quotes one local imam, warned of the potentially lethal consequences of his defiance, as saying, 'How dare you say you are going to "teach us Islam"? We were born with Islam. We have had Islam in this city for a thousand years' (p. 143).

By January 2013, the French-led forces had retaken the city. Hammer's book is a poignant reminder that the key battle for hearts and minds is within Islam, and that violent jihadists, for all the lurid headlines they generate, are losing.

Closing Argument

President Trump

Dana H. Allin

I

This journal goes to press three days after Donald Trump was elected president of the United States (and most of its articles were finalised before we knew the result). Mail-in ballots on the West Coast, and provisional ballots throughout the country, are still being counted. It looks certain, however, that Hillary Clinton, not Trump, will win the popular vote by a margin of between one and two percentage points, or somewhere between 1.5 and 2 million votes. So this is the fifth time in American history that the winner of the popular vote has lost the electoral college and therefore the presidency. And it is the second time it has happened in the past five presidential elections. By historical standards, the popular-vote margin was not even especially close: Clinton's winning margin is on the order of four times larger than Al Gore's, and Gore won the national vote by a larger margin than Richard Nixon's over Hubert Humphrey in 1968, or John Kennedy's over Richard Nixon in 1960.

Beyond any solace of moral vindication that Democrats might cling to, the mismatch between votes and victory is significant because it is tied to the structural reason that Trump won and Clinton lost, offering at least a partial insight into the motivations of Trump's voters. A complete analysis is not yet available, but Trump won over rural, small-town and working class white voters without a college education, in comparison to Clinton's

Dana H. Allin is Editor of *Survival*, and IISS Senior Fellow for US Foreign Policy and Transatlantic Affairs.

Survival | vol. 58 no. 6 | December 2016–January 2017 | pp. 237–248 DOI 10.1080/00396338.2016.1257206

more racially mixed and more highly educated urban voters. Or, as others have put it, the losers versus the winners of globalisation.

The designations are relative and somewhat subjective. The plight of American blacks has been bad for centuries, but has gotten steadily better since the 1960s. They credit the Democratic Party for their improvement, and remember that Barry Goldwater's opposition to the civil rights act of 1964 morphed into a Southern Strategy. Hispanics' progress has been geographic – their parents or grandparents came to the US for a better life and, though that life remains tough, it is better than what they left behind and they know it. Other minorities – Asians, Jews – are economically natural Republicans, but they smell prejudice and racial fear-mongering, and have the muscle memory to know that the scapegoating of one minority usually ends badly for others. And they, too, are winners of globalisation.

For congressional races, Clinton's voters are naturally gerrymandered – they are packed more tightly together in urban districts where the preponderance of Democratic votes is wasted. There was also, obviously, a mal-distribution of Democratic voters in the presidential electoral college. Certainly, many Hispanic votes are likewise wasted because of their concentration in California, safely Democratic, and Texas, for now safely Republican.

The difference from Trump voters was therefore at once ethnic, cultural and geographic. Rural, working class and less educated whites are objectively losing out, and certainly feel themselves losers of an economic transformation which benefits vibrant cities to which they cannot move, and which they may associate with changes in the very complexion of American society.

Trump's campaign appeal was overtly racist, which is not quite the same thing as saying that the anger and motivation of his voters was predominantly racist. It might better be called white-ethnic anxiety, and has to be understood in the context of communities that really feel they are slipping – a slippage that was hinted at in research published more than a year ago that indicated an astonishing rise in white, middle-class mortality, a phenomenon utterly at odds with any comparable wealthy society and more reminiscent of post-Soviet Russia.[1]

The racial subtext of American politics is enduring and difficult. One of its most powerful documents was the speech that Barack Obama gave just over eight years ago when his candidacy was threatened by a racial firestorm ignited by the sermons of the black preacher at the Chicago church that Obama and his family had attended. Obama spoke of the trials and tribulations of American blacks since slavery, but he also expressed a profound empathy for whites such as his grandmother – 'a woman who helped raise me, a woman who sacrificed again and again for me, a woman who loves me as much as she loves anything in this world, but a woman who once confessed her fear of black men who passed her by on the street, and who on more than one occasion has uttered racial or ethnic stereotypes that made me cringe.' And then he said this:

> Most working- and middle-class white Americans don't feel that they have been particularly privileged by their race. Their experience is the immigrant experience – as far as they're concerned, no one handed them anything. They built it from scratch. They've worked hard all their lives, many times only to see their jobs shipped overseas or their pensions dumped after a lifetime of labor. They are anxious about their futures, and they feel their dreams slipping away. And in an era of stagnant wages and global competition, opportunity comes to be seen as a zero sum game, in which your dreams come at my expense. So when they are told to bus their children to a school across town; when they hear an African-American is getting an advantage in landing a good job or a spot in a good college because of an injustice that they themselves never committed; when they're told that their fears about crime in urban neighborhoods are somehow prejudiced, resentment builds over time.[2]

Genuine empathy for this resentment has a logical corollary that the conservative party in a two-party system is likely to be *racially conservative* as well, and the natural home for resentful whites. It follows that the strategic decision to embrace the disaffection of southern whites after the civil rights revolution of the 1960s was not fundamentally culpable. It put Republicans on the wrong side of history – yet, in a two-party system, it could be argued that someone had to be there. Richard Nixon may have done his country a service in siphoning votes from the overtly racist George Wallace without embracing Wallace's overt racism.

But now Donald Trump has used Wallace language rather than Nixon language, and he has won the presidency. Here the Republican Party *is* culpable. The ground was laid for Trump in the exploitation of Tea Party rage that was so clearly directed against America's first black president, in the pursuit of a policy of blanket obstruction throughout his presidency, going so far as to use the credit-worthiness of the United States as a means of extortion for political ends, and in the refusal to repudiate the odious 'birtherism' – a feverish conspiracy theory that the black man in the White House could not be a legitimate president because he was not a real American. Where was the birth certificate? (Ironically, whereas Obama was irrefutably born in the American state of Hawaii, his opponent in the 2008 campaign was in fact born in the Panama Canal Zone.) The most prominent and energetic birther was one Donald Trump.

Many Republican leaders did recoil when it became apparent that Trump would win their party's nomination for president. Some refused to support him and have maintained that refusal. Most, however, rallied around. And their decision has paid off, for they are about to take control of all three branches of the federal government.

II

This is another important reason that Trump won. In a polarised country, the decision of the party institutions and its elected officials to back him made it acceptable for many Republican voters who had their doubts, but were driven by animus against the Democrats, to follow suit. Trump was normalised by this Republican support. When some piece of outrageous rhetoric or behaviour drove some of his voters away, the institutional backing of the party allowed them to come back in good conscience.[3]

As did their animus towards Hillary Clinton. A large mystery of this campaign was how a woman whom polling showed to be extremely popular when she finished her service as secretary of state just four years ago could have become such an object of distrust and even hatred.

The post-factual generation of that enmity is at least part of the explanation for how the American system could install a manifestly authoritarian and illiberal candidate into the presidency of the United States. The narrative towards the end had been at least mildly reassuring. Trump's unfitness extended to the conduct of an even minimally competent campaign. He wasted irreplaceable campaign weeks on such erratic behaviour as attacking, via Twitter, the Muslim parents of a martyred American soldier, smearing a pageant winner who had gained a little weight after he took ownership of the Miss Universe Contest, and threatening to sue more than a dozen women who stepped forward to confirm that he had in fact assaulted them in the manner a 2005 video recording had captured him bragging about. Meanwhile, to fill out a policy platform that included various war crimes, mass deportations, extorting Mexico to finance a great border wall and banning Muslims from the United States, he vowed, dictator-like, to jail Hillary Clinton upon assuming office, and said he would keep America 'in suspense' about whether he might accept an election defeat. With more generally bizarre behaviour in the three national debates, these statements appeared to destroy his candidacy. Two weeks before the election, polling averages gave Hillary Clinton a lead of more than five percentage points. The system seemed to be working.

And then it didn't. Part of the normalisation of Trump was the absurd equation of Hillary Clinton's careless email practices with deep corruption and even criminality. The conventions of media coverage were hard to surmount: if reporters covering the Trump campaign were going to press Donald Trump on the countless bizarre and dangerous statements emitting from his lungs, then the different set of reporters covering the Clinton campaign would have to pursue her about something. Her use of a private email server while secretary of state was the best they could come up with. A small portion of the emails passing through it contained classified information, though the level of secrecy in these was in fact trivial.[4] The system was set up for admittedly frivolous reasons of convenience. But there was zero evidence that she used it to hide anything untoward. That was the conclusion of the FBI Director James Comey who, after his bureau investigated, declared in July that 'no reasonable prosecutor' would bring charges based on such evidence. He also said she had been careless with classified communications. The Trump campaign and Republican leaders in Congress expressed fury that the director was letting Clinton off the hook, and it turns out that many FBI agents were angry too, so when a separate investigation (into the bizarre and lurid sexting habits of former congressman Anthony Weiner, who happened to be married to Clinton's trusted aide Huma Abedin) turned up a computer that seemed to contain more Clinton emails, Comey sent a letter informing Congress that these would be examined as well. This was 11 days before the election. Comey's letter violated decades-old Justice Department guidelines to avoid any statements on ongoing investigations that might affect the outcome of an impending election. If he felt compelled to inform Congress before his anti-Clinton and pro-Trump agents leaked the information, this says a lot about the FBI's own discipline and carefulness with secrets. In any event, Comey at the time had no idea what new evidence the unexamined computer contained – and the answer turned out to be none. This episode came in the context of a steady drip of Wikileaks's release of other emails hacked from Democratic National Committee and Clinton campaign computers, according to US intelligence agencies, by groups associated with the Russian state, with the aim of interfering in the American election.[5] These leaks revealed that the emailers in question talked and behaved like normal human beings, which is to say that they wrote things that they might not want to see published. Such was the post-factual environment in which Trump's repeated claims that Hillary Clinton was the most corrupt and criminal candidate in American history, and belonged behind bars, could be taken seriously by many of his supporters.

III

Earlier this year, the American journalist Anne Applebaum wrote that 'right now, we are two or three bad elections away from the end of NATO, the end of the European Union and maybe the end of the liberal world order as we know it'.[6] The elections she had in mind were a British vote to leave the EU, the election of Trump as president of the United States, and the election of Marine Le Pen as president of France. Only the third has not yet happened; France votes next year.

In the American case, we now step onto terra incognita – we have not had a genuinely illiberal president in any living person's memory. Certainly since the Second World War, Democrats and Republicans have conformed to a basic liberal consensus. George W. Bush, notwithstanding his administration's unilateral impulses, was a liberal internationalist – arguably to a fault. Richard Nixon, though privately an anti-Semite and beset by other personal demons, pursued domestic and international policies well within the mainstream of American politics.

On the eve of Trump's election, Francis Fukuyama, in conversation with *Vox* editor Ezra Klein, sounded very worried:

> We went through a period like this in the 1930s after the Great Depression where you had a lot of economic distress and a lot of radical policies being pursued, and Germany and Italy went off in this authoritarian direction and the United States chose Franklin Roosevelt – a radical in the context of American politics, but [he] stayed well within the political frame. I think people thought that just reflected a very different kind of American political culture that is deeply democratic and liberal. I think this election year has suggested that maybe we were just lucky back then and there was nothing deeply constraining that kind of move other than just good leadership.[7]

What kind of leadership should we expect from President Trump? There is not much to go on except what he said in the campaign that he would do as president: reverse President Obama's climate-change regulations, because climate change is a Chinese hoax designed to ruin the US economy; deport 11 million undocumented immigrants ('humanely', he has said, but this is a definition of humane that includes breaking up thousands of families); build a great wall with Mexico and extort the Mexican government into paying for it by threatening to cut off remittances and applying other economic pressures; reinstitute torture for terrorist suspects and make it worse than waterboarding because, even if it doesn't work in terms of intelligence gathering, they deserve it; kill terrorist family members because that is the only effective deterrence against terrorists who are willing to sacrifice their own lives; ban Muslims from entering the United States; if intervening in places like Syria or Iraq against the Islamic State, do it in a smart way for American interests which means, at the very least, seizing the countries' oil; tear up the nuclear agreement with Iran; take a more transactional approach to the American alliance system, which means, for example, if the Baltic states cannot pay adequately for American defence, then, 'congratulations, you will be defending yourself'; impose 35% and 45% tariffs on Mexican and Chinese imports; sue the women who have come forward to accuse him of sexual assault; and instruct the anti-trust division of the Justice Department to go after Amazon's Jeff Bezo, the owner of the *Washington Post*, because Trump was unhappy with the *Post*'s coverage of his campaign.[8]

Against this dire programme, there are two thin hopes. First, maybe it was all a kind of grievance theatre for his much-aggrieved followers, and one that we do not need to take seriously as a plan for governing, not least because much of it is logically impossible. Second, President Trump will operate within the institutional checks and balances of the American constitutional system, which will act to restrain excesses.

The first hope requires us to ignore everything we saw and heard over the past 16 months – but who knows? On the second hope, some of the agenda, obviously, constitutes war crimes. The former head of the CIA and various retired generals have stated that America's spies and soldiers will refuse to carry out such orders. Trump's first response was: if I order it, they will do it. Then he backed off a little. So maybe that is a fight he would not seek. In more general terms, Congress is in Republican hands. There are elements of this agenda – the trade wars and the abandonment of NATO – that are at odds with Republican consensus. Other elements – the mass deportation of undocumented Hispanics – are at odds with Republicans' long-term political interest in not permanently alienating the fastest-growing segment of the American population. So Congress could fight him on these issues, although it is not clear why we would expect their calculation of interest and ideology to be any different now that he has won than it was when he was a candidate.

Those campaign promises that fit with the Republican agenda are very likely to be implemented. These include an abrogation of any action against climate change; appointments of conservatives to the Supreme Court; and very significant, regressive tax cuts, which will require draconian cuts to discretionary domestic spending. With countervailing increases in defence spending, these fiscal policies will almost certainly bring a return of massive structural federal-budget deficits. We can also expect in many Republican-controlled states a further restriction of voting rights, under the guise of combatting practically non-existent 'voter fraud'. These will include measures such as requiring certain forms of photo identification that may sound innocuous but are actually more expensive to acquire in real terms than the notorious poll taxes of the segregated South.

'Leadership' is an oft-used and somewhat vacuous mantra, but we are about to understand its more precise meaning by virtue of its absence from the liberal West. As Applebaum perceived, the disintegration of that community predated Trump's ascent. Institutions such as the EU and NATO may survive, but they are likely to be robbed of credibility and solidarity. Britain's strong, if prickly, position as a leader of the European Union is finished; it will now spend many years in collective contemplation of its navel, a dispiriting but unavoidable exercise of figuring out the values and technicalities of its new place in Europe and the world. The political dynamic that caused Brexit is the same as that which carried Trump. Certainly, Nigel Farage, Donald Trump and Marine Le Pen all welcomed Brexit because they are positively hostile to the EU. President-elect Trump has expressed similar hostility towards NATO.

Maybe there is enough memory of liberal purpose and recognition of stark interest in individual middle-ranked powers to bridge, selectively, part of the abyss. At the beginning of this century the French parties of left and right cooperated to deny Marine Le Pen's father the presidency; this required socialists to stifle their distaste for Jacques Chirac. They could do it again. Britain will leave the EU, but a High Court decision has required a greater role for Parliament in setting the terms; since most MPs were against Brexit, perhaps this majority will find a programme for privileging common European hopes over tabloid exploitation of baser fears and resentments in negotiating their departure. Germany will not abandon its destructive anti-Keynesian orthodoxy, but maybe in this era of prolonged crisis German leaders can accept that the harsher forms of austerity are corrosive to what is left of broader European solidarity. The community of Western values will not be enlarged in the foreseeable future; indeed, 'enlargement' projects were part of the overreach that led to the current crisis. But NATO has the conventional and nuclear means to defend its members, including Baltic states, and even if the leader of its leading power might be indifferent, treaty obligations mean something.

The military defence of NATO members is easier than restoring their solidarity, and both are lesser challenges compared to two truly existential threats. The first of these is a social, technological and moral threat to capitalist democracy. Brexit and Trump rode the currents of resentment against globalisation; yet globalisation may be only a smaller part of technological transformation that will increase the already huge disparities as autonomy and artificial intelligence devastate the viability of a jobs-based distribution of income. Maybe this nightmare scenario springs from a Luddite failure of imagination about the jobs of the future. But maybe not. As we stand on the cusp of a revolution in driverless automobiles, to take one example, we might consider how many people earn their living as drivers.

The second threat is environmental: catastrophic climate change. Technology in clean energy has advanced more quickly than we could have hoped for a few years ago, and that advancement allowed the presidents of the United States and of the People's Republic of China to reach a bilateral agreement that was the basis for a truly meaningful Paris agreement. The global-governance challenge, as my colleague Jeffrey Mazo has long argued, was always going to be at least as difficult as the one faced by the founders of the Bretton Woods institutions at the end of the Second World War. In fact, it is more difficult, because Bretton Woods was among allies, where as China and the US – the world's leading carbon polluters – are developing a relationship of rivalry, if not enmity.

Bretton Woods required American leadership, but it is hard to avoid the conclusion that, at least on this threat, such leadership will be absent for the next four years. And four years is a fairly large share of the time that is left to humanity to bend the curve of global emissions downward, before truly catastrophic temperature increases become irreversible. European states, for all their troubles, are not governed by political parties that deny the science of climate change. Perhaps they remain wilful and coherent enough to seek accommodation with China, and other big developing states such as India, to bridge the time until America comes to its senses. There could be geopolitical peril in such accommodation. Yet, if they could pull it off, the Europeans would have performed a worthy historical service and repayment of genuine debt for America's past sacrifices: the old world stepping forth to the rescue of the new.

Notes

1 See Julia Belluz, 'Nobel Winner Angus Deaton Talks About the Surprising Study on White Mortality He Just Co-Authored', Vox, 7 November 2015, http://www.vox.com/2015/11/7/9684928/angus-deaton-white-mortality; and, for the original study, Anne Case and Angus Deaton, 'Rising Morbidity and Mortality In Midlife Among White Non-Hispanic Americans In the 21st Century', *Proceedings of the National Academy of Sciences of the United States of America*, vol. 112, no. 49, 8 December 2015, http://www.pnas.org/content/112/49/15078.full.pdf.

2 Barack Obama, 'A More Perfect Union', speech to the National Constitution Center, Philadelphia, PA, 18 March 2008, http://constitutioncenter.org/amoreperfectunion/docs/Race_Speech_Transcript.pdf.

3 Ezra Klein, 'Donald Trump's Success Reveals a Frightening Weakness in American Democracy', *Vox*, 7 November 2016, http://www.vox.com/policy-and-politics/2016/11/7/13532178/donald-trump-american-democracy-weakness.

4 Fred Kaplan, 'The Hillary Clinton Email Scandal Was Totally Overblown', *Slate*, 6 July 2016, http://www.slate.com/articles/news_and_politics/war_stories/2016/07/hillary_s_email_scandal_was_over-hyped.html.

5 See Nigel Inkster, 'Information Warfare and the US Presidential Election', *Survival*, vol. 58, no. 5, October–November 2016, pp. 23–32.

6 Anne Applebaum, 'Is this the end of the West as we know it?', *Washington Post*, 4 March 2016, https://www.washingtonpost.com/opinions/donald-trump-and-the-end-of-nato/2016/03/04/e8c4b9ca-e146-11e5-8d98-4b3d9215ade1_story.html.

7 Francis Fukuyama, interview with Ezra Klein, *Vox*, 26 October 2016, http://www.vox.com/2016/10/26/13352946/francis-fukuyama-ezra-klein.

8 On climate change, see Donald J.

Trump, 'The concept of global warming was created by and for the Chinese in order to make U.S. manufacturing non-competitive', tweet, 5 November 2012, https://twitter.com/realDonaldTrump/status/265895292191248385. On immigration and the border wall, see 'Donald J. Trump's 10 Point Plan to Put America First', https://www.donaldjtrump.com/policies/immigration/?/positions/immigration-reform. On torturing terror suspects, see 'Trump on Torture', Factcheck.org, 28 July 2016, http://www.factcheck.org/2016/07/trump-torture/. On killing terrorists' family members, see Peter Holley, 'Former CIA Director: Military May Refuse to Follow Trump's Orders If He Becomes President', *Washington Post*, 28 February 2016, https://www.washingtonpost.com/news/morning-mix/wp/2016/02/28/former-cia-director-military-may-refuse-to-follow-trumps-orders-if-he-becomes-president/. On seizing countries' oil, see Julian Borger, 'Trump's Plan to Seize Iraq's Oil: "It's Not Stealing, We're Reimbursing Ourselves"', *Guardian*, 21 September 2016, https://www.theguardian.com/us-news/2016/sep/21/donald-trump-iraq-war-oil-strategy-seizure-isis. On the nuclear agreement with Iran, see Yeganeh Torbati, 'Trump Election Puts Iran Nuclear Deal on Shaky Ground', Reuters, 9 November 2016, http://www.reuters.com/article/us-usa-election-trump-iran-idUSKBN13427E. On NATO and the Baltic states, see 'Transcript: Donald Trump on NATO, Turkey's Coup Attempt and the World', *New York Times*, 21 July 2016, http://www.nytimes.com/2016/07/22/us/politics/donald-trump-foreign-policy-interview.html?_r=0. On imposing tariffs on Mexico and China, see David Lawder and Roberta Rampton, 'Trump's tariff plan could boomerang, spark trade wars with China, Mexico', Reuters, 24 March 2016, http://www.reuters.com/article/us-usa-election-trump-trade-idUSKCN0WQ0WG. On suing his sexual-assault accusers, see Jeremy Diamond and Eugene Scott, 'Trump Says He'll Sue Sexual Misconduct Accusers', CNN, 23 October 2016, http://edition.cnn.com/2016/10/22/politics/trump-says-hell-sue-sexual-misconduct-accusers/. On Jeff Bezos and the *Washington Post*, see Eugene Kim, 'Trump Warned Amazon Would Have "Problems" Under His Presidency – Here's What Could Happen', *Business Insider*, 9 November 2016, http://uk.businessinsider.com/how-trump-presidency-will-affect-amazon-2016-11?r=US&IR=T.